PIUS XI
THE POPE AND THE MAN

"He was second to none"
CARDINAL LUALDI

PIUS XI

THE POPE AND THE MAN

by Zsolt Aradi

HANOVER HOUSE, GARDEN CITY, NEW YORK

Nihil obstat: JOHN A. GOODWINE, J.C.D.
                  Censor Librorum

Imprimatur: ✠ FRANCIS CARDINAL SPELLMAN
                  Archbishop of New York
                  November 7, 1957

Excerpt from Virginia Cowles' Winston Church-
hill *used by permission of the publishers, Harper &
Brothers.*

TO
PIO BONDIOLI

Contents

Introduction

WHEN Pius XI, Achille Ratti, died on February 10, 1939, the world was already gripped by the fear that World War II was in the offing. Dark clouds spreading over the entire political horizon signaled the impending storm. Every day, almost every hour, from February 1939 on was charged with electric tension. Nations and individuals were filled with thoughts of how to save themselves, how to remain alive, or even how to exploit the situation for selfish purposes.

The biographies of Pius XI that have been published were all motivated by the best intentions, but with very few exceptions these biographies saw the light of day under adverse circumstances. Those published in Italy and in Germany were necessarily biased because their evaluation had to take into account the existing climate of the two police states. Other biographies, published in the Western democracies, had to confine themselves to data available in their own countries, because the war made communications impossible. In addition to these obstacles, the immediacy, the lack of historical perspective, impeded his biographers from seeing the real Pius XI. The constant theme of these biographies was that Pius XI was a great Pope. All the Popes of the modern age ever since the pontificate of Pius IX can be considered great Popes. All lived irreproachable, saintly lives, and helped to bring about an unprecedented revival of spirituality. Their lives have been described and evaluated, and we now can measure the dimensions of their greatness.

The more we become separated in time from the age of Pius XI, the stronger become the conviction and proof that Pius XI was indeed one of the greatest Popes that history has known, a Pope who opened a completely new chapter in Church history. In fact, it can be said that Achille Ratti was a man of genius. His life seemed to consist of great contradictions; writers who dealt with his life and activity were unable to overcome this obstacle. What were the contradictions?

How was it possible that a quiet librarian, well in his sixties, within four years' time suddenly became an active diplomat, a Nuncio, an Archbishop, a Cardinal and then Pope? There was no easy answer, so the question was totally evaded. Many writers contented themselves with other approaches: some stressed his scholarly qualities or his sense of command. Others took refuge in the annoyingly repeated phrase that Pius XI was the Pope of the concordats. Even his best biographers failed to recognize many important facts in the life of Pius XI up to the time he became sixty-five. And because this life was apparently passed in a drab, gray simplicity, few people took the pains to look into the real background of the Pope and the motives underlying his actions. Those actions were decided upon by him alone and not by others; behind those actions there stood a man whose physical, mental, material and spiritual stature did not rise up automatically on the day of his election to the papacy. His actions were the result of his education, his study of human events, the contacts with men from all walks of life.

I do not fancy that I have filled all the gaps left by other biographers. Nevertheless, I have made an honest effort. I was not totally unfamiliar with the subject and with the life of Pius XI; nevertheless, I was surprised to find so much evidence of the complexity of Achille Ratti's character. If I experienced any difficulty while writing this book, it was the difficulty of overcoming my temptation to expand it.

It was a privilege to recreate the life of Achille Ratti, and

I feel that certain explanatory notes are in order, to tell why and how this biography came to be written.

As a young man of seventeen I saw Pius XI for the first time in Rome in 1925. From 1936 to February 10, 1939, when Pius XI died, I was present at several general and special audiences, but I never had the privilege of talking directly with him. My formative and very active years (1931–1938) were spent, however, very much under the spell of this Pope and the atmosphere he created within the Catholic Church.

During those years, in our native Hungary, my friends and I helped to found newspapers, magazines and publishing houses that bore the stamp, often unconsciously, of the great personality of Pius XI.

Though I never met him, he was a close friend of some of my closest friends and associates. Some of these persons are still alive. Under their guidance I participated in several international Catholic movements sponsored by Pius XI. I consider it a great privilege to have lived more than a decade in Italy, most of the time in Rome, but also in Milan. For one year I lived at Lake Como, commuting daily to and from Milan through the township of Desio where Pius XI was born. I was in Rome when Pius XI died.

I have kept a diary from early youth, and in it I noted many events and conversations concerning Pius XI, related to me by the friends and associates of Achille Ratti. Yet I never planned to write a biography of Pius XI, or of anyone else for that matter.

Upon being approached to undertake this task I was not enthusiastic. When I consented and was confronted with the material, I was most dismayed, for, though I knew the subject, I was overwhelmed by the magnitude of the task. The reason there are no biographies besides those written eighteen or more years ago—two of which are of particular excellence: by Msgr. Philip Hughes and by Msgr. Joseph Schmidlin—is that the death of Pius XI coincided with the beginning of World War II. It was only natural that, faced with the problems of the postwar period and the beginning of the atomic age, many people should assume that the dead Pope had no message for the world. This is a great mistake. The message of a great man is always valid, for its value is not limited in time.

I should like to express my deepest gratitude to His Excellency Archbishop Carlo Confalonieri, former secretary to Pius XI, and to His Excellency Fr. Agostino Gemelli, O.F.M., Rector Magnificus of the Catholic University of Milan, Italy, and president of the Pontifical Academy of Sciences. I also wish to thank Fr. Robert Leiber, S.J., Professor of the Gregorian University in Rome, for his unfailing friendship and assistance. In addition, I wish to thank Count Giuseppe Dalla Torre, editor-in-chief of *Osservatore Romano;* Monsignor Giovanni Bandera, Dean of Desio; Dr. Pio Bondioli, historian, of Milan; Fr. Ferenc Monay, of the Penitentiary Fathers of St. Peter's Basilica; Mr. Dan Sullivan, Professor of Philosophy at Fordham University, New York; Monsignor André Bouquin, Rome; Fr. James J. Tucek, chief, NCWC-News Service, Rome; Dr. Liana Bortolon, Milan; and Mr. Salvator Attanasio, of New York City, for his invaluable editorial assistance.

Though I have added a bibliography, I wish to acknowledge my indebtedness to three books in particular. One is Schmidlin's *Papstgeschichte* (History of the Popes). Since the book was published in 1939 in Hitler Germany, the evaluation of the personality and policy of Pius XI is obviously incomplete. Prof. Schmidlin, whom the nazis imprisoned, died as a result of his sufferings in a concentration camp. The second, more recent, was written by the former secretary of Pius XI, Archbishop Carlo Confalonieri. It is a well of information and the best book on Pius XI. The third is a charming sketch written by Msgr. Arborio Mella di Sant' Elia, who spent his entire life in the service of four Popes, one of them Pius XI, at the Vatican.

It is rewarding to try to revive the life of a great person,

for one identifies one's self constantly with his destiny and
would like to preserve his image for mankind. I hope that
the readers will feel the same attraction I do for the personality of Achille Ratti.

New York, New York
May 31, 1957
One-hundredth anniversary of
the birth of Achille Ratti

PIUS XI
THE POPE AND THE MAN

CHAPTER ONE

Younger Days in the Brianza

ACHILLE RATTI was as much a product of Northern Italy, more specifically of Lombardy, as Erasmus of Rotterdam was a product of Holland. There were few greater humanists than Erasmus, who lived in an age of controversy, yet he was able to keep his identity not only during his lifetime but through the centuries that followed. Erasmus had a global view of international affairs; he never became a narrow-minded nationalist; he had understanding for the views of violently opposing parties of different nations. But he had deep roots. He was Erasmus of *Rotterdam,* so Flemish that the prototype of the quiet, sometimes cool, well-mannered Dutchman could be carved out from his figure. His attachment to his roots did no harm; on the contrary, it broadened his universality and his thinking.

So with Achille Ratti. He cannot be understood unless we know the native soil from which he sprang: the environs of Milan. His roots were so deep and his attachment to Milan so great that in an earlier age he would have been called Achille of *Milan,* and known as such through the ages.

Desio, where Achille Ratti was born on May 31, 1857, is a village in the lowlands of Lombardy in the northwestern tip of Italy, dominated by the massive and majestic Alps. The village whose history goes back to Roman times—historical documents indicate that Desio was an important Christian center in the sixth century—forms the center of the larger Brianza region, and sits on the main road between the famous

St. Gotthard Pass and the great industrial city of Milan only fifteen miles away.

Despite its closeness to Milan, where the industrial revolution and the social and political transformations of the nineteenth century found their most advanced expression in Italy, the Brianza region, of which Desio is the most important community, managed to keep relatively immune from these swift and bewildering changes.

The silk and textile plants that dot this area did little to modify the traditional landscape or the character and folkways of the people. The inhabitants of the plains of Brianza live in a close, vital relationship with the mountains, whose snow-capped peaks they can see on clear days, and with its dark, mysterious valleys and swift torrents that eventually find their way to the River Po.

Up to the beginning of the twentieth century most inhabitants of the area still worked as agricultural day laborers on the vast estates of the local gentry, and the region still preserved its reputation as the home of Italy's finest carpenters and cabinet-makers.

The family of the future Pope, the Rattis, belonged to the relatively newly created lower industrial middle class. Before the industrialization of the area around Milan they had been artisans and peasants.

At the time that Achille Ratti was elected Pope—in 1922— the inevitable attempt was made to link the Ratti family to the great aristocratic families of the region, an attempt that naturally was unsuccessful and which in no wise was encouraged by the Pope, amused over the pretentiousness of the project.

The family of Achille Ratti, however, can be traced in documents that go as far back as the sixteenth and seventeenth centuries in Rogeno, upper Brianza, in the vicinity of Lake Como. Most of his antecedents were peasants, as was the progenitor of the Ratti family, a certain Gerolamo.

Later, the family occupation shifted from the soil to the

workshop. Members of the Ratti clan became skilled lathe operators, specializing in wood and later in metal, and toward the end of the nineteenth century some of them worked as metal lathe operators for the state railway. Other relatives became spinners and weavers in the silk mills, but they stubbornly held on to small properties and farms.

In a word, the Rattis were a hard-working, simple, industrious folk. By Italian standards, however, they were relatively well-to-do, as is indicated by the generous gifts they made for charitable purposes or for the embellishment of local churches and monasteries registered in the church annals of Rogeno and Massiola.

In the birth certificate of Achille Ratti, his father is listed as a landowner. The elder Ratti did own some land, but he also worked as a weaver in the small silk factory in Desio owned by the Count di Pusiano and his brothers. Later, he became its manager.

The house in which Achille Ratti was born is a three-story building on Via Lampugnani (now Via Pio XI)[1] with a center section. Two wings of the house are connected at the end of the courtyard by a covered bridge. The house did not belong to the Rattis, but to the Pusiano family. In fact, the "factory" was located on the same premises and the hum and din of the spinning and weaving machines were familiar sounds to the Ratti children as they romped and played about the big house.

Achille Ratti was the fourth child of Francesco and Teresa Ratti. His mother, neé Galli, came from the neighboring township of Saronno, and she had already presented Francesco with three boys: Carlo, Fermo and Eduardo. A girl, Camilla, was born in 1860.

Signora Ratti was a dark-haired, medium-sized woman, with lively dark eyes. There was no question about the fact that she ruled the Ratti roost. In a sentimental poem written

[1] Pius XI disapproved of the change of name, because of his personal modesty and his sense of history and affection for mementos of the past.

by her son Achille on the occasion of her birthday in 1882, the spankings received by the children are humorously remembered, and Achille himself was no exception, even though she treated him with special care because he was the youngest son.

On June 1, 1857, the day after his birth, the Rattis took their fourth-born son to the nearby cathedral in Desio, where he was baptized as Ambrosio Damien Achille. The boy was named in honor of an early Christian martyr whose name is still venerated on the Via Appia in Rome in the little church of St. Nereus and Achilles. According to the Desio parish records, Ambrosio Ratti of Rogeno, from which the family originally came, was godfather to the child, and Luigia Zappa of Desio, a friend of Signora Ratti, his godmother.

Teresa Ratti, who had married Francesco in 1850 when she was twenty, had all the traditional virtues of the Italian women of her time. From the moment of her marriage she dedicated herself completely to the welfare of her husband and the growing family, despite her delicate health and constitution. Signora Ratti frequently suffered from headaches, so much so that her son, who never had a serious illness until his seventy-ninth year, remarked that her pains and sufferings must have included the share that should have been his.

The Rattis lived an orderly, well-regulated life. Francesco left the house early each day to supervise the work at the factory, or to see business associates, very often in Milan, to arrange for sales and purchases of silk products. Milan at that time was a booming business center; the grain and wine markets were jammed with people and humming with activity. But whenever he stayed at home in Desio, Signora Ratti made it a point that the family should take its meals together.

The house of the Rattis in Desio was well furnished, in a style typical of the lower bourgeoisie of the nineteenth century. Many of the objects and furnishings in the house had great sentimental value for Achille Ratti. Among other things, for example, he kept a music box from the paternal home in his room until the end of his life.

Since the family was neither poor nor wealthy, Francesco Ratti was able to maintain the traditional independence of his forebears. Although he was an employee, this was possible because he owned enough land and had enough savings. Hard work and constant activity were the basis of the family's well-being. This was a lesson that was not lost on Achille Ratti who later, as Pope, once asserted that *"La vita è azione,"* "Life is action."

Francesco Ratti allowed himself no luxuries. The education of his five children was for him a primary goal and he was determined to make any sacrifice in order to put the children through the higher schools. And his wife never failed in her thrift and was as alert in running the household as her husband was in conducting his business.

Young Achille was very much influenced by his mother and much devoted to her. Although Achille was a normal, active and very good-humored child, he was still the most serious of the five, and prone to solitude and meditation. It was for this reason that his schoolmates called him "the little old man." Otherwise, Achille was just like any of the other boys in the village, sharing their games, pranks and experiences. In church he often served as an altar boy, and even learned how to ring the church bells. The bells of Lombardian churches have a tonality peculiar to them. Young Achille was so fond of the sound of the bells, when one church seemed to respond to the other in a harmonious obligato that faded into the distance, that when he became Pope a recording was made of the bells of Desio and presented to him as a gift. He kept this recording until the end of his life, playing it often whenever nostalgia for his old home town came over him.

Achille's first teacher was a simple country priest named Don Giuseppe Volontieri. He was a truly remarkable man, who had a deep influence on the pupils who were entrusted to him. At that time there was no religious instruction in the schools, and Don Giuseppe, as he was called, taught the children of Desio, ranging in age from six to ten, the elements of religion in his own home.

In addition, it was his custom to discuss the daily problems of life that arose in the village with his "class," especially during the frequent trips to the surrounding countryside where he would patiently and lovingly point out to them the wonders and beauties of nature. In explaining the events that impinged at some point or other on the lives of his young charges, whether it was a trivial family dispute or the behavior of the soldiery, Don Giuseppe never tried to varnish reality. Yet he always discussed such matters in the context of his own deep faith and natural goodness in a way that, instead of dismaying the youngsters, actually strengthened their belief in the essential goodness of life and man and the inscrutable ways of God. He would often counsel his young audience, among whom Achille was an avid listener, to live according to the principle of Ignatius Loyola: "Pray as much and as deeply as if everything depended on God. Work as hard and as strenuously to achieve whatever spiritual or other aim you have, as if everything depended on you."

Through his pupils Don Giuseppe was always sending gifts of food and money to the poor of the village. And his pupils' parents were often the surprised recipients of large bouquets of flowers gathered for them at his tactful suggestion. Don Giuseppe taught for forty-three years in the village of Desio and, in a sense, exerted a greater influence on the townspeople than did the political events that were also shaping their lives, or the other priests attached to the local parish. As late as 1956 there were still old residents in Desio who remembered his name because their fathers and grandfathers had so often extolled his lofty qualities as a man and as a priest.

When Don Giuseppe died, in 1884, it was Achille Ratti who delivered the funeral oration and who wrote the still legible inscription on his tombstone in the cemetery of Desio:

"Giuseppe Volontieri was full of enthusiasm for the honor of the Church and school, and educated children to love both."

The climate of Desio is much like that of Milan. Winter can be very cold, autumn is always beautiful, but the summer is dreadfully hot and humid, unrelieved by refreshing breezes or showers. Between noon and four o'clock in the afternoon the hot streets, otherwise so bustling with life, are deserted and the shutters on the houses are drawn tight.

But life in Desio was not exactly idyllic. It was the time when the unity of Italy was being forged. Achille Ratti was born in the days of the Risorgimento and his growing intellect and imagination, from the earliest days of his life, had been crammed with the images and rhetoric of this romantic era influenced by European liberalism and nationalism.

The earliest event that Achille Ratti remembered was also one of the great historical events in Italian and European history. He recalled that one day in 1859, when he was only two years old, his father rushed into the house breathlessly, shouting: "The Germans are at Desenzano!" This was at the time of the Franco-Italian war against the Austrians, as a result of which the Hapsburgs were driven out of Lombardy and Venice. This event set off a chain reaction that ultimately ended with the occupation of Rome by the forces of the revolution and completed the unification of Italy.

Achille Ratti remained ever aware of the "two" Italies within the unified country. He knew that northern Italy is different from the rest of the peninsula, clearly distinguishing between Italy *north of the Po* and *south of the Po*. In his opinion, people north of the Po were more enterprising. This was why, as Pope, he never would send help if a routine request came from north of the Po. He would explain that "People there should help each other because they are able to do so." To be sure, he loved the Brianza people and they in turn loved him. Like any other Italian, Achille Ratti also kept strong ties with his native region.

As a child, Achille Ratti spoke two languages: Italian and

the *meneghino* dialect used in the family and among his play-
mates. In his later years he loved to use the dialect with his
intimates, particularly when talking about matters Milanese,
so that he could give full scope to the colloquialisms reminis-
cent of his beloved Milan and Brianza. He spoke the *meneghino* dialect well, with the correct tonality and expression, a
skill which put him in good company. Among this company
were Manzoni, the great Italian novelist of the nineteenth
century, Antonio Stoppani, one of the teachers of the future
Pope, who was also a famous geologist and author of *Bel
Paese,* and Msgr. Ceriani, Ratti's predecessor at the Ambrosiana in Milan. All three men wrote poetry in the *meneghino*
vernacular. Achille Ratti followed their example. One of his
poems in dialect, containing forty-three stanzas, was dedicated to his mother as a birthday tribute on October 15, 1882.

Achille Ratti's love for the Brianza ever remained a strong
emotional factor in his life, a concrete and perennial proof
of how deep were his roots in the soil, the spirit and the history of this region and its people. In 1922, for example, when
the Brianza region showed itself to be less than enthusiastic
toward fascism in the elections, the fascists were enraged.
In revenge, the Blackshirts destroyed the locals of the *Partito
Popolare* (People's Party), offices of Catholic Action and parish halls. The fascists held these three groups responsible for
their defeat. In a letter to his Secretary of State, Cardinal
Gasparri, Pius XI strongly deplored the violence and van-
dalism, particularly that against the parish halls, and he immediately gave half a million lire for the relief of the victims
and reconstruction of the damaged properties. It was at this
time that he earned the sobriquet, *"Il Papa Brianzolo,"* the
Pope of Brianza.

In addition to his family and his teacher, Don Giuseppe,
two other men exercised particularly great influence on the
boy Achille: his uncle, Don Damiano Ratti, and Archbishop
Calabiana of Milan. Achille spent his summer vacations with
this uncle whom he loved. Don Damiano was the same kind

of priest as Don Giuseppe: devout and full of a sense of humor. Moreover, he was a pastor with a broad knowledge of the world. He loved youth and knew how to kindle its idealism and imagination.

Don Damiano was well liked by his fellow priests and by his superiors, too. One of his great friends was Archbishop Calabiana, who would often come to spend several days in the delightful atmosphere of Don Damiano's house. It was here that the young Achille frequently met older seminarists who took him on walks, and where he also met the Archbishop. This particular meeting was one of the most important, if not decisive, regarding his future.

During the summer season Don Damiano's house was the gathering place of young students and seminarians, a veritable youth hostel. Archbishop Calabiana liked and encouraged this atmosphere charged with youthful spirit and energies, above all because the young guests shared his ideas of Italian patriotism.

Archbishop Calabiana was no ordinary figure in the fights for Italian unity. Born in 1808, he had become Bishop of Casale at thirty-nine. A member of the Piedmontese aristocracy, he had been given an important post in the court of King Carlo Alberto, with the title of royal almoner. Calabiana was a man of impeccable conduct, an exemplary priest, and a defender of the rights of the Church. But at the same time he was an unswerving supporter of the cause of the Savoy dynasty, whose divine mission, he thought, was to carry out the unification of Italy. Other great patriots, though they abhorred the violent and anti-Church ideas of Mazzini and Garibaldi, shared Calabiana's opinion. He was a strong-willed man, kind, but accustomed to command, and he knew how to exercise the authority given to him.

In 1848, Count Calabiana became a Senator of the Kingdom of Piedmont; thus, his career as a politician coincided with the actual beginning of the Italian struggle for unification. The overwhelming importance of the Risorgimento and

the ideas of nineteenth-century liberalism on the character
and development of Achille Ratti can be traced to his first
encounter with Calabiana, in 1867.

For his part, Don Damiano did not fail to call Archbishop
Calabiana's attention to his young and talented nephew,
whom the Archbishop also called "our little old man."

During that very year Calabiana became Archbishop of
Milan. At that time he was fifty-nine years old and, though
of a pragmatic bent, he was also a man of vision. That is to
say, he liked to make long-range plans. In 1867, Calabiana
had to wrestle with one of the most difficult tasks of his life.
The clergy in Lombardy were divided into two camps. On one
side were the so-called intransigents, who refused to cooper-
ate with the Savoy dynasty and its government because it
threatened the sovereignty and independence of the Papal
States. Furthermore, the intransigents refused to consider
any compromise or understanding with the new political
and liberal trends then sweeping Europe. The liberals
among the clergy, who were in the great majority—without
giving up any Catholic principle or minimizing ideological
difficulties—were of the opinion that sooner or later it would
be possible to reconcile the point of view of the Pope and the
Italian government. Their hope lay in the ultimate victory of
common sense. The two clerical groups fought each other
bitterly. *Osservatore Cattolico,* edited by Don Albertario,
was the organ of those who were strongly in favor of re-
establishing the Papal States. This militant Catholic newspaper, published in Milan, answered the attacks of the anti-
Church radicals and liberals in the most outspoken manner,
sometimes becoming as vitriolic and as intransigent as Garibaldi and his followers, sworn enemies of the Pope and the
Church.

On the opposite side, Archbishop Calabiana, who abhorred
both violence and bad taste, did his best to reduce the tensions between the two clerical groups because he knew that
the Church would need a balanced, harmonious priesthood

untorn by dissension. Don Damiano Ratti was one of the moderates who sided with the Archbishop. Calabiana was very fond of the Ratti family, precisely because of their sense of proportion about such matters. Their deep religiosity and patriotism were in perfect equilibrium, complementing each other.

As has been said, the Rattis had five children. It had been for centuries the custom in Europe to dedicate one member of a family to God. On the basis of his friendship with young Achille, the Archbishop, who undoubtedly perceived the future sacerdotal qualities latent in the boy, strongly suggested to him and to his family that he become a priest. And the simple village boy took the advice of his older friend.

Upon finishing his first schooling with Don Giuseppe, Achille Ratti entered the seminary after a final consultation between Don Damiano and his parents. According to the rules of the Church, young Ratti needed the affidavit of the local pastor before acceptance by the seminary. Pastor Don Rovida declared in his affidavit that the ten-year-old Achille was a boy of great intellect, persevering and industrious in his studies, and of excellent moral character. Thus armed, Achille Ratti entered the seminary of St. Peter the Martyr in Seveso in September 1867. And on December 7 of that year he donned ecclesiastical garments for the first time. To be dressed in the cassock did not necessarily mean that the young student would take holy orders; many did not complete the preliminary training and did not go on to a major seminary.

It was here in the Seveso Seminary on May 24, 1868, that Achille Ratti received his first Communion. As a student he more than lived up to the praise of Don Rovida. It was a custom at the seminary that the best students each year received a medal with the portrait of St. Charles Borromeo in bas relief on one side, and the inscription "Humilitas" on the reverse. Achille Ratti received his at the end of his first year.

Achille Ratti remained at Seveso for five years. Here he

received the first part of Italian higher education that is given in the *ginnasio*. He spent the next two years in the seminary at Monza, and completed the second part of Italian higher school education, called the *liceo*, at the College of San Carlo in Milan. This was followed by another three years in the great seminary of the archdiocese of Milan.

These long years of seclusion might give rise to the impression that the education of Achille Ratti and his fellow seminarians was an extremely isolated one. Yet no greater mistake could be made than to view these young seminarians as unhappy, isolated victims of a backward and joyless educational system. To be sure, they were subjected to a unified discipline, yet all were treated as individuals, according to the needs of their personalities. The schedule was rigid, but it served the purpose of imparting solid knowledge. The teachers were experts in their fields. In addition to the regular staff, there were special instructors. These were young priests, or older youths, seminarians themselves, who were heads of small groups into which the student body was divided. Each group became a kind of "family," with an authentic family spirit. The entire system was based on the pedagogical principles of St. Charles Borromeo, the great sixteenth-century Archbishop of Milan, who had laid down the rules for asceticism and study followed by the institutes that educated Achille Ratti.

The young Achille adjusted easily and amiably to strict but salutary routine. It would be another mistake to imagine that the young Ratti, whom his teachers and the Archbishop called "our little old man," was withdrawn or introverted. The excellent sportsman who later was to climb Monte Rosa and Mont Blanc got his training while in the seminary, where he excelled as a sprinter. Only once, at the age of fifteen, was he sick during his seminary years. He suddenly became pale and tired, that summer at home, alarming his mother, but the family doctor pointed out that the boy was entering adolescence, and that school strains were having an adverse physical effect on him. The doctor told Signora Ratti that her son was in good health, but needed more physical exercise, walks, and lots of fresh air.

Nothing could have been more welcome to the young Achille. He undertook a long-distance hike with other seminarists from the school and they visited famous shrines and holy places in the neighborhood. Sometimes they would hike sixty miles, visiting the important sanctuaries of Lombardy.

There were summers when the entire Ratti family went into the mountains on vacation. For Achille this was a welcome break in the routine of his studies. Though he liked to study, his days did not consist of study alone. In his leisure time he read many books which were the favorites of two continents. Among his favorite authors was Jules Verne, whose works he read avidly, literally absorbing them, so that he remembered even the remotest incidents in this early science-fiction. Another author whom he liked very much and reread often was Mark Twain. He identified himself so deeply with the problems of Mark Twain's Negro figures that his fellow students for a while called him *l'Africano,* "the African." Achille was particularly pleased, since at that time he expressed the hope that he would sometime be sent as a missionary to Africa.

It was during his seminary years that he became familiar with the great classics of Italian literature. He learned Dante's *Divine Comedy* by heart while vacationing with his family one summer in the mountains, and was equally well acquainted with Manzoni's works and could quote whole pages from them.

Achille Ratti's education in the seminary was a well-rounded one. He was also interested in music, for which he had a good voice and an excellent ear. He studied the cembalo and harmonium, the cembalo at the insistence of his mother and the harmonium because it could always be useful to a priest.

All the great qualities and characteristics of the future

scholar and scientist blossomed during his high-school years in the seminary. His mathematics teacher once asked him to solve a particularly difficult problem during the three-month summer vacation. Great was the teacher's surprise when young Achille solved not only that problem but all the other problems he found in the book. When asked why he had done this, Achille answered, "Just for fun."

Seminarians were not exempt from government examinations. An examination, which would be the equivalent of our college-board examination, was held before a committee of extreme anti-clerical persuasion. One of the professors questioned Ratti on a subject in botany that was not in the curriculum, hoping that he would fail. To the great embarrassment of the examiner, Ratti gave correct answers, talking for about half an hour, to the delight and wonderment of other members of the commission. What the examiners did not know was that again "for fun" the young Ratti had become a part-time assistant to one of the curators in the botanical museum in Milan. Because of his great curiosity about the natural sciences, the youth grasped every occasion to deepen his knowledge. This was how he also learned the elements of geology. His innate curiosity led him always to more and more research, not for the sake of research itself, but to find out what lay at the distant end of these sciences. Things that seemed remote had a great attraction for him.

Achille Ratti spent ten years in continuous study, away from his family and native village. All this time he lived in a community of other boys without too much privacy. They slept in dormitories, studied, ate, played and prayed—always as a group. He was always among the first of his class. The high school and the seminary provided him with a sound theological training and a basic knowledge of Western culture. His education was a sound mixture of humanistic and progressive education. It involved a thorough knowledge of Greek civilization, particularly of the Greek philosophers and classic authors. This was followed by a thorough study of

Latin literature and civilization, centering on Virgil and Horace. Seminaries at that time, following secular educational institutions, greatly stressed the natural sciences. Achille Ratti had an inclination for both classics and the natural sciences. He particularly excelled in mathematics and philology. And his accomplishments in Latin were so unusual that, upon finishing the prescribed courses for the high school and upon entering the theological seminary proper, he taught these two disciplines in one of the lower grades.

Achille Ratti was only twenty years of age when he ended his studies at the seminary. Thus, he was too young to be ordained. His professors did not want the talents of so excellent a young scholar to go to waste. Some suggested he study mathematics at the University of Turin; others, that he go to Rome and implement his studies of theology.

As reported by Archbishop Confalonieri in his recent book on Pius XI, Signora Ratti decided in favor of Rome. When she expressed her wish that her son go to Rome, she said jokingly: "To be sure, one might also become a Pope by studying mathematics, but theology is a more direct route."

CHAPTER TWO

The Formative Years

THE decision made, 20-year-old Achille Ratti was sent to Rome with great expectations on the part of all concerned. He enrolled in the Lombard College, founded by St. Charles Borromeo, which was under the jurisdiction of Archbishop Calabiana of Milan, who was delighted to see his protégé proceed to the eternal city. At that time there was already a railway connection between Milan and Rome, so Achille, who liked to travel and was fascinated by technical progress, arrived quickly and happily at his destination.

Achille had a robust, medium-sized figure, and thin blond hair. But his high, broad forehead and the eyeglasses he had begun to wear betrayed the scholar. Alert as he was, young Ratti gave no outward sign of the great intellectual and spiritual energies that stirred within him. There was a calm, almost philosophical, about his behavior, the calm of a healthy, physically strong, self-assured person. Achille was not at all loquacious; when he spoke the words came slowly, sometimes even with difficulty; not because words failed him, but because of his almost fanatic determination to be exact and precise. By this time, he already had acquired a great respect for the spoken and written word. Achille Ratti had the awe and reverence for the word that is the hallmark of poets. Anybody who might have interpreted his restrained behavior as a result of the wait-and-see attitude of a shrewd person or of one unsure of himself was disabused of this notion after a few minutes. Everything about the young theology student was genuine: his physical strength, his smile, his modesty of bearing, his inconspicuous piety, and his tremendous knowledge of literature, theology, mathematics, and the natural sciences.

The Lombard College, originally known as the Seminary of St. Ambrose and St. Charles Borromeo, was situated next to the Church of San Carlo Borromeo at the Corso. The Corso was, and in certain respects still is, the most important thoroughfare of Rome. Running in a north-south direction, it connects the Via Flaminia in the northern part of the city with the Via Appia that starts at the southern end. Until railway connections altered the traditional pattern of the flow of traffic to the city, most tourists, pilgrims, merchants and travelers entered Rome through the Porta del Popolo at the northern end of the Corso. Even though the railway linking Rome with northern Italy was already in existence, the Corso still preserved its great importance and glamor. In order to get to the center of the city, people had to pass before the Church of San Carlo, and this coming and going of the colorful *popolo* of Rome gave the street an exceptional attraction. Though lined on both sides with magnificent Renaissance palaces, the Corso was a rather narrow thoroughfare. Its side streets provided thrilling views of the remnants of medieval Rome; at its southern end the visitor came upon the Capitoline Hill from which he enjoyed a breath-taking glimpse of the Colosseum and the ancient city below him. During Achille Ratti's three-year stay in Rome, the expansion of the city northward and westward had not yet begun. These were the first years of Italian administration. It should not be forgotten that only eight years before Rome had been not only the capital of Christianity but the administrative center of the Papal States. The center of the city, around the Corso and the Colosseum, and also around St. Peter's Church, consisted of a conglomeration of buildings, with romantic exteriors and façades, not matched, however, by their interior appointments. This was also the case with most of the colleges and

institutes, the Lombard College being one of the few exceptions. The Milanese, though full of reverence for the papacy
and admiration for Rome's history, would not tolerate unhy-
gienic, disorderly living conditions.

Achille Ratti remained in Rome from 1879 to 1882, eventually graduating from the Gregorian University and the
Academy of St. Thomas Aquinas, after studies in law, theology and philosophy. There were about fifteen seminarians at
the Lombard College while he was there. These seminarians
had their own rooms and studied under dedicated instructors. But the actual courses were taken at the Gregorian University and at the newly established Academy of St. Thomas
Aquinas. The Gregorian University, founded by Gregory
XIII, is the most important institute of higher learning in
Rome. Originally, it developed from the Collegium Romanum
of the Jesuits and it increased in importance as an educational institution with the passing years. At first, only theology and philosophy were taught there. Under Pius IX,
canon law and history were added. Students who entered
the Gregorian University became, not only auditors, but participants, in the academic process from the first day of their
studies. They were obliged to discuss the subjects under
study with their fellow students and to participate in dispu-
tations with their professors—all this, by the way, in Latin.
The problems touched upon were not only theoretical, but
were often concerned with the application of canon law or
the pastoral duties of the priest. At the time of Achille Ratti's
enrollment there were 415 students at the university, 32 of
whom were studying law.[1]

Achille Ratti's three-year stay in Rome was marked by intellectual and spiritual growth. The years spent in the minor
and major seminaries of Milan had given him the kind of

[1] During the academic year 1921–22, when Achille Ratti became Pope, the
number of students in the Gregoriana was 995. In 1955 it was over 5,000.
For both 1879 and 1921, the comparatively low number was due to the
chaotic postwar situations in Europe.

education that befitted a young priest. The study and research in Rome not only broadened his education, but deep-
ened and transfigured the personality of the young priest.

The age in which he lived was an age of pioneering effort
everywhere. Seminal ideas represented by the greatest spirits
of the age were abroad and in headlong clash with traditional views and ways of thinking. It was Achille Ratti's good
fortune that he had teachers of such a caliber that they could
prepare him to engage in the struggles of his time with the
requisite intellectual and spiritual armament.

At the Gregorian University, Achille Ratti studied canon
law under the direction of the Jesuit priests, Sanguineti, Lu-
gari, Baldi, and Querini.

Fr. Sanguineti was one of the most important jurists of his
time and he became a consultant to the commission that set
up the Vatican Council. During its sessions he was one of the
theologians who acted as adviser to the Pope. Sanguineti had
started his career as an instructor in the North American
Seminary in Rome. Because of his knowledge of English, he
was sent for a while to Roehampton, England, where he
taught theology. This eminent jurist and international authority had a great influence upon Achille Ratti.

Although his studies in canon law were extremely important, it would be a mistake to consider Achille Ratti as a
jurist. They were important primarily because they familiar-
ized him in detail with the constitution and administrations
of the Church. Every period of human history has been
marked by some degree of friction between Church and state,
regardless of how well defined the tasks of both may have
been. In the latter decades of the nineteenth century the
state, though not totalitarian in today's sense, claimed an
ever-increasing number of prerogatives in the shaping and
direction of society. According to this philosophy of "stat-
ism," of Hegelian origin, the Church was considered useful
only if it furthered the aims of the lay state. Young Achille
Ratti knew from his own experience and from history itself

that Church interference in the tasks and functions of the state could be as harmful as well-intentioned state interference in the affairs of the Church. The lectures on canon law by Sanguineti served admirably to confirm and strengthen his own beliefs on this all-important matter.

Another of his teachers at the Gregoriana was Fr. Francis Xavier Wernz, a German Jesuit. Many authorities consider Wernz to have been the most eminent canonist of the late nineteenth century. His clarity, moderation and profound sense of law had made him, at the age of forty-four, the consultant of the important Congregation of the Council, Congregation of the Holy Office, and Congregation of Extraordinary Ecclesiastical Affairs. Later, he became a member of the commission appointed by Pius X to codify canon law. His *Jus decretalium*, on which he worked for sixteen years, became a classic among the commentaries on canon law. In 1906, Wernz became General of the Society of Jesus.

While Ratti's teachers at the Gregoriana were all Jesuits, he studied philosophy and theology at the Academy of St. Thomas. His teachers here were no less important. One, Francesco Satolli, was adviser to and collaborator with Pope Leo XIII in his effort to restore Thomism in Catholic schools. In 1892, Pope Leo XIII sent Satolli as his delegate to the World's Fair in Chicago. It was Satolli who convinced the Pope of the exceptional importance of American Catholicism. Pope Leo XIII appointed him the first Apostolic Delegate to the United States; he also lectured at the Catholic University in Washington, and his *Loyalty to Church and State* was published in 1895 in Baltimore. He became a Cardinal that year and returned to Rome. At the conclave of 1903 he played a very important role as one of the most important supporters of the election of Cardinal Sarto as Pope Pius X.

The beginning of Leo XIII's reign had been marked by the introduction of a new system for the education of priests, and a new approach to the study and propagation of Thomism in the schools. Up to the end of the nineteenth century the teaching of theology in seminaries and theological schools was directed and defined by the Jesuits. The philosophy of St. Thomas was taught, but often only in the revision of the great Spanish Jesuit, Suarez. During the preceding five centuries Aristotelian philosophy had almost been abandoned and theology taught on a somewhat eclectical basis.

After the great revival of Thomism in the twentieth century, several authors sought to trace historically the origins of this movement and of the revival itself. The first to throw a stone into the placid waters of eclectic theology was the Italian Jesuit, Fr. Vincenzo Buzzetti of Piacenza. In 1798 he was a seminarist in his native city. During one of the classes he felt that the teacher had inadequately refuted certain articles of Locke and the French-Italian Condillac, and he attributed this inadequacy to the failure of the teacher to employ St. Thomas's argumentation. Buzzetti decided to look more deeply into the matter. The result of his research and study was a work entitled *Institutiones sanae Philosophiae juxta Divi Thomae atque inconcussa Dogmata*, which remained in manuscript. When Buzzetti became a professor of philosophy he exerted a great influence on other Jesuits, so that he can be considered the father of neo-Thomism.

Fr. Liberatore, another teacher of young Ratti, became one of the founders of the authoritative *Civiltà Cattolica*, was a pupil of one of Buzzetti's students. Reading the history of the age, one is struck by how serious were the ideological contrasts among the professors of Catholic theology. Further, one is agreeably surprised at the freedom that was theirs in expressing their ideas. Since Achille Ratti was taught by just such teachers, it is fitting and also of interest to make some remarks on the general ambience in which they moved and had their being.

After the 1848 revolution, the Italian Jesuits felt the necessity of establishing a Catholic magazine that would communicate their religious and political and social ideas to a larger strata of intellectuals. Thus, *Civiltà Cattolica* was founded in Naples in 1849, its first issue appearing in April 1850. Fr. Liberatore, one of the founders, was not a Thomist at this time. The rest of the editorial staff was almost entirely composed of ardent Thomists. Four years later, Fr. Liberatore "surrendered" to the Thomists and fully and sincerely accepted their ideas. Thenceforth he declared that Catholic philosophy should make St. Thomas Aquinas its point of departure. Meanwhile, Fr. Liberatore studied Thomism more profoundly and revised his works accordingly.

The man who had the greatest influence on Liberatore was Fr. Seraphim Sordi. And he exerted an equal influence on another Jesuit, professor of philosophy at the seminary of Perugia, Fr. Joseph Pecci. Pecci also became a Thomist about 1850. His brother, Joachim Pecci, was then the Archbishop of Perugia. And in 1878 this Joachim Pecci became Pope Leo XIII, whose encyclical *Aeterni Patris* re-established Thomism as the basis of Catholic theology. Since Leo issued this encyclical less than a year after becoming Pope, it is clear that he was deeply convinced about the importance and future role of Thomism even before his election as Supreme Pontiff.

Salvator Talamo, another of Achille Ratti's teachers, became famous when, at the age of twenty, he published *Aristotelianism in Scholastic Philosophy*. In recognition of his great qualities, Leo XIII appointed him secretary of the St. Thomas Academy, a post he held for more than fifty years. Achille Ratti stood very close to Talamo, who was a man of vast erudition, open to the ideas of the modern world. He was particularly interested in social problems. Talamo was one of the founders of the *International Review of Social Studies* and remained its editor-in-chief for thirty-three years. The other founder of this review was Giuseppe Toniolo, whose activity revolutionized Catholic social thought and whose influence was largely responsible for the issuance by Leo XIII of the encyclical, *Rerum Novarum,* which was, and remains, the great answer of the Catholic Church to the crucial social questions of the modern world.

It is also of interest to note that Cardinal Mercier of Belgium, a great supporter of the candidacy of Achille Ratti at the conclave in 1922, was a pioneer Thomist like Leo XIII. After Leo XIII became Pope, he directed the Catholic University of Louvain, one of the most important institutes of the Catholic world, to establish a chair of Thomist philosophy. The Belgian Bishops, though agreed in principle, raised some objections on practical grounds. But Leo XIII threatened to send his own appointee, an Italian professor of philosophy. The Belgian Bishops appointed Abbé Desire Mercier to be "professor of philosophy according to St. Thomas Aquinas." In order to assure an adequate number of students for the course, the Bishops decided to make the course free, accessible to all, but compulsory for students of theology and for candidates for the degree of doctor of philosophy and those seeking degrees in the political sciences. Leo XIII knew how to put his convictions into practice without hesitation, and Achille Ratti, whose personality was similar to that of Leo XIII, acted the same way in comparable situations.

These were the years when, under the guidance of Leo XIII, Catholic social thought and philosophy were revitalized. These were the years that saw the formation and rise of Christian political parties. These were born out of the necessity of coping with the change of government systems that had occurred all over the world. Up to the middle of the nineteenth century, the Church had kings, princes and emperors—in other words, authoritarian rulers—as its allies or partners. An agreement made with a monarch or prince was valid, and no democratic process was required to approve or confirm it. With the emergence of democratic societies in which the fate of society and government was in the hands of parliaments and representative governments, Catholics were urged to enter the arena of politics; otherwise, they would run the risk that an ill-informed and an ill-disposed

majority might pass laws harmful to the freedom of the
Church and of themselves. This age was the age of revolutionary transition and painful adjustment for many long-es-
tablished institutions, including the Roman Catholic Church.

Fr. Antonio Stoppani, one of the representatives of the so-
called Catholic liberals, was a teacher of Achille Ratti. He
was a world-famous geologist and also an ardent supporter
of Antonio Serbati Rosmini, one of the greatest minds of
nineteenth-century Italy—priest, theologician, philosopher
and politician, whose name was synonymous with heated controversy over the entire peninsula. Stoppani wrote, among
others, three important works: *Geological and Paleontologi-
cal Studies of Lombardy;* the four-volume *Lombard Paleon-
tology,* which made him world-famous; and a populariza-
tion of geological and geographical facts about Italy, *Il Bel
Paese.* This last combined a description of the Italian soil and
landscape with an ardent patriotism.

Rosmini was the scion of an aristocratic family, a philosopher, an indefatigable organizer of works of charity, and an
Italian patriot, eager to bring about a reconciliation of the
controversies between the interests of the Holy See and the
Italian movement for unity. He undertook a mission on behalf
of King Carlo Alberto of Piedmont to Pius IX in 1848 and
was supposed to have exerted a great influence on the Pope.
His philosophical works were misinterpreted by some of his
followers and as a result some of his works were placed on
the Index. A later decree removed the prohibition, but, after
his death in 1887, forty of his theses were again condemned.

In those Catholic circles of Italy which were against a continued hostility with the Savoy dynasty, such decisions became a political issue. Such circles tried to make a hero out of
Rosmini on false grounds. During his lifetime Rosmini had
always obeyed the decisions of the Pope, and nothing was
more alien to him than hot-headed polemics. Rosmini's influence, however, continued to spread and at the present
time it is actually undergoing a revival because of his far-

sighted views on Church-State relations, and his understanding of secular society, as well as because of his works of charity.

Achille Ratti studied geology, botany, and zoology, too. He also spent many hours during his seminary years, and later as a young priest, at the municipal museum in Milan, of which Stoppani became director, not only studying with him but helping him in his tasks. They shared a love for science and enjoyed a common understanding with respect to questions of philosophy and national politics. Rosmini's influence on Ratti was, though indirect, greater than Ratti's contemporaries thought or imagined.

Even as Pope, Achille Ratti kept on his desk a Bible, *The Imitation of Christ*, a pocket edition of the *Divine Comedy*, Manzoni's collected works, and the poetry of an Italian priest-poet, Zanella, entirely unknown to the non-Italian world. Zanella's ideas appealed to the young Ratti more than anything else he read during the first thirty years of his life, except for Dante and Manzoni. Zanella was a Catholic priest, born in 1820. He had been an ardent patriot who, in one of his sermons in Vicenza in 1848, praised fervently the five-day upheaval in Milan, the stirring *cinque giornate*. Zanella, who was on excellent terms with the men who later created Italian unity, became rector of the University of Padua. His great influence on Achille Ratti lay in his approach to the questions of science and faith, questions which interested Achille Ratti most deeply throughout his life. The themes of Zanella's poetry are faith, patriotism and science. Science had opened a new view for humanity, said Zanella. He extolled the harmony of science and faith, refusing to accept the positivist assertion that faith and science cannot be reconciled. Zanella's famous ode "On a Fossil Shell" is considered his masterpiece; in it he speaks about the duties of man toward God in understanding that both material progress and faith come from God. Some titles of his poems give us even more insight into his spiritual and mental make-up: "Industry," "On the Opening of the Suez Canal," "Microcosmos and the Telescope," "Milton and Galileo." Alongside these poems are a filial homage "To the Madonna of Monte Berico" and a meditation "After Reading The Imitation of Christ."

The most important feature of the humanistic education of the late nineteenth century was not its transmittal of a great store of knowledge to the student, but the fact that this knowledge was integrated and harmonious. It was not sufficient, for example, to know mathematics; the student also had to know the life and times of the great mathematicians. Students learned an enormous amount of facts because they recognized the interrelations between them. History played a great part in the humanist curriculum.

This was something that Achille Ratti never regretted, because his broad views on history helped him later in life to act wisely and to respond to good and bad events as they occurred, with the equanimity that befitted one acquainted with the endless vicissitudes of history.

Curiously enough, Dante's *Divine Comedy* had a great appeal to Achille Ratti as a guide to the philosophy of history. Ratti began to read Dante when he was a young seminarist. Before he was twenty he had read all the works of Manzoni, not only *The Betrothed,* but the odes and his great *Observations on Catholic Morality.* Ratti read different authors for reasons as varied as the authors themselves. He admired Dante as one admires a genius whose height one is unable to reach. He read Thomas à Kempis for practical religious reasons. And he was enthusiastic over Zanella because Zanella expressed his own views. For Achille it was a joy to read someone who in some mysterious way articulated thoughts that were also his.

But Manzoni absorbed him totally. The special appeal of this great Italian writer lay in the fact that communicated a way of life and an atmosphere. To become a "Manzonian" meant that one used Manzoni's insight, phraseology, and approach to problems. In this sense Ratti became a "Manzonian," as he himself made clear to Fr. Gemelli, rector of the University of the Sacred Heart in Milan, another "Manzonian." Manzoni "and I understood each other always. Achille Ratti made it a point to read Manzoni before making any decision. Above all he read Manzoni before writing encyclicals and before receiving people in audience. For him, Manzoni was a practical guide in a world strange and sometimes hostile. Upon becoming Pope he relied more than ever upon the inspiration, strength and guidance—so rooted in Catholic sentiment and wisdom—that came from his readings of Manzoni."

Ratti was so fond of Manzoni that he would often read him aloud when alone, a habit he continued after he became Pope. One day his master of ceremonies, Msgr. Arborio Mella di Sant' Elia, entered the Pope's study. As required by ceremony, he knelt while awaiting the papal orders. But the Pope did not notice him. Pius XI was busy reading aloud—indeed, declaiming with gusto—a famous passage from Manzoni's *The Betrothed*. The monsignor remained on his knees for about twenty minutes before the Pope became aware of his presence. He apologized most profusely and then said with a smile: "These are pages that it is worth listening to on one's knees, Monsignor!"

After fifteen years of continuous study and semi-seclusion under the discipline of instructors, headmasters, rectors and the supervision inherent in student bodies themselves, Achille Ratti at last became something of his own master.

Achille Ratti was ordained in the Lateran Basilica, along with fifteen other seminarians, on December 20, 1879. His entire family participated in the festivities, including his uncle Damiano Ratti who helped place him on this path. He also received a congratulatory telegram from Archbishop Calabiana of Milan, that great patriot and Church leader whose ideas on the reconciliation between Church and state had left such indelible marks on the mind of his young admirer.

Although he had been ordained in the Lateran, Fr. Ratti celebrated his first Mass in the Church of San Carlo Borromeo, the church of the Lombards and the Milanese with which he felt a close kinship.

Few realize what the life of a Catholic priest means if he takes his vocation seriously. Fr. Achille Ratti took his vocation seriously, and with the grace of God and the help of his teachers he used his talents to the highest degree, ever training his mind, elevating his soul, and sharpening his wisdom and judgment. He took his vocation seriously in the sense that he was prepared to become a servant. He was also aware of the danger that every priest has to face. Each status in this life has inherent joys and dangers peculiar only to it. From the very start Achille Ratti knew that one of the greatest dangers besetting a priest was the human—all too human—weakness of identifying his own person with the dignity of the sacerdotal status, and thereby demanding or expecting respect for his own person rather than for the status. In his view, respect for the clergy should be spontaneous and directed toward the sacerdotal status and toward the man, the individual. He knew well that the quality of his own life as a servant of God would be the measure of how others would respond to the sacerdotal dignity of his office.

Achille Ratti, through study, meditation and discipline, had deliberately cultivated an authentic priestly mentality. He was determined to perfect himself as a priest for the exclusive benefit of the faithful; no ecclesiastical authority can force a priest to do this. It is an act of free will and the consequence of constant, unremitting spiritual exercise, and, of course, the grace of God.

One of the most important books Achille Ratti read daily, and with great spiritual satisfaction, was Vendrick's *Sacerdos devote celebrans SS. Missae Sacrificium*. This book, containing prayers for each day of the year, was a spiritual preparation for priests before the celebration of Mass. Another cherished volume was a small manual entitled *Regolamento di vita per un Sacerdote, allo scopo di mantenere il frutto dei santi esercizi* (*Suggestions for a Priest on How to Gain Much from Spiritual Exercises*). These were practical suggestions on virtues of the priestly life. A third daily reading was *Methodus meditandi et examinandi quotidie conscientiam* (*A Plan for Meditation and for Daily Examination of Conscience*).

In addition, Achille Ratti never neglected to recite three special prayers each day: one was for a good death; the other two were for his status as a priest.

Ratti's spiritual readings during his years in the seminary, the books that he perused daily as a priest, and his membership in pious associations gave a new spiritual dimension to his personality. These memberships and pious exercises were unknown until after his death. They were finally disclosed by Archbishop Carlo Confalonieri, who had been secretary to Cardinal Ratti and to the Pope for eighteen years. They throw a revealing light on the quality of his spirituality.

In his early youth Ratti joined several pious associations and kept the vows connected with the members until his death. In his early seminary days he became a member of the Archconfraternity of the Honor Guard of the Sacred Heart of Jesus. Ever since 1882, no matter where he found himself between five and six o'clock in the afternoon, he managed to retire and pray for this special purpose, because of a vow he had taken, a vow kept until his death. He also became a member of the Sacred League of Reparation to the Divine Heart of Jesus, which he entered in August 1883. Once a month the members of the League had to offer Mass for the intentions of the League. Achille Ratti's day was the fifteenth of each month, an obligation which he observed meticulously. Another pious association to which he belonged was the Angelic Militia of St. Thomas Aquinas, which he joined in Rome in 1881, most probably when he studied at the Academy of St. Thomas Aquinas.

In 1876 he became a member of the Third Order of the

Franciscans (according to the Capuchin rules), and eight years later, in 1884, he made his final vows as a tertiary.

At home and in the seminary Achille Ratti grew up in an atmosphere of devotion to the Blessed Virgin. Later, when Pope, his private chapel and private chambers were bedecked with images of Mary. His devotion was principally directed toward three Marian shrines: the Madonna of Lourdes, Maria Bambina of Milan, and the Virgin of Loreto. Since 1875 he had been a member of the Confraternity of the Sacred and Immaculate Heart of Mary for the Conversion of Sinners, associated with Loreto.

He was also a devoted son of the Madonnina and Maria Bambina of Milan. It is said that the citizens of Rome, in time of tension and distress, personal or public, used to console themselves by looking once a day toward the church of St. Peter to assure themselves that the "cupolone," the big dome of the basilica, was still there. Once reassured, they felt better because as long as St. Peter's remains intact the world of the Roman is endurable.

The people of Milan have a more personal relation to those celestial forces which becalm earthly mortals. The Milanese is wont to take "due passi," (a little walk) around the Cathedral ("Il Duomo") for a little chat "quattro chiacchere." Here he meets people walking leisurely about. The "Galleria" literally hums with excitement and animated discussion. Reassured that his friends are alive, and that life and business are going on as usual, the Milanese utters a thankful prayer while looking heavenward to the top of the Duomo where, amidst the hundreds of statues, there emerges, ever so much higher than the rest, the Madonnina. This is the statue of the Madonna whom the Milanese love and whom they address affectionately and familiarly as the *Little Madonna*.

The Cathedral of Milan, the Duomo, is a Marian church because it is dedicated to the infancy of Our Lady. The actual shrine of the child Madonna is in the Via Fatebenefratelli connected with a congregation of nuns dedicated to welfare work. The Madonnina, the *Little Madonna*, statue on top of the cathedral represents a young gentle-appearing Mary, looking toward the Alps. It was before her image that Achille Ratti, upon finishing his studies and preparing to depart for Rome, came to perform the ritualist *due passi* around the Piazza before the cathedral, and to look up for reassurance at the smiling Madonnina.

Achille Ratti received his final degrees in 1882, three years after his ordination, and there was a welcome surprise in store for him. He and one of his associates, Fr. Lualdi, who later became Archbishop of Palermo and a Cardinal, were received by Pope Leo XIII in private audience after their graduation. It was this great Pope who had founded the Academy of St. Thomas Aquinas to increase the influence of Thomism, and Achille Ratti and Lualdi were the first graduates.

At this audience Ratti and Lualdi were introduced to the Pope by one of their professors, and they were accompanied by a monsignor who served in the papal court and had become a friend of Ratti's because he, too, came from Lombardy. This monsignor had invited the two young priests to lunch with him in his apartment at the Vatican. During the luncheon a papal footman, in spectacular red uniform, appeared suddenly, bringing a box of nougat candy as a personal gift of the Pope to the newly ordained priests. It was characteristic of Leo XIII to make such a gift, just as it was characteristic of Ratti to take the empty box with him to the Vatican and keep it among his souvenirs. Upon his graduation he had received from his mother a gold ring with a blue precious stone. He also kept this ring for decades and separated himself from it only to give it, when he was Pope, to a newly graduated doctor who had been a good friend of his family.

CHAPTER THREE

A Priest and Citizen of Milan

AFTER Achille Ratti finished his studies in Rome the
Archbishop of Milan appointed him curate and vicar of the
little parish of Barni di Valassina. He remained there only
four months.

The parish of Barni is in the Valassina, near Asso, a region
that Ratti knew very well from his childhood. It was a wise
move on the part of the Bishop. The young priest was now
twenty-five years old. Regardless of the greatness of his talents, his first duty was to care for souls, and Barni was a
beautiful place in which to begin his pastoral duties. This territory, lying between the two branches of Lake Como, where
he knew every road and every mountain peak, had always
seemed to him an earthly paradise. It was far from the main
roads, almost cut off, like an island.

His duties here were exclusively spiritual. Archbishop Confalonieri mentions that not too many years ago there were
still people in Barni who remembered the sermons of Don
Achille. The people liked the fact that he talked to them,
even in his sermons, in *meneghino,* the local dialect. These
simple people praised their former curate very highly for his
simplicity and modesty, expressions that were true and sincere and had nothing to do with the fact that the curate later
became a Pope. Some of his former parishioners considered
him to be "another San Luigi." Ratti the priest must have
made these deep impressions, because, on another occasion,
some mountain people to whom he had preached while trav-

eling through their village had asked the Bishop to send them this "good priest"; after his appearance, they declared, "even we at last became human beings."

Achille Ratti was ready to stay right there, not out of obedience, but because he was a man and a priest whose soul rested in God. Here was the first occasion to realize his sacerdotal mission. He did not suspect that his superiors had other plans for him. Nor did his relatives or his mother at any time interfere with Archbishop Calabiana on his behalf. They were too religious and sensible to seek special favors for him. Besides, it was customary for a young priest to start in a rural parish, and, as far as Archbishop Calabiana was concerned, he energetically discouraged people from making recommendations on behalf of favorites. Calabiana acted only according to his conscience and in the light of his understanding of the needs of the Church. It was said that he had a "strong hand," and that he never tolerated his clergy seeking recommendations from anybody, particularly from politicians whom the Archbishop knew so well from his association with the liberal party. Later, as Archbishop of Milan and as Pope, Achille Ratti acted similarly.

After four brief months Ratti was brought in to Milan. He plunged fully into the maelstrom of life in a big city, where great and disturbing ideas were abroad, amid a thriving industrial and material progress. Some attention must now be given to the Milan and the Italy of this time.

Achille was ten years old when Garibaldi marched on Rome. Although at that age he could hardly appreciate the significance and importance of the event, he did hear talk, two years later, about the opening of the Vatican Council— the council that brought to Rome the Bishops of the whole world. Rome fell in 1870, marking the end of the Papal States, the end of the 1500-year-old temporal sovereignty of the Bishops of Rome. In that very same year the dogma of papal infallibility was proclaimed in Rome. Pius IX, in the midst of a rationalist liberal era, had stirred up an issue that scandal-

ized the world. Even some Catholics found it difficult to accept the dogma. Some could not forget that this was the same
Pius IX who just a few weeks before still had an army which
fought bloody battles, bringing death and destruction in their
wake. Now this man, as the Pope, declared himself to be infallible.

The subsequent years were to a large extent dominated
by the polemics, disputes and quarrels this pronouncement
engendered. The parliaments of Europe denounced the papacy as the arch-enemy of progress. Voltaire's star again rose
rapidly, and in his wake the fame of Karl Marx whose *Das
Kapital* had been published in 1867. Developments of the
ideas of Charles Darwin on human evolution had already
been spread throughout the intellectual world. Darwin,
whose *Origin of the Species* had been published in 1859, died
in 1882, the year in which Achille Ratti returned to Milan as
a young priest.

The world then seemed to be enamored only of its great
patriotic leaders who, in each and every country, fought military campaigns in the name of one main idea: liberal nationalism. It was Gambetta, the idol of the French masses, who
originated the slogan that united them all when in the French
parliament he cried out: *"Le clericalisme, voilà l'enemie!"*
(Clericalism is our enemy!) All Europe seemed to applaud
his outburst.

Like Calabiana, Don Ratti and most of his teachers were
considered "anti-clerical"—not in the Voltaire-Gambetta
sense of the word, to be sure, but in the sense in which the
entire Catholic Church in its essence is anti-clerical by its distinct separation of the secular from the spiritual power.

The dilemmas that faced Catholics, and particularly Italians, deserve not to be underestimated. E. E. Y. Hales says
rightly that Macaulay, in his essays on Ranke's *History of
the Popes*, designated the Enlightenment and the Revolution as the fourth and the most dangerous onslaught
launched, in all its long history, upon the Catholic Church.

It was Pio Nono's fate, after his original sympathy with liberalism, to be forced, though he was not by nature a fighter, to challenge and fight its pretensions. It was his glory that "he confronted the tempest without flinching, and was faithful to the end. He died a hero to his followers, but to the world a failure. Few thoughtful men, in 1900, considered that he might have been right. It was necessary then to find excuses for the famous *Syllabus*—better, even, to forget it. But today, when the world has come face to face with children and grandchildren of European liberalism and the mythic revolution, and has seen the gentle Mazzini turn into a Mussolini, and the idealistic Herder into a Hitler, and the early socialists into the intransigent communists, a new vantage ground emerges from which to consider once more whether Pius IX, or the optimistic believers in an infallible progress, like his cultured friend Pasolini, will have the better argument in the eyes of eternity."

When Achille Ratti returned to Milan he found a booming city, sowing the wild oats of capitalism, liberalism and socialism. It was a city where liberals, socialists and Catholics fought out great ideological battles at all levels. Yet there was no unity within any of these three distinct groups who also engaged in intramural quarrels on their own in the city of Milan, from which the Austrians had been driven less than twenty-five years before.

The fertile land of Lombardy between the Alps and the Po was for thousands of years the cause of wars and the much-desired goal of conquerors because of its wealth. Lombardy got its name from the Longobards who settled there in 568. They came from the regions around the lower Danube and Panonia, present-day western Hungary, followed by other Germanic tribes, in one of the great migrations of all time. Many were still pagan, but most of them embraced Arianism. For about 200 years the Longobards ruled this area. Then Charles the Frank subjugated them, but the Lombards never really made peace. Much later the Guelfs and Ghibel-

lines fought fierce battles in Lombardy, raging from village
to village, often house to house.

The meeting of mountain people and peoples who dwell
on the plain creates tension; different ways of life clash, and
finally merge into a type of man and culture that is a blend
of the formerly opposite elements. In this sense Lombardy
was the meeting ground of the European north and the European south, or, more precisely, of the Germanic and the
Italian. This contact exerted a great influence upon the various dialects of Lombardy, and upon the formation of a distinct
type of Italian. During the sixteenth century Lombardy became a part of the Hapsburg empire. This, of course, brought
in new elements from the west and east of Europe through
the soldiery stationed there. The Hapsburg domination
lasted more than two centuries. Then came Napoleon, who
created the Cisalpine Republic, which lasted for only twenty
years.

The fall of Napoleon left the people of Milan in a state of
indescribable excitement. During the French rule each city,
each province, had become a miniature republic, or they
had their kings or viceroys. But none of the Italian cities and
provinces went as far as the Cisalpine Republic created by
Napoleon. And this republic, during its twenty-year existence, saw the emergence of men of great spiritual and political qualities. It was during these twenty years of Napoleonic rule that the first glimmerings of the idea of national
unity sparked the imagination of the masses.

This was the situation when the troops of the Hapsburg
empire reoccupied Milan and the province of Lombardy in
1815. Some people in Milan—very few, indeed—greeted them
as liberators. The rural population, still remembering the lax
and benevolent Austrian rule of 1796, was friendly. But in
1815 Metternich was in the saddle; the benevolence of Joseph
II was no more.

The reactionary Vienna Congress which opened in 1815
did its best to liquidate the heritage of the French revolu-

tion and Napoleon. Those of the *ancien régime* who survived fancied that they would inaugurate a new golden age. The exhaustion following upon the Revolution and the Napoleonic wars helped to create an atmosphere of false security. Between 1815 and 1848 the European bourgeoisie, led by their Austrian and southern German counterparts, passionately dedicated themselves to a static, ultraconservative way of life. The armchair and the long-stemmed pipe were its symbolic reply to the dynamic frenzy of progressives and revolutionaries. The people, too, welcomed this way of life because it promised peace and tranquility. Yet this world was bound to fall apart. Its peace and calm were based upon the violent suppression of an idea, and the rulers knew this well. They had to protect themselves against the resurgence of this idea by an elaborate police system.

It is not surprising that most of the European secret police systems came into being after the Vienna Congress. The Austrian police in Milan seemed harmless at the beginning. By 1840, however, they worked with a huge staff, whose jobs ranged from opening letters to spying upon young lovers sitting in the park or strolling under the moonlight. The fact that these police systems made themselves ridiculous did not alter the effect on the population. But they were not always ridiculous. The ideas of the French Revolution were not wholly dead. Brutal and arbitrary police action evoked greater and greater reaction, eventually becoming active resistance.

The first manifestations of this movement found expression in literature. This was the birth of Italian romanticism. People became increasingly enthusiastic about those poets and writers who praised the sovereignty of sentiment. Milanese poets and writers like Ugo Foscolo, Carlo Porta, Tomaso Grossi, Silvio Pellico, Sismondi, and Manzoni above all, became the heroes of popular imagination. Many were thrown into jail for their ideas.

The greatest among them was Alessandro Manzoni, without whom, perhaps, there might not have been a modern Italy, either in a literary or in a political sense. Italy is the country *par excellence* where geniuses rise suddenly and then rule over the tastes of the country for generations, creating new styles in sensibility, thought and manners. In other countries the shifting of public opinion and taste takes place in a different and more intricate pattern. In Italy new ideas must first catch the fancy and emotion of the people. Manzoni's writing and his life expressed everything about the Risorgimento movement that made it appealing and desirable to the Italian people. The genius of Manzoni ruled over Milan from the very beginning of the Risorgimento up to World War I. The Manzonian spirit can be described as humanitarianism leavened by philosophy and an unbreakable and unfailing Christian faith, expressed in a literary style that illuminated and transfigured the realities, great and small, that it described. Manzoni was the great mediator between the European spirit and Italy in a measured harmony of expression that was peculiarly Italian. It speaks highly for the Risorgimento that it revered a man like Manzoni, who in time of injustice and brutality could speak in the tones and live in the spirit of justice, for whom forgiveness and compassion were great virtues.

The Austrian oppression which started with a routine police censorship, not taken too seriously by the Milanese, grew during the next two decades into a nightmarish persecution. From 1821 to 1848 Milan experienced all manner of oppression and the reaction this engendered: house searches, daily arrest of patriots, conspiracies, clandestine newspapers, secret societies, prisons literally overflowing with inmates, and the ever-busy gallows. It was the brutal rule of the *Soldatesca*, a regime based on sword and bayonet. There was no law, not even martial law.

In other parts of Italy the population reacted during these twenty years in a manner different from that which moved the Milanese. These were the years of preparation of Italian unity, and both the popular indignation and enthusiasm burst out in minor upheavals, the creation of provisional governments and partisan movements. The Milanese, no less Italian than the rest of the peninsula, were not easily given to emotionalism. The impact of the Austrian oppression can be measured in terms of the reaction of the phlegmatic Milanese, who took twenty years to act. When they did, their reaction was such that it rocked the very foundations of Austrian rule in Italy. In fact, the *cinque giornate,* the five-day revolution of March 18 to 22, 1848, was the beginning of the end for the Hapsburgs.

The repressed fury of the Milanese people had a greater impact than did the smaller conspiratorial uprisings. And it was the boundless fury of those persons who are usually quiet or who talk in understatement. Heine, the German poet, who had been in Milan just before the *cinque giornate,* felt the rising tension during a visit to the La Scala Opera House.

The troubles actually started in early 1847 and had religious connotations. Gaisruk, the Austrian Archbishop of Milan, died in 1846. The Austrian government—expressing the stubborn will of Metternich—insisted that his successor be of German origin. But Pope Pius IX, who was aware of the nationalist movement, appointed Msgr. Bartolomeo Romilli, an Italian. His entrance into Milan on September 8, 1847, was a triumphant tour amid cheering tens of thousands. The Austrian administration was irked and, though the crowd on the Piazza of the Duomo could do no harm to the police or to the authorities, it was asked to disperse before the Archbishop imparted his blessing from the steps of the cathedral. The crowd remained menacingly silent and did not budge. Without warning, the police then opened fire on the crowd and wounded sixty people. The tension constantly mounted, and on February 22, 1848, the Austrian government put Milan and Lombardy under martial law and a curfew. A few weeks later Metternich was dismissed as Chancellor of the Austrian empire and the people felt now was the time to act. Similar

developments took place in other countries of Europe: in
Paris, in Berlin, in Vienna and in Hungary.

The Milanese uprising started on March 17, 1848. The
Milanese took up the fight with one of the strongest and best
equipped military garrisons of Austria, and defeated it, one
might say, with bare hands. The "five days" marked the beginning of a national and ideological outbreak, chaotic in its
details, but well-organized so far in the determination of
individuals. Many pamphlets, leaflets and newspapers suddenly appeared. The Milanese had a program; they were
ready, in short, to fight for the unity of Italy.

It was a historical hour, for at the moment of the outbreak
in Milan and the defeat of the Austrians the Kingdom of
Piedmont was ready to take over the leadership of the fight
for Italian unity. But, when the Milanese realized that they
might have to exchange Austrian rule for that of the Piedmontese, their enthusiasm momentarily cooled. In addition,
Piedmont seemed to be under too much French influence.
The centuries-long division of Italy had not changed the basic
traits of the Italian character. The inhabitants of a little state
or even a city or village were *campanilists*—their only concern
the land around the belfry tower of the local church. The
Milanese realized that they had won against the Austrians
because they were united, because they were tough and were
able to set aside personal and party considerations. They recognized that the future of Italy's struggle for unity required
from them the same determination and non-partisan attitude.
Thus, they forgot about the "danger" of a Piedmontese rule
and a temporary government of Milan and Lombardy concluded an agreement with Carlo Alberto, King of Piedmont.
This paved the way to the final victory. It took another ten
years, and it required the help of Napoleon III and the
French army, to drive out the Austrians from Lombardy.

And twenty years from the outbreak of the "five days" had
to go by before the troops of Vittorio Emanuele and Garibaldi occupied Rome, completing the unification of Italy.

There were, of course, adversaries among their own people. A number of priests tried to convince the faithful that it would not be Manzoni, but Mazzini and Garibaldi, whose ideology would ultimately triumph. They pointed out that the latter were anti-Catholic freemasons and that their liberalism was directed against the Pope. But the self-confidence of the Italians, who distinguished between secular and ecclesiastical interests, gave them an assurance that the righteousness of their actions did not depend upon the nature or reputation of their allies. Either their cause was just and in accordance with natural and divine law, or it was not. The motivations of their allies could not change the rightness of their cause. Other churchmen agreed with the aims of the revolution and with the cause of Italian unity. They backed Carlo Alberto and his successors in their fight for unity, and at the same time they opposed them when they sought to carry out an ideological program tainted with Voltairianism and basically directed against the Church.

To understand the dilemma of the Italian who wanted to be a Catholic and a nationalist, and at the same time to understand fully the genius of persons like Manzoni who found the right solution to this problem, one must know not only the patriotic aspect of Italy's Risorgimento, but its ideological and religious attitudes. Freemasonry, which the people called *la marianna*, inspired by the anti-clerical and anti-religious directives of the French lodges, was quite active. The first article of the new Italian constitution recognized that Catholicism was the official religion of the state and that other religions were to be tolerated. In practice, however, the situation was quite different. It was the Catholic Church which was subjected to odious vexations, often ridiculous, while minority religious groups received special favors. For instance, the largest religious minority was that of the Valdese church, with 21,000 communicants. This group received money to launch a widespread propaganda campaign, and in a short time it was able to build new churches in Turin.

Further, its priests were exempted from military service, while for the Catholics only one priest out of 20,000 was liable to such exemption. In 1861 all cemeteries were removed from ecclesiastical jurisdiction. Priests and bishops were hindered in exercising their ministry. The Bishop of Mondovi, for example, was sent to prison for three months because he read the *Syllabus* from the pulpit. Many such instances could be cited to show that the new state was intent upon secularizing Italian life and imposing anti-Church and anti-religious laws and practices. It was not the free church in a free state that had been hoped for by those advocating the separation of Church and state. The state was free, but no freedom was given to the Church.

Subsequently, religious orders were suppressed; their houses, rents, and properties confiscated and sold at auction. Monasteries and convents were transformed into prisons, and sometimes into schools. Many churches were converted to profane use. As far as financial support was concerned, nuns received one lira and former monks one lira and twenty-five centesimi for their daily subsistence.

The Church was in a grave situation. This was the time when Bishop Luigi Calabiana of Casale advanced a proposal on behalf of the episcopate of Lombardy and Piedmont. He suggested that the government withdraw its anti-Church laws and at the same time suspend payments to the clergy. The episcopate would obligate itself to pay the pastors and the curates. Bishop Calabiana's proposal was not accepted, and the anti-Church laws of 1855 became effective.

After 1859 this anti-clerical legislation was extended to other territories as they were occupied by the forces of the national revolution. Like Piedmont, the rest of Italy became hostile to the Church in the legislative, judiciary and executive branches of government. One can imagine the dismay and desperation of millions of faithful who had not expected such anti-Church measures from the new leaders. These masses were sincerely patriotic and genuinely in favor of unification, but at the same time they were faithful to the Church. The vexations and irritations did not stop. In 1866, *Osservatore Cattolico* suspended publication of the names, even of the smallest donor, of those who gave money for the Pope, lest the police question and harry them. In 1869, other religious circles became the target and were attacked—even the so-called *Santommasini*, members of philosophical groups dedicated to the study of Aquinas, were assaulted and beaten. Religious processions were disturbed or dispersed; the Eucharist was violated (in Bologna in 1873); statues of the Blessed Virgin were stoned; even Good Friday was profaned. Catholics were prevented from visiting the tomb of St. Francis; masses of the faithful who went in silent pilgrimage to the shrines in Assisi and Loreto were dispersed by violence, by the police or infantry using drawn bayonets.

Garibaldi in these years wrote: "No freedom should be given to assassins, gangsters, wolves and their companions; are not priests more harmful to our country than wolves and assassins?" Gavazzi, another leader of the Risorgimento, told an audience in Leghorn in 1873 that Pius IX was a crowned reptile.

In 1875, the government refused to allow thirty-three Italian Bishops to take possession of their sees, because they had not presented their credentials to the government. That same year the government and the anti-clerical forces gave orders to organize hundreds of meetings under the motto: "Extirpate the cancer of Italy." By this they meant the papacy and the Catholic religion. In 1878, a few days after the death of Pius IX, during a violent manifestation in Leghorn, Abignente, a member of the radical party, demanded that the Catholic religion be destroyed immediately and with one stroke.

It was a deplorable state of affairs, because it did not stop with demonstrations. Officials and private citizens were protected by the law while destroying ecclesiastical monuments, breaking into monasteries, convents, parish buildings, reli-

gious institutes and libraries for purposes of plunder and rap-
ine. At the end of 1887, Prime Minister Crispi suggested that
the confiscated patrimony of religious institutions be legal-
ized. The value of this confiscated patrimony amounted to
about 100 million lire and was composed of hostelries for pilgrims, retreat houses, hermits' dwellings, as well as trust
funds and foundations.

Direct interference in everyday life meanwhile continued:
one day it was the prohibition of processions outside church
grounds. Cardinal Ferrari, Archbishop of Milan, during his
twenty-six years of office, was not allowed to organize any
Eucharistic processions, not even during the National Eucharistic Congress at Milan. Processions were allowed in the
villages, but not in the cities. The government and municipal
authorities felt that any religious procession would "dese-
crate" the clean, liberal streets of the city. On another day
an organized campaign would be waged against the law of
guarantees, assuming the most violent forms. The insults did
not stop at the parish rectories and the blasphemous made
no distinction between rich and poor. Bartolo Longo was the
simplest, poorest country peasant south of Naples, yet he was
brutally beaten because he started to build a sanctuary for
the Madonna at Pompei—now one of the greatest shrines of
Italy.

In 1881 a mob attempted to throw the coffin holding the
body of Pius IX into the Tiber. Pius IX had died in 1878
and had requested in his will that he be buried in the Basilica of San Lorenzo, about two miles from the Vatican. He
was first laid to rest in one of the niches in St. Peter's Basilica,
because the tense atmosphere existing between the Holy See
and Italy did not permit the transfer of the body before 1881.
At that time it was decided to move the Pope's remains to
San Lorenzo under a fitting and proper escort. As the funeral
procession arrived at the bridge over the Tiber facing Castel
Sant' Angelo, it was attacked by a small group of anti-Catholic desperadoes, who had planned to seize the coffin and

throw it into the river. In the ensuing battle eight persons were killed. The coffin was rescued, but it had to be rushed to the Church of San Lorenzo without further ceremony. Garibaldi wrote the following: "The celebration of the Sicilian Vespers offered the Italian democracy the precious occasion of demanding the destruction of the shrewdest of all tyrants, the corrupter of peoples, the patriarch of the lie who is located at the right bank of the Tiber." He meant the Pope.

Typical of the climate of the government and certain circles was the celebration of Voltaire's centenary. In 1882, almost every large Italian city seemed to vie with the others to see which would provide the greatest celebration for the centenary and which would be more insulting to the Church and its representatives. At the celebration in Rome representatives of the king, the government and the parliament applauded the anti-religious speeches and the recital of poems in praise of Satan. Satan was the hero in celebrations in Genoa, in Brescia and in Milan.

By 1898 the increasing industrialization of Milan and the Lombardy created a new industrial-worker class that was not yet organized and did not receive adequate protection. European unionism, until the present day, was a product of ideological battles fought out along classical Marxist class-warfare lines. In 1898 it created the first social revolt in Italy, fomented by both socialists and anarchists. The government was forced to act against the socialists.

The action of the government was preceded by violent discussions within the liberal groups. The outcome of the discussion was an agreement that not only the socialists, but the Catholics, had to be "annihilated." For this reason the government delivered blows against the socialists, the republicans, and the so-called clericals; it suppressed their newspapers, closed their associations and circles, dispersed their membership, and arrested their leaders. It was the execution of Garibaldi's "suggestion" that Catholicism be destroyed in one stroke.

It is true that, after 1898, Italian Catholics fought valiantly against the anti-Catholic legislation and atmosphere. Nevertheless, the fundamental conflict remained. The government and the liberal bourgeoisie wanted to eliminate the Catholic tradition and give the country a new concept and image of authority. It wanted not only the separation of Church and state, but it also wanted to endow the state with a new mystical meaning. In short, it wanted a state without God.

In 1878 Leo XIII, an aristocrat, succeeded Pius IX. With Leo began the reassertion of Catholic spiritual, moral and intellectual power that was to rally the disheartened and scattered forces of the faith against the rising might of the armies of materialism. Deprived of all natural resources, ignored by nearly all governments, and strongly opposed by the most powerful among them, Leo XIII at once began to speak as one having legitimate authority, not only to the peoples directly under his spiritual jurisdiction, but to the entire world. On the very day of his election in 1878 Leo notified Germany and Russia of his ascent to the papal throne and expressed the hope of re-establishing relations with them. Russia sent the more cordial reply, but both governments were noncommittal. The world gave slight attention at first to this voice that so calmly but powerfully now spoke from the "prison" of the Vatican.

Leo's voice soon compelled attention; his utterances began to produce their effect. Bismarck speedily found that he was unable to govern without Catholic support. He began his pilgrimage to Canossa that very year. Several of the most odious of the Prussian laws against the Church were relaxed. The Center Party, the Catholic political bloc formed because of necessity, won battle after battle at the polls. By 1883 Bishops were being appointed by Rome to various long-vacant German sees. And in the following year diplomatic relations with the Vatican were resumed. Three years later state and Church in Germany composed the main points of their quarrel. In 1882, Bismarck even proposed Leo as arbitrator in the dispute over the Caroline Islands.

Yet Germany was but one item in the score of problems which confronted Leo, such as the ups and downs of the struggle in Russia, with its effects in Poland and other countries bordering on the Czar's dominions. In 1879, after the attempt on Alexander's life, Leo held out hands of friendship to the Czar. When Alexander III ascended the throne in 1883, a temporary agreement was reached. A few episcopal sees were tolerated and the more stringent laws against the Catholic clergy were slightly relaxed.

The great storm brewing in France did not break in its full force until after Leo had passed from the scene. He remained on good terms with the government of France through his entire pontificate, despite manifestations of the spirit of opposition to the Church. Leo called on all French Catholics to accept the republic. The powerful monarchical party would not pay heed. But Leo's wisdom was greater than theirs, and his policy was to stand the Church in good stead in later years.

In Belgium, also, there were storms over educational questions leading to the breaking off of relations between the Vatican and the Belgian government in 1880. But in 1885 the new Catholic government restored diplomatic relations. In Italy, Leo maintained the attitude of protest forced upon Pius IX with regard to the Kingdom of Italy and its usurpation of Rome, and the seizure of the property of the Church. He desired the complete independence of the Holy See and its restoration as a real sovereignty. He upheld the prohibition against Italian Catholics taking part in political elections, in the hope that the government would be obliged to come to terms.

Cursory mention should be made of Leo's activities in connection with the Church in other countries. In England, for example, where the hierarchy had been reconstituted by Pius IX in 1850, there were such important events as the elevation of John Henry Newman to the cardinalate. There was the investigation of the crucial problem of the validity of Anglican orders, and the decision confirmed by the Pope that Anglican orders were null and void. There was the restoration of the Scottish hierarchy in 1878. Ten years later, the hierarchy was established in British India. In Ireland, in 1879, there began the gradual recognition of Catholic rights in the field of education. The passing of the Intermediate Education Act, which appropriated money for prizes, exhibitions and the like, irrespective of creed, was a decided step in favor of the Church, since the state had previously given no assistance whatever to Catholic education. In 1888, there was a message to the Bishops of Brazil on the abolition of slavery. The following year, the first Plenary Council of the Church of Latin America was held in Rome. Leo's activities covered the entire world.

Such was the general situation when Achille Ratti became Professor of Sacred Eloquence and Theology at the Grand Seminary of Milan at the age of twenty-five. Teaching was not an unfamiliar job for him, since he had given courses in mathematics and theology during the last two years of his seminary studies. But now he was a full-fledged member of the faculty.

A teacher of rhetoric selects and comments on appropriate passages, as examples to follow, from the great sermons and speeches of all time in literature and history. Ratti was admirably fitted for such a task and his students still praise his impeccable taste in selecting these examples. In teaching Christian oratory he first acquainted his pupils with the lives and personalities of the orators of a given school, then he selected one for special study. The class would read the text of the sermons of one orator for weeks. Several passages had to be memorized. After all important members of a given school were considered, he would point out the salient similarities or dissimilarities of the school and place it within its specific historical context. He was known as *il dotto parla-*

tore, the learned lecturer—high praise for a young professor. Former students recall that his speeches were terse and thoughtful, interspersed with striking images already showing the literary qualities of the encyclicals to come.

Achille Ratti, like the Milanese and Lombards in general, was not loquacious. Yet he could hardly be classified as being silent and withdrawn. He expressed his opinions only after careful consideration, and tended to conceal his emotions if such emotions were purely personal. Ratti was fond of silence and meditation. He would urge his students to withdraw often into solitude as a way of strengthening their concentration and will and of deepening their knowledge, temporal and spiritual, of the world. As a teacher he stressed rigorous methodical training. He abhorred generalizations, a characteristic that remained with him through life. He never gave broad, general surveys of the subject under study before analyzing it in great detail. Only after every possible avenue of approach to the subject was exhausted, sometimes after several months of work, did he permit himself to sum it up and place it in a general context.

Fr. Ottavio Marchetti, who was a pupil of Achille Ratti in the seminary, has thus described his teacher:

"The courses of the professor of eloquence were few during the scholastic year, because he had only one hour each week. Several times, however, for some reason or other, even this one hour was omitted. The lessons of Professor Ratti were perhaps not brilliant and sparkling, but were full of original and congenial observations, and often accompanied by quotations from Italian and foreign authors. The latter were translated fluently and at first sight by the professor himself from the original language.

"One could say that Ratti, the learned professor of eloquence, himself was not very eloquent. The slowness of his speech and the continuous self-corrections in order to find the right word to express in a more perfect way his thoughts broke the free and uninhibited flow of his lecture and made us think that he had difficulties in expressing himself. But, once we overcame our first impressions, his sermons proved attractive because they were always most original."

The center of his pastoral activity was the convent of the Sisters of the Cenacle. This religious congregation was entirely dedicated to works of charity. Fr. Ratti first became its spiritual director and celebrated his daily Mass at the convent. He showed particular interest in and concern over all the people, especially the children, who came to the convent for aid. In 1883, one year after his arrival in Milan, Fr. Ratti founded an association for Catholic women teachers. Since the Convent of the Last Supper was also the center of a women's Marian congregation, he was asked to give the sermons during the May devotions. In later years he organized pilgrimages to neighboring Marian shrines, especially to the Sacro Monte of Varese, twenty-five miles north of Milan, close to the Swiss border. This ancient Marian shrine is one of the most important in Italy, and its history is closely connected with the Christianization of Lombardy.

Achille Ratti took a great interest in helping Catholics whose mother tongue was German. He spoke fluent German, in addition to French, to which later he added Spanish and English. But since Lombardy is the meeting place between the Germanic and the Italian worlds in Europe, the German language had a considerable importance. Ratti had learned German while in the seminary and he had a chance to improve his knowledge of it by his student trips to Switzerland. Such student exchanges were customary between the seminaries in upper Italy and in Switzerland. Toward the end of his seminary studies he knew German so well that Don Ambrogio Amelli, a learned Benedictine monk who was responsible for the restoration of the Gregorian chant in Italy, gave him several German essays and two or three books to be translated into Italian.

In Milan, thanks to his knowledge of German, he became the German confessor at the cathedral. Later, he became the spiritual adviser and leader of the German colony in the capital of Lombardy.

At the time of Fr. Ratti's activity in the 1880's there was no organized pastoral work for Germans or for any other nationality. He was especially touched by the situation of German servant girls in the city, numbering two hundred, whom he organized into two groups. One group met in the sacristy of the cathedral, the other in the church of San Sepulchro, where they had occasion to meet socially as a group and to make their confessions in their native language.

Ratti realized that these German domestics needed a sort of club where they could relax and feel completely at home. Within a year his efforts in this direction were crowned with success. A congregation of Italian nuns, at the urging of the young priest, provided the girls with two rooms for this purpose. And three years later the German domestics of Milan had their own *heim*, run by German nuns.

At the same time Fr. Ratti ministered to German Catholic children, to whom he gave religious instruction in the sacristy of the church nearest their home, preparing them for their first Communion. Such an activity required great love and patience since most of the children belonged to poor families, and spoke neither German nor Italian fluently.

In 1898, when the German population of Milan grew to several thousand, not counting the Swiss who resided in the city for business reasons, Achille Ratti's work load and reputation increased simultaneously. At that time he gave the Lenten sermons three times weekly in German. Many Italians who were familiar with German went to hear Mass here and to listen to the young priest about whom so much was being heard.

In addition, Fr. Ratti was deeply interested in the welfare of the youth in and around Milan. He gathered the chimney-sweep apprentices, most of whom came from the neighboring city of Bergamo, gave them religious instruction every Sunday, and also prepared them for Holy Communion. One of these youngsters, who later became a prominent member of the Catholic *Partito Popolare*, wrote the following about his former pastor:

"I remember Monsignor Ratti very well, since I am one of the youngsters he instructed. He would celebrate Mass for us in the little chapel of the Sisters of the Last Supper. Not only did chimney-sweep apprentices come to this Mass, but others, too, who heard about Fr. Ratti. There was no religious instruction in the Italian schools at that time and we certainly were not angels during classes. In fact, we were always bent upon mischief. But Fr. Ratti never became the stern disciplinarian. Instead, he talked to us kindly, without the slightest condescension. He took us seriously. He liked to teach us as we strolled with him in the garden of the Sisters. I still remember the day he explained the mystery of the Eucharist to us."

If it be borne in mind that Ratti began his pastoral work in 1882, which he then continued for twenty-nine years, it comes as no surprise that Achille Ratti, as Pope Pius XI, was so familiar with the practical questions concerning the relationship between the priest and the faithful. In his view, the priest's dignity should be rooted in the spontaneous respect, lovingly given to him by the faithful. "We are not rulers, we are servants," he declared.

In a society which looked upon a priest with suspicion because it feared that he might "rule" minds and thus halt progress Achille Ratti was a welcome figure.

It soon became known that the young professor at the archdiocese and the seminary, in addition to being an educator, was also an indefatigable research worker. He had a passion for detail, and collaborated in the preparation of two scientific works. This is how Achille Ratti came to the attention of the directors of the Ambrosiana Library. The prefect of the Ambrosiana, Msgr. Ceriani, needed a young and promising scholar to work under him. Achille Ratti was the perfect choice, and it was Ceriani who invited him to join the library staff in 1888.

The Ambrosiana Library is one of the great spiritual monuments of Italian and Christian scholarship. It was founded by Cardinal Federigo Borromeo on December 8, 1609. "Federigo Borromeo," wrote Manzoni, "was one of those rare men —whatever the age in which they live—who used their great talents, their entire wealth and the advantages of their privileged status as noblemen or aristocrats untiringly to seek and to realize the best for the benefit of the community." It had been Federigo Borromeo's idea to lay the foundation for a library for scholars and writers. For this purpose he sent emissaries to countries all over Europe, the Middle East, and even farther, in search of books and manuscripts. Achille Ratti was especially fond of Federigo Borromeo's observation that "One should live two lives: one at daylight for one's daily business; the second at night for one's studies. Only such people who love solitude can do this." It is remarkable how the description of Federigo Borromeo's character fits Achille Ratti's. One of the biographers of Cardinal Federigo says that he had a very lively personality, and was emotional, yet not given to sudden outbursts. He had a very delicate soul and was easily offended, sometimes even melancholy, but he made an effort to control his emotions and he succeeded in doing so. He lived in serenity of spirit and studies and in contemplation and communion with God.

The Ambrosiana Library, at the time of Achille Ratti's assignment there, consisted of 250,000 books and 15,000 manuscripts; it also contained an important gallery of pictures and statues. The manuscripts included the correspondence of St. Charles Borromeo, fragments of a Homeric codex from the third century, a fragment of a manuscript of Virgil, many letters of Leonardo da Vinci. The art gallery had several pictures by Raphael, Titian, Botticelli, Leonardo and others. The Ambrosiana was not strictly a Church institution, and enjoyed considerable independence because the original funds had been set aside for the library specifically and were not to be used for anything else. The administration of the Ambrosiana was in the hands of members of the Borromeo family and representatives of the Archbishop and the chapter of the cathedral and of the parish priests of the city. Immediately, it was run by a *collegio dei dottori*, presided over by a prefect or director of the institute. Fr. Ratti became one of the *dottori*.

Achille Ratti's background and degrees exceeded by far the requirements for becoming a librarian. He knew Latin and Greek; his French was almost as good as his Italian; he knew German and could read and converse in English. At the time he was twenty-five years old he undertook his first research project dealing with the origin of man, which appeared in a book on theology written by one of his colleagues in the Milan seminary, Don Federigo Sali. Prior to this work, Ratti had collaborated in writing a chapter of a book dealing with volcanic phenomena in Italy. He was asked to do the research on the history of earthquakes, a task that required a knowledge of history as well as familiarity with the problems of geology.

Cardinal Tisserant has described the future Pope's career as a librarian: "As a student in the theological seminary, Don Achille Ratti had been in charge of the reading room (1877) and was accustomed to help his fellow students, who, more than likely, were provided with very poor notions of bibliography. He considered that his chief task as assistant librarian of the Ambrosiana was to assist visitors in their research involving manuscripts or rare books. He tried to know the resources of the library as completely as possible. Since he had an excellent memory, he succeeded so well that many years later, when he was Pope, he remembered titles with their locations in the Ambrosiana. He preferred not to specialize too much. For many years he was only one of the assistant librarians, and, like his colleagues, he spent most of his time in the preparation of publications. The director of the Ambrosiana inclined more and more to leave the contacts of readers and the care of the material organization to him."

Thus, while Ratti prepared the publication of scholarly books, he also found time to reorganize the Ambrosiana. He arranged that the floor in the rooms above the library should no longer be used as living quarters, thus diminishing the risk of fire in so old a building, which had been a cause of concern. Then he rearranged the painting gallery and the Museo Settala, a private seventeenth-century collection. He also wrote a descriptive article on the Ambrosiana Library for the official guide to Italian libraries, as well as a 160-page guidebook to the library for the general public, which was published anonymously.

The Ambrosiana scholars were obliged to publish the results of their research. The older type of librarian was primarily a researcher servicing scholars. The modern librarian does this in some measure, but he is more of a technician. Ratti can be said to have been a blend of the old and new. Thus, Ratti participated in the publication of two monumental works. One was the publication of the sources of the Milanese church, *Acta Ecclesiae Mediolanensis*, four volumes containing documents from the first to the eighteenth century. The other was a liturgico-historical work, *Missale Ambrosianum Duplex*, a commentary on the Milanese Missal.

The Milan archdiocese, although it belongs to the Western patriarchate, has kept its own rite as established by St. Ambrose. This rite was greatly influenced by the Byzantines, because Ravenna, one-time center of the Byzantine emperors, is only one hundred miles distant from Milan.

In 1910, at the three-hundredth anniversary of the canonization of St. Charles Borromeo, Ratti helped to produce the memorial *St. Charles Borromeo and the Third Centenary of His Canonization*. Most of the historical articles in this volume were written by him.

Ratti was also a frequent contributor to the historical archives of Lombardy and to the Lombardy Institute of

Science and Literature, both secular institutions. These contributions are of interest. One describes Milan in the year 1266, giving the names of more than 2,000 citizens of that period. Another is an essay on an important Lombardy poet of the thirteenth century, Bonvesin da Riva.

Ratti showed a great interest in the Renaissance Pope, Aeneas Silvius Piccolimini, called Pius II, and published forty-two of his original letters.

Drawing on his knowledge of Greek and Latin, he also published the fragments of the so-called Milan *Ilias* and the satirical poems of Juvenal.

But all these writings were only secondary to the real scholarly aim of his life—to learn as much as possible about the *Liber diurnus*, the oldest known register of the papal chancery. It had been started in the eighth century and for a long time it was used daily. Because it contains all kinds of documents issued by the papal chancery, the *Liber diurnus* is one of the most important sources of papal history and that of the Roman curia. Unfortunately, Ratti was unable to complete this task, and he discontinued his researches in 1911. However, he maintained a continued interest in this work and assisted in its publication.

It is quite impossible to list the entire literary output of Achille Ratti, both before and after his election as Pope. The most detailed list has been made by Msgr. Galbiati, Ratti's successor as prefect of the Ambrosiana. Galbiati's book contains information on Ratti's works published up to the time of his election. Yet not even this list is complete, because he wrote many articles in magazines under pen names, or anonymously. As Pope, he made many extemporaneous speeches, and all of them were not reported in *Osservatore Romano* in their entirety. All in all, one could say that he published more than one hundred books, long essays and articles up to 1921.

After nineteen years at the Ambrosiana, in 1907 when Msgr.

Pope Pius IX (1846–1878)

Pope Leo XIII (1878–1903)

Pope St. Pius X (1903–1914)

Pope Benedict XV (1914–1922)

The four predecessors of Pope Pius XI. He was born during the pontificate of Pope Pius IX, became a priest during Pope Leo XIII's reign, was appointed prefect of the Vatican Library by Pope St. Pius X, and became cardinal under Pope Benedict XV.

Achille Ratti in 1888, when he became Doctor of the Ambrosiana Library in Milan.

MILANO - CORTILE DELL'AMBROSIANA
E ABSIDE DI SAN SEPOLCRO

The courtyard of the Ambrosiana Library, Milan. Achille Ratti worked
at the Ambrosiana Library from 1888 to 1912.

Milano - Pinacoteca Ambrosiana - Esedra Superiore

Entrance to the Art Gallery of the Ambrosiana.

Achille Ratti (third from the left) on the Rothorn glacier in Switzerland, August 31, 1897.

The Breithorn (over 12,000 feet) in the French-Italian Alps, which Achille Ratti climbed.

Achille Ratti leads the Corpus Christi procession in Warsaw in May 1918.

Achille Ratti, newly appointed archbishop and cardinal, arrives in Milan and is escorted by civil authorities from the railway station to his palace. May 1921.

Achille Cardinal Ratti inaugurates the Catholic University in Milan, 1921.

Partial view of the Catholic University of Milan.

Achille Ratti, shortly after he became cardinal, in discussion with two experts of the "Vulgata" in Rome. June 1921.

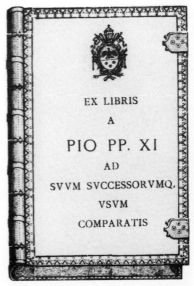

Ex Libris of Pius XI.

Pius XI in the first year of his pontificate, 1922.

Ceriani died, Ratti was the most obvious choice to succeed him and was appointed *prefetto*.

At this time Achille Ratti lived at 26 Via Moneta, which belonged to the Ambrosiana Library. He received 1,200 lire a year as salary, and free lodging. Ratti rarely entertained in his apartment. His time was divided between his work at the Ambrosiana, his pastoral duties at the Sisters of the Last Supper, and the diocesan seminary where he taught history. Ratti never used a carriage, always walking from the Ambrosiana to the seminary or to the convent. Respected by everyone who knew him in Milan, Ratti lived, looked and behaved just as any ordinary citizen.

When Achille Ratti became director of the Ambrosiana his mother organized his household. She sent him her housekeeper,[1] who stayed with him during all his years at the Ambrosiana and later when he worked in the Vatican Library.

His contact with the intellectuals of Milan and his unbiased attitude did not mean that he shared the opinion of a narrow-minded, anti-religious bourgeoisie that did not believe in anything. In the religious realm there still raged the old quarrel between the intransigents and liberals, and in the world of philosophy the Thomists and followers of Rosmini —whose works were again condemned—disputed endlessly. Partisanship seemed a more important issue than truth itself, even among fair-minded, balanced people. In such an atmosphere so-called progressive liberals considered every priest an evil reactionary. On the other hand, religious persons considered progressive liberals as the minions of Satan. Amid all this rancor, bitterness and bigotry, Ratti seemed to be an exception. One of his contemporaries, Theodor Moneta, a dis-

[1] From 1922 to 1926 this woman, Signora Banfi, was also the housekeeper in the papal household until Pius XI reorganized it by commissioning the Franciscan Tertiaries of the Holy Cross to take over all papal household duties. This is a religious congregation of German origin whose members remain lay brothers. They serve as waiters, housekeepers, nurses, etc. Their hostel, Villa San Francesco, in Rome is one of the most famous and best run hotels for ecclesiastics.

tinguished Milanese layman, once declared: "All these priests are full of anger, even Albertario and Stoppani— But wait a minute. I have to correct myself. All but one: Ratti."

The story of the conversion of Eduardo Gemelli, a young doctor who later became a Franciscan and an intimate friend of Pius XI, dramatically highlights the spirit of these times. Eduardo Gemelli was twenty-five years old in 1903, and already an established psychologist and physician, as well as an ardent Marxian socialist and a violent, intolerant, anticlerical. The violent articles he wrote as an editor of the socialist weekly aroused indignation in ecclesiastical circles. He was arrested several times by the police, who, though anticlerical themselves, could not let this young man go too far in insulting the local Archbishop. Suddenly, however, Gemelli started to see the light as the result of the influence of a pious and God-fearing friend of his. Unknown to anybody, he then began to take religious instruction and spiritual counsel from a member of the Ambrosiana Library. Suddenly, he disappeared from Milan.

Two or three weeks after his disappearance, Gemelli wrote to his father that he had decided to become a priest, and that to achieve this aim he had entered the Franciscan monastery at Pavia, near Milan. Eduardo Gemelli's conversion was one of the greatest "scandals" of the time in Milan. Both his parents belonged to the wealthy and "enlightened" bourgeoisie for whom religion was nothing but superstition, the Pope the great inquisitor, and members of religious orders— particularly the Franciscans—low, cunning folk whose only aim was to stultify people's minds in order to dominate them. Now their gifted son, once so "progressive," wanted to become a member of this hated and despised crowd.

Gemelli's father immediately had the newspapers publish the letter, while in a separate statement he accused the Franciscans and the Archbishop of misleading, even of kidnaping, his son. The press in Milan, with the exception of *Corriere della Sera*, launched a campaign against the Church, the priests and the Franciscans for "turning the head" of the successful ex-socialist.

These press attacks culminated in an unprecedented move. Gemelli's father expressed the wish to visit his son in the monastery. The Franciscan priests gave permission. The father and his son had a long conversation. The son was adamant, so the father began to take his leave coldly. Young Gemelli accompanied him to his carriage which was waiting in front of the monastery. The Superior followed, a few steps behind. When both Gemellis got close enough to the carriage, two men jumped out, and with the help of the father grabbed young Gemelli and tried to force him into the carriage. The Superior and the monks rescued the new brother only after a long and severe tug-of-war.

This irresponsible assault on the freedom of conscience of his own son on the part of Signor Gemelli was also reported in the press. Editorial comments and letters to the editors were divided on the question of whether or not the elder Gemelli was justified in his attempt to kidnap his own son.

In the midst of an atmosphere that generated more heat than light, Ratti was indeed a welcome exception. It was refreshing to come upon a man who did not judge people according to their ideological affiliations, but according to their inner values. He maintained contact in all social circles, regardless of how their members stood politically or otherwise. He had many friends among the aristocracy and among the bourgeoisie, most of whom did not belong to the camp of the intransigents, whose aim was to force the new Italian state "to go to Canossa." In turn, everybody liked Ratti, especially those who knew about his scholarly achievements. This is why, despite the anti-religious atmosphere, Ratti became a member of many secular scientific and learned institutions. He was elected member of the Royal Lombard Institute of Science and Letters, the Royal Italian Historical Society, and to the Commission of the City of Milan which was responsible for all historical archives of the city. In addition, he was a member of the Italian government's royal delegation in charge of historical research in upper Italy, and after 1905 a member of the examining board for the School of Paleography and the School of Archivists. Upon his election as Pope in 1922, the Royal Lombard Institute of Science and Letters was somewhat "embarrassed," because no member of the Society had ever been elected Pope. After long discussion it decided to request that Pius XI remain an honorary member, an honor that Pius XI gladly accepted. But the librarians in far-off Iowa acted more quickly. They sent a congratulatory message: *"Unus ex nobis factus est Papa"* (One of us has become Pope).

It would be a great mistake to conclude that Achille Ratti was "tolerant." He was more than tolerant, in the routine, liberal sense of the word. His open-mindedness was something greater, rooted in a deep understanding, which did not always imply approval of the manifold possibilities of human deportment. For example, when the Royal Lombard Institute of Science and Letters, once an ecclesiastical foundation, which later became secular and even tainted with anticlericalism, elected Achille Ratti to membership, he was asked to deliver the customary eulogy on the defunct member to whose place he had been elected. This was a very delicate task, because the defunct member had been passionately anti-Catholic. Ratti did not make the slightest reference to the ideological convictions of his predecessor. Instead, he praised the man and recalled his good deeds—and they were many—on behalf of his fellow men.

The appreciation that Achille Ratti's objective intellectual stand found in the controversy-ridden city of Milan can be inferred from the fact that in 1898 he was entrusted by the Italian government to reorganize the library in the Carthusian monastery in Pavia which was under the supervision of the state. The Italian government, at that time, was anything but friendly to ecclesiastics, and there were certainly many Italian lay librarians available for such a task. And in 1906 the government made him a "Cavalier" for his reorganization of the Ambrosiana.

Scholarly interests and activity never caused Achille Ratti to deviate from his constant aim of improving his pastoral activity. It was for this reason that he joined the Oblates of St. Charles Borromeo, an association of priests founded by St. Charles in 1581. At the time he joined it had only 200 members. Members of this Oblate association swore to accede to the request of the Bishop to undertake any kind of pastoral, educational, or charitable work, including missionary work, within the diocese, in addition to their regular tasks. By coincidence, the Ambrosiana Library, from its founding in 1609, was entrusted to the Oblates, who, during the first fifty years, traveled to distant parts of the world to locate and purchase ancient Armenian, Syrian, Hebrew and Chaldean manuscripts.

At the time Ratti entered the Oblates, the association did not meet the requirements of modern life. He was instrumental in reorganizing it, assisting Cardinal Ferrari in the revision of the statutes endorsed by Pope Pius X in 1905. But he had joined the Oblates primarily to obtain the spiritual benefits inherent in such a priestly association. Constant contact with like-minded priests and participation in religious retreats were important sources of spiritual strength and stimulation. His thoughts about spiritual exercises were expressed in an article, "St. Charles and the Spiritual Exercises according to St. Ignatius." In it he recalled that St. Charles had founded a retreat house in Milan and had entrusted the Jesuits with its direction. St. Charles himself preferred the Ignatian form of religious exercises. Ratti summarized this method as follows: "The spiritual exercises of St. Ignatius do not consist of any teaching, but, rather, of a series of practical suggestions based upon experience of a delicate mind and spirit." Ratti preserved his high opinion of the methods of the Jesuits. Upon becoming Pope, he entrusted them with some of his most important projects.

On September 4, 1905, Achille Ratti celebrated the twenty-fifth anniversary of his ordination. He celebrated it in the company of many of his former colleagues in the beautiful setting of the Sacro Monte di Varese. There he gave an address, "Modern Culture, Science and Faith." The following excerpt is of interest because it summarizes much of his future policy:

"The twenty-five years that have passed since our ordination have not been ordinary years. Africa and Asia, the North and South Poles, the highest mountain peaks, have been forced to reveal their secrets. Humanity can now imagine how many square miles are available for its expansion. Human life unfolds itself in a manner truly gigantic in new roads, underground passages and above the clouds. Luxury trains speed through landscapes where yesterday there was naught but virgin forest or deserts of sand and snow. The miracles and terrors of an overwhelming culture come face to face with the crude expressions of primitive life. Babylon and Susa, Troy and Olympia, the archives of all civilized peoples and of the Vatican at the pinnacle, have unveiled their limitless treasures of the past, to enable us to rewrite the history of mankind and of the Church, in honor of God and of His anointed.

"Such and such great things have we seen occur before our eyes, that you, together with me, express gratitude to Divine Providence which has deigned to allow us to live and experience the greatness of progress. For, despite the misuse or the faults, we can perceive in this development the upward move toward truth, toward happiness, that is, toward God."

Our concern with his intellectual and pastoral activity should not allow us to overlook one of his activities that played a central role in his life, and for which he was famous; namely, his mountain climbing. This, too, was part of his spiritual life. As a child he saw the blue ridge of the Alps from Desio, or from other localities of his beloved Brianza, only from a distance. The closest was about twenty or twenty-five miles. Desio lay on the flatland and there was no tradition of mountaineering in his family. At the time of his birth, sports were not popular. Yet, his father was a nature-lover; he enjoyed taking long walks in the blossoming fields and meadows. And Ratti's interest in Alpinism can be traced back to these walks with his father, and his old teacher Don Giuseppe, and the talk about the mountains that loomed above them in the distance like a challenge.

Italian Alpinism was at its beginning during the second part of the nineteenth century, and Achille Ratti became one of the first members of the Club Alpino Italiano, joining its Milan chapter. Despite the infancy of Italian Alpinism, the Club Alpino admitted only experienced Alpinists as members. Achille Ratti met this qualification. His first mountain-climbing attempts were made in the neighborhood of Asso, in the Valassina region between the Como and the Lecco branches of Lake Como. He climbed Monte San Primo (over 5,000 feet high), and, later, Monte Resegone in the neighborhood of Lecco, a site particularly dear to Don Achille because some of the action in Manzoni's novel takes place in those pre-Alpine peaks rimming Lake Como.

Later, he started to negotiate the peaks of the real Alps, preparing his every ascent with the greatest care. He was familiar with almost every arete and crevasse, since he had studied detailed military maps of the area. He even studied the history of the mishaps that had occurred on other ascents, in order to avoid repeating the same mistakes. Ratti said once that real Alpinism is not just a walk up a hill, but a question of prudence, courage and endurance, all combined with a reverent feeling for nature and its beauties.

In a period of twenty years he made a hundred Alpine ascents, all above the 8,000-foot level. Among these were Monte Rosa, Monviso, the Grand Paradiso, the Cervino (or Matterhorn), the famous Marmolada, queen of the Alpine peaks, and the highest mountain peak in Europe—Mont Blanc.

Ratti never went mountain climbing alone. His constant
companion in his wanderings was the Milanese priest Berto
Grasselli, a teacher at the seminary. Equipped with anaroids,
rucksacks and their breviaries, they would take a train to the
climbing area a day before the actual start of the climb, sleeping overnight in a village at the foot of their goal. They always started their climb before dawn.

Their adventures very often began in the afternoon as
they walked through woodland no higher than 3,000 or 4,000
feet. The rocky part of the mountain would be reached
around evening. Ratti and his companion were bold but cau-
tious when they clambered up the barren land of the giant
peaks. They would reach the Alpine refuge about seven or
eight o'clock in the evening. There they would pray, and
after their devotions sleep on wooden benches, wrapped in
blankets. The real climb began at two or three o'clock in
the morning.

Achille Ratti was the first to traverse a new path, starting
from the Italian side in the locality of Macugnaga, over the
Zumstein of Monte Rosa on the Swiss side. He undertook
the venture to conquer this mountain, 13,000 feet high, in the
company of Prof. Grasselli and two local guides, Gadin and
Proment.

To understand the importance of this feat and the enormous difficulties it involved, some remarks on Monte Rosa
are pertinent. Toward the east, Monte Rosa looks like a giant
fortress wall with four battlements. There are four peaks: Sig-
nalkuppe, Dufour, Zumstein and Nordend. From the Swiss
side Monte Rosa appears beautiful and alluring. But from
the Italian side, particularly from the great plain of the Lombardy, "one does not know whether the Monte Rosa invites
or challenges you," to use the words of mountain-climber
Ratti. He planned this expedition very carefully, the prepara-
tions alone taking three weeks. On July 29, 1889, he and Grasselli arrived in Macugnaga around noon. Their first act was

to visit the little church and the pastor of this Alpine village. Then they took lodgings in the ancient inn.

After a two-hour rest they followed the known and fairly comfortable mountain path up to the Marinelli refuge, built on one of the rocks that cuts into the glacier like a dike. They cooked their extract of meat in snow water to make a strong bouillon. Here is an excerpt from the report that Ratti wrote for the magazine of the Italian Alpine Club: "The silence was solemn. The infinite stars glittered most vividly against the deep, almost velvet blue of the sky: I felt the overwhelming power of the towering mass of mountains and peaks, the movement of giant shadows upon the white surface of the snow and ice."

It was with this impression that the Alpinists lay down to sleep. At one o'clock they arose, lit their two lanterns, and proceeded immediately toward the famous and feared Marinelli Corridor, where three years before three persons had been killed instantly by a sudden avalanche. The four were roped together: first, Gadin, one of the guides; second, Achille Ratti; third, Proment, the other guide; and last, Grasselli.

The glacial corridor was at this time full of deep furrows and crevices and covered with ice, making the hike difficult and tiring. It took them about an hour to reach the glacier, which was covered with a very thin layer of snow, so Gadin and Ratti had to cut steps into the ice. Hours and hours went by as they zig-zagged their perilous way upward. About noon they were close to the end of the glacier, and the first rocks of the Dufour side of Monte Rosa looked as if they were within reach of their hands. This was but an optical illusion that so often occurs at great heights. "Up there," Ratti wrote, "everything is out of proportion; the mountain masses which surround you and the distances which separate them from each other, both the general outlines of the landscape and its details. This does not mean that the relation of measures of space and volume cease to exist, but they are concealed in the harmony of the whole as in the really great works of hu-

man art. Take, for instance, the Church of St. Peter which
does not disclose its real proportions immediately to the
viewer. So is it with structures of God, the primal artist of all
beauty."

The rest of the climb was no less difficult; the snow drifts
became deeper, and when they finally reached snowless
rocks, Prof. Grasselli skidded and lost his ice pick. At seven-
thirty in the evening they reached the immediate path to the
eastern peak of Monte Rosa. It took them a full hour to climb
up the peak and then to descend to their last station because
a storm was brewing. The little island rock at the end of the
glacier was not wide enough for the four of them to lie down
on. So they were forced to stand up all night at an altitude
of 13,800 feet. Sleep was impossible; their coffee froze, the
hard-boiled eggs burst. They fed on some chocolate, however. During the long hours of the night the climbers were
constantly exposed to the danger of avalanches—they were
expecting one and they actually witnessed the beginning of
an avalanche below them. Its initial slow rumble grew into
deafening thunder lasting several minutes. When morning
came, the quartet, sleepless and tired but elated by the sight
of the triumphantly rising sun, ascended the highest peak still
before them and around noon they started down the mountain into Swiss territory.

During one of his mountain-climbing expeditions with
Msgr. Grasselli they arrived one Saturday at the little village
of San Rhemy in the valley of the great San Bernard. It was
the eve of the Assumption, and for some reason there was no
priest in the village. For many months the villagers had been
unable to participate in the sacrifice of the Mass or to take
the sacraments. It was a very poor village and its inhabitants
felt that everybody had abandoned them, including the
Church authorities who failed to send them a new pastor.
Nevertheless, each Sunday they gathered in the church and
sang and prayed together. The villagers asked the priests
whether they would say Mass and preach the sermon. Achille

Ratti, of course, consented. To him this was certainly more important than mountain climbing. He celebrated Mass and mounted the pulpit. The *dottore* of the Ambrosiana, philosopher, historian, and great intellectual, spoke slowly, simply, to these simple villagers. At the end of his sermon the peasants gathered around the two priests and asked them to stay on forever. In fact, a commission was sent to Milan to invite them formally!

Alpinism and mountains were more than physical exercise for Ratti. It was a spiritual ascent in the highest sense of the word. Atop the peaks he felt truly uplifted, prepared to conquer the highest and most difficult tasks in life that would be assigned to him.

It has been mentioned that as a seminarian he became a member of several pious associations. In two of them he obligated himself to perpetual adoration of the Sacred Heart of Jesus. When, in 1899, Leo XIII expressed the wish to consecrate the twentieth century, looming on the horizon, to the Sacred Heart, Achille Ratti warmly welcomed this idea of the Pope's. He decided to share in it in his own characteristic way. He organized a night mountain-climbing party to the crater of Vesuvius. When the little group arrived at the summit, the Italian sky was divided in two—a dawn phenomena peculiar to Naples. Toward the west the sky was dark, but the stars shone brightly. The smoke of the volcano was wafted by gentle breezes from east to west. The eastern part of the sky became slowly radiant. This was the dawn of the twentieth century. The group knelt and prayed there in silence for more than an hour. Don Achille said they prayed surrounded by a "glorious triumph of beauty."

During his frequent trips he encountered not only mountain villages without a priest, but villages whose priests were cut off from contact with the world—simple parish priests who lived in poverty, sacrificing themselves to the needs of their flock. Ratti remembered them, and whenever he could, after becoming Pope, he sent them help. In 1925 he canonized St.

John Vianney, the famous Curé of Ars, one of the greatest
figures of the nineteenth century, who lived in just such a
remote mountain village with a population of unbelievers
whom he gradually converted. When Pius XI canonized the
Curé of Ars, he invited the priests of the entire Italian, French
and Alpine dioceses to attend the ceremony. The selection
of the priests was at the discretion of the respective bishops,
but the expenses of their travel and stay in Rome were borne
by the Pope. Pius XI received them in a special audience
and greeted them most affectionately.

There were many other occasions when the Pope referred
to his mountain-climbing experience. In 1929, for instance,
talking to a pilgrimage from Milan composed of university
professors and students, he discussed strenuous negotiations
that finally led to the conclusion of the Lateran Treaty. And
he said, with a smile: "One needed perhaps an Alpinist Pope
to solve the Roman question; an Alpinist who was immune
to vertigo and was accustomed to facing the most arduous
ascents." This time he was not speaking figuratively, but from
actual experience.

That same year he received a pilgrimage of mountain
guides. He told them that in the natural order he had never
seen the greatness of God better documented than up in the
mountains. And he told the story of a young Alpine guide
who, after his first great exploit, arrived at the summit and
exclaimed spontaneously: "One is moved to pray here!" He
then proclaimed St. Bernard of Menton as the patron saint of
Alpinists. Later, Pius XI instituted a new ritual in the *Rituale
Romano,* a ceremony for the blessing of all the instruments
and tools that are necessary *"ad montes conscendendos"*—to
mountain climbing.

In 1911, Fr. Ehrle, director of the Vatican Library and a
great German Jesuit scholar (whom Pius XI later elevated
to Cardinal), expressed a wish to retire and dedicate himself
to scientific work. The Vatican began looking around for a
successor. When asked to suggest a successor, Fr. Ehrle de-

clared: "There is only one man who could do the job—Achille
Ratti, prefect of the Ambrosiana." But the Ambrosiana
needed Achille Ratti, too.

There were some difficulties to overcome. Achille Ratti was
bound to the Ambrosiana by a contract and its supervisory
board had no reason to release so excellent a librarian. The
problem was finally solved by permitting Ratti to act as dep-
uty librarian of the Vatican, while remaining prefect of the
Ambrosiana.

Ratti literally became a commuter between Milan and
Rome. Rome is 400 miles from Milan and in those days trans-
portation was not so rapid as now, to say nothing about the
smoke, dust and dirt of the trains which were not yet elec-
trified. The journey was quite strenuous and took almost an
entire day, yet Ratti made the trip twice a month.

Pope Pius X welcomed the suggestion to appoint Ratti
to the Vatican Library, for the Pope knew him. Their first
encounter was a memorable one between two truly saintly
priests. It had taken place toward the end of the nineteenth
century. Pius X, at that time Msgr. Giuseppe Sarto, was
Bishop of Mantua. One morning, presumably very early,
someone knocked at the door of the Bishop's residence. His
household was managed by his three sisters, as simple-man-
nered and good-hearted as the Monsignor himself. This
morning, however, for some reason the Bishop himself opened
the door and greeted an ecclesiastic who introduced himself as Dottore Ratti, prefect of the Ambrosiana. Ratti had
come to the Bishop for permission to do some research
work in the archives of the episcopal chapter. Monsignor
Sarto invited his early-morning visitor to stay for a cup of
coffee and, without waiting for an answer, went toward the
kitchen to prepare it. Ratti tried to dissuade the Bishop, im-
ploring him not to trouble himself. Sarto, however, assured
him that he would enjoy making it better if somebody helped
him drink it. The Bishop spoke in the Venetian dialect—Ratti
in a mixture of *meneghino* and Venetian. Then both sat down

in the kitchen and sipped their morning coffee, while talking of sundry matters, and specifically of the research Ratti was doing.

Pius X always found Ratti likeable, so, when Fr. Ehrle's proposal came, he welcomed it heartily. Thus, in 1914, after Fr. Ehrle's complete retirement, Ratti became prefect of the Vatican Library, but he had already taken quarters in Rome two years earlier.

Achille Ratti was a new type of librarian and a new type of scientific researcher, imbued as he was with the ideas of his time. The nineteenth century cultivated an almost adoring attitude toward science. Although Achille Ratti did not share the blind faith of those who expected from science the solutions to all problems, he was convinced that science is given by God to be used by man. His education and his contacts with the intellectuals of Milan and Europe now began to bear fruit. Each year he traveled to all the great centers of learning in Europe: Vienna, Munich, Berlin, Paris, Budapest, Riga, Warsaw, Freiburg, Oxford, London, and other places. He studied the library systems in these cities and talked with many scientists.

Cardinal Tisserant, who was attached to the Vatican Library at the time Achille Ratti became its prefect, gave an interesting account of Ratti as librarian: "He resolved to begin at once the work on a main catalog of all the Vatican printed books. Those of the attendants who had tolerable calligraphy and were careful in their transcriptions were invited to give extra work for copying on cards the entries in the ancient catalogs. The effort was not conceived as a definitive one, because the original entries were too lacking in uniformity, but to have all the titles in one card catalog would have been a decidedly great advancement.

"Unfortunately, the period of the war was not a propitious time for the undertaking; the men were anxious to procure food for their families and some of them had found more remunerative work outside the library. However, the prefect did not lose courage and after obtaining permission from the Pope, on December 15, 1917, to turn over the library court-yard to the staff members of the lower grades for the cultivation of vegetables for their families, he asked, on February 10, 1918, that the copyists, in order to accelerate the work, be allowed to carry home every evening some of the ancient catalogs."[2]

When Fr. Tisserant, as a French citizen, was called to arms and had to leave Rome, he wrote: "After that date I received post cards or letters almost every month which kept me informed regarding my colleagues and the life of the library. The librarian of the Vatican was very human!"

Cardinal Tisserant evalued the work of Achille Ratti in relation to the Vatican Library as follows: "The great objective for which Pius XI as librarian had worked was not forgotten. The old, untrained personnel had been replaced by hard-working catalogers who attacked the stock of uncataloged books with gratifying results. In the beginning of 1926 a very favorable circumstance arose—the Carnegie Endowment for International Peace indicated that it was ready to assist the Vatican Library to give more efficient service to the public, quite properly considering the library an important international center, where representatives of many nations meet. The idea had its inception in a chat between the late Prince Gelasio Caetani (then the Italian ambassador in Washington) and Mr. Samuel H. Church. After a thorough discussion of the problem by the trustees, Mr. Henry S. Pritchett arrived in Rome and was received on May 10, 1926, by the Pope, to whom Mr. Pritchett made the proposal to assist in the preparation of a main catalog of the printed books. The Pope thought over and accepted the offer. Next year, on March 12, when there was under construction a room for the catalog and catalogers—the first special room for any department or officer, except that of the secretary and disbursing officer—there arrived, as consulting library expert of the Carnegie En-

[2] *Library Quarterly*, Oct. 1939.

dowment, Dr. William W. Bishop. Since the primary problem concerned the printed books, Dr. Bishop began, on March 14, with an examination of the printed collections. The trustees, however, had given to him very broad instructions and, with the agreement of the Vatican authorities, he soon extended his inquiry to the other services of the library, including manuscripts and incunabula. Pius XI, who had been informed the day before by Msgr. Mercati of all the technical problems considered, received Dr. Bishop on March 30, and on the morning of April 2 accepted as a first measure the invitation to send one of the officers of the library to visit American libraries. On Palm Sunday, April 10, the Pope received me, and in twenty-five minutes gave me his instructions and counsels, both general and technical. . . . There followed, on my return from the visit to the United States and Canada, his approval, in the main, of a scheme of organization corresponding to the probable increase of the collections and services during a long period, say, of fifty years."

As head of the Vatican Library, Ratti remained objective and as helpful as ever during the war, of service to belligerents and neutrals alike. He did as much as he could to catalog the printed books of the Vaticana and sponsored essential projects to save the manuscripts. In 1907 he accompanied Fr. Ehrle to the International Conference of Librarians held in St. Gall, Switzerland. Here he learned how to repair paper manuscripts corroded by ink. Since this involved the weaving of a special kind of silk, he promptly asked the operators of the family mill, still working in Desio, to prepare the necessary thin silk tissue needed for the repair of the many volumes of corroded manuscripts. This was an example of how scholarship and practical sense always complemented each other in Achille Ratti.

Pope Benedict XV recognized the great qualities of the head of the Vatican Library. There is every reason to believe that the Pope, who had a sharp eye for the abilities and characters of men, kept Achille Ratti in mind as someone whom the Holy See could use for other and more important tasks. On October 28, 1914, Achille Ratti received the title of Protonotary Apostolic. The life he now led for the next four years was a quiet one, marked by hard work. But his days were well organized and he had many occasions to meet other officials of the Vatican since he now belonged to the Pope's official family. Then suddenly in 1918 Msgr. Ratti was thrown into the chaotic world of international politics.

CHAPTER FOUR

The Crucial Task

OUTWARDLY, nothing could be more surprising, indeed confounding, than the appointment of Achille Ratti as Apostolic Visitor to Poland, Lithuania, Latvia, Estonia, Finland and, later, to Russia. Why was this scholar removed from the calm of the Vatican Library and from the way of life that had been his for so long? Many people were mystified as to why Benedict XV selected this quiet Milanese. But it was no mystery to those who knew Ratti's exceptional ability to lead and influence others. And many persons in the Vatican knew this. There were many people who would like to have seen Ratti in a post more responsible than those he held in the Vaticana or the Ambrosiana, because of his abilities to make responsible decisions and to lead. Such opportunities did not come until his sixty-first year. Nobody knew that even during his seemingly drab years at the Ambrosiana Library in Milan Ratti had been very much interested in political questions. Cardinal Ferrari of Milan and other important leaders of the Church consulted Ratti regularly because of his sharp judgment and ability to make quick decisions. Ratti solved many knotty political problems which were put before him by ecclesiastical authorities in Milan. Public opinion and the clergy did not know that it was Ratti who stood behind those decisions. And nobody was able to find out about his political views. He did not join either the liberals or the so-called intransigents, the two camps that divided Italy during those years. There was no opportunism in this attitude; he enjoyed the respect of both camps because people were aware of the fact that Ratti stood above the political battles of the day.

The librarian of the Biblioteca Vaticana himself felt that the people might consider him inadequate for this task, and he therefore asked the Pope to send someone else. He himself, to be sure, entertained no feeling of inadequacy. He was quite aware of the difficult mission upon which he was sent. It was evidence of the completely balanced character of Achille Ratti that he was prepared—not only spiritually, but physically—to undertake a mission almost adventurous in nature, so late in life.

As far as the "adventure" such a mission involved, he welcomed it. In 1917, when the Italian army suffered a tremendous setback at Caporetto, Achille Ratti was the prefect of the Vatican Library. He declared then that if the army would take him he was prepared to go to the front as a chaplain. Msgr. Confalonieri writes that Ratti always became enthusiastic when reading about heroic deeds in history. Now he was faced with a situation that involved a kind of frontline defense of the Church's interests in its struggle with the new forces unleashed in the twentieth century.

The reason for sending an Apostolic Visitor to Warsaw, then still occupied by the Germans, was to help the Polish hierarchy and clergy in the reorganization of the material and spiritual administration of the Church. The problems in Lithuania, Latvia and Estonia were somewhat similar.

Before World War I, Poland was divided between Austria, Germany and Russia. During the fall of 1916 Germany and Austria granted a semi-independent status to those Polish territories under their jurisdiction, in order to avoid a more hostile attitude on the part of the population, which, of course, expected the defeat of both the German-Austrian allies and the Russians. A victorious Franco-British alliance, they hoped, would help the Poles. In 1917 a council of regents was formed, headed by Archbishop Kakowski of Warsaw; the territory of Poland, however, was under German-Austrian occupation. The year 1917 ushered in great events in eastern Europe. Russia had been on the verge of collapse since 1916. The German general staff, in order to hasten the disintegration of Russia, smuggled Lenin into St. Petersburg (now Leningrad). In return, Lenin promised to agitate for a separate Russian peace with the Central Powers. Secretly, Lenin was certain that the Austrian monarchy, as well as Germany, would collapse and that, once Bolshevism was in power in Russia, it would spread to Germany and Austria. Lenin arrived in St. Petersburg in April 1917. The revolution swept away the moderate Miliukow and the liberal Kerenski, and by the end of 1917 great areas of Russia were in the hands of Lenin and his associates. On March 3, 1918, a separate peace was signed between Germany, Austria and the new Russian Bolshevik regime.

The problems of Central and Eastern Europe seem to be much too complicated for Westerners. Basically, these problems are as ordinary as the problems of the West: social, religious, national and racial. Since the nations lie closer to each other and because Central Europe is the real dividing line between two mentalities, the problems are fought out with passion and conviction, and sometimes with great cruelty. In order to understand Ratti's mission to this part of the world, and the point of view of the peoples with whom he dealt, a brief historical survey is necessary.

In April 1918, World War I was still going on. In the West, though the Germans were in retreat, all the victories of the Entente were almost doubtful victories because of the terrible cost in men in Flanders, at Verdun, and on other bloody battlefronts. The great and bloody battles at the Piave drained the strength of both the Italian and the Austro-Hungarian armies.

The Eastern front and the territories behind it were on the brink of chaos. The picture was brighter in the West. The entry of the United States meant not only fresh divisions

and supplies, but new spirit and a promise of total cooperation of the New World in the reorganization of battered Europe. President Wilson's famous Fourteen Points were a
beacon light of hope and promise to the war-torn people, but
in Central Europe people could hardly believe that such pro-
posals could be applied to them, too.

The German Reich and the Hapsburg monarchy still existed, but in Russia the Czar had already been deposed and
shot. Kerenski, the liberal democrat, had fled, and the power
in Russia was held by two obscure men who had spent a great
part of their lives in conspiratorial activity: Lenin and
Trotsky. Germany was tottering. The Hapsburg monarchy
had been shaken to its foundations. The nations of which it
was composed demanded their independence at any cost,
even at the cost of destroying each other.

The Poles recognized the advent of the historical hour that
would help them regain their unity. Since the Russian revolution weakened the great Eastern empire, the Poles hoped that
the weakening of Germany and the Hapsburgs and their impending defeat would enable them to put the three parts together and mold them into one nation.

The people of Central and Eastern Europe were silent, worn
out, and terribly depressed. There were only two hopes for
them. One was their religion. The majority of these people
were Catholic. They saw in Benedict XV a real successor of
the Apostles, a man who suffered with them while working
untiringly for peace. On the temporal level, the peoples of
Central Europe clung hopefully to the messages that came
from the New World and from the practical suggestions submitted to the belligerents by the Pope.

This was the situation when Achille Ratti received his appointment. He left Rome on April 25, and arrived in Warsaw
on May 30, 1918.

In Poland the hierarchy knew nothing about Ratti's appointment, inasmuch as they were completely out of contact
with Rome.

On his way, Msgr. Ratti's first stop was Munich. Bavaria, though a part of the German federation, was an independent kingdom, ruled by its ancient Wittelsbach dynasty. Old Leopold III was approaching his end. Bavaria maintained most cordial relations with the Holy See, and the Nuncio in Munich at that time was a young Roman who spent his entire life in the service of Vatican diplomacy, Eugenio Pacelli. The meeting between Achille Ratti and Eugenio Pacelli was extremely important, because Pacelli briefed him carefully on the situation in Poland and Central Europe. The German Reich and the Austrian government consented to his mission in Warsaw. Nevertheless, he wanted to be sure that the Holy See was not going to increase Polish expectations by sending an Apostolic Visitor.

In Munich, Ratti was faced with an immediate problem. Nuncio Pacelli invited the highest Bavarian officials and the ambassadors of Prussia and Austria to dinner. Fr. Ehrle, the Jesuit predecessor of Ratti at the Vatican Library, was also present. In a way, the Austrians and the Germans welcomed Ratti's mission, because they hoped it would have a pacifying effect on the Poles. It is curious that so many excellent men, endowed with a wide historical knowledge and good will, were unable to understand that the Holy See at this time was not pursuing power-politics, nor were they able to perceive that in the person of Achille Ratti they were face to face with a man who knew how to strengthen the Church's position and assert its rights without recourse to intrigue and arms.

Two days later Ratti continued his journey—this time to Vienna. The Hapsburg capital was living its last days of imperial, though very shabby, grandeur, on the verge of revolution. Again Ratti's education as a historian, particularly his knowledge of German language and history, came to his aid. If the Prussians were suspicious that the Pope's representative would strengthen papal influence, the danger in dealing with Austrian officials was that they still might live in the past, and that the Emperor of Austria and King of Hungary might consider the emissary of the Pope their political ally. The Emperor of Austria was still the Emperor of the imaginary Holy Roman Empire and welcomed the help of any Pope at any time to realize a dream. As King of Hungary, he held the title of Apostolic, with the right to take part in ecclesiastical affairs.

Ratti avoided Emperor Charles VI whose wife, Empress Zita, was openly under attack by extreme nationalists. It was rumored that, being half-French and half-Italian, she had betrayed her oath of allegiance as queen. This was not true, but it was true that her brother, Sixtus of Parma, had carried out a very important peace mission at that time. The representative of the Vatican did not want to be involved in intrigues and domestic troubles. Therefore Ratti took his papers, said good-bye to Vienna, and boarded the Orient Express through Bohemia to reach Berlin.

Berlin was no less chaotic than Vienna. German socialist and Christian democratic opposition against the continuation of the war was on the rise. There were demonstrations by workers and by students.

The German Chancellor was most anxious to know from Ratti what the Holy See's attitude was toward the peace offensive of the neutral countries. His interest was acute, because Erzberger, a member of the Reichstag, was involved in this peace offensive. Ratti made it clear that the Holy See would do everything possible for peace, but that it was not involved in any conspiracy. He received his permit to proceed to Warsaw.

At Wloclawek, where the Polish administration began, he was received by an enthusiastic throng headed by the local bishop. His entrance to Warsaw was triumphal. He arrived on Corpus Christi, 1918 and celebrated high Mass in the cathedral, after which he carried the Eucharist in the traditional procession through the streets of the Polish capital. The Corpus Christi procession is one of the most moving and beau-

tiful spectacles in Eastern Europe. Regardless of religious af-
filiation, the entire city turns out to see or participate in the
procession. The streets through which the Eucharist is borne
are strewn with flowers by young girls. It is always a colorful
pageantry, regardless of how poor the city may be. The uni-
forms and costumes, ancient and modern, are bright. The
clergy turns out in full regalia. The blare of brass bands alter-
nates with the Gregorian chant as the procession moves
slowly through the city. The church bells ring constantly from
the moment the procession starts until it returns to the altar
steps.

Msgr. Ratti first stayed in the house of Cardinal Kakowski.
After the arrival of his secretary, Msgr. Pellegrinetti, they
moved to the house of Msgr. Brzeziewicz, a local pastor who
placed an apartment at the disposal of the Apostolic Visitor.

His first and immediate task was to help the people in a
material way. His second, no less important, was to help clar-
ify the situation of the Church. The provinces around Warsaw were not incorporated into Germany after they lost their
ties with Russia; the administration was a military one. But
since the establishment of a new Polish state was expected,
and the Holy See certainly expected the end of the German
and Austrian power in the East, they envisaged the future
problems of constitutional, material, national and spiritual
nature that the Church in Poland would have to face.

Benedict XV had chosen wisely by sending Ratti to Warsaw, because Ratti was a historian, familiar with the most
intricate relationships between states, peoples and religions
in that area. He had traveled there previously when he had
visited famous libraries. And his ideas about the relationship
between Church and state had been forged in the crucible
of his personal experience with this problem in Italy.

An Apostolic Visitor has no diplomatic status. Achille Ratti
was not obliged to get in touch with secular authorities or
to produce credentials. Nevertheless, he had various contacts
with Polish officials and with foreign diplomatic representa-

tives. His contacts were marked by sincere and warm-hearted cordiality. In short, he was the same person he was in Milan or Rome; he did not assume a new face to go with his new semi-diplomatic task.

It was, of course, important that he acquaint himself with the situation in Poland, and later in the Baltic nations, by personal, first-hand contact. This meant that he had to travel all over Poland and the Baltic nations.

Upon arriving in Warsaw, he immediately started to learn the language of the country. His knowledge of German, French and English was very helpful. He spoke in Latin with the clergy in Poland, but soon he made great progress in Polish and was able to understand it and to read newspapers and books in that language.

His first journey was a visit to the shrine at Czestochowa, the national shrine of Poland, on July 15, 1918. The history of the Polish national shrine of Czestochowa mirrors the tormented and troubled history of the nations of Central and Eastern Europe. The Polish nation attributed its very existence to the help of the Virgin of Czestochowa. The veneration of the picture of the Madonna was the expression of the Polish nation's faith and gratitude. Thousands of pilgrims gathered there daily to pray.

The Czestochowa shrine was under the care of the monks of St. Paul the Hermit, a Polish-Hungarian religious order. The great sanctuary was the heart of a great complex of churches, hostels, ancient fortifications, arcades and shops, dominating the rocky hill below which modern industrial Czestochowa sprawled. Upon becoming Pope, Achille Ratti made Czestochowa into a bishopric and the image of Our Lady of Czestochowa adorned his chapel and his bedroom.

Msgr. Ratti had to inspect each diocese to determine the needs of the clergy and the faithful, and to bring living proof of the care of the Pope. According to the custom of the country, his visits were always made in conjunction with some religious function. The appearance of the emissary of the

Pope in these tiny villages and cities, which considered themselves desolate and abandoned by everyone, was, to the inhabitants and the clergy, a great occasion.

No papal representative ever arrived in war-torn countries
during and after World War I and World War II without
bringing material relief. The Holy See knew very well that
in times of disaster secular authorities very often are unable
to cope with the material needs of the population. Though
secular authority was very strong in peacetime in Eastern
Europe, it seemed to collapse during the numerous wars
that beset this territory during the centuries. It thus was a
welcome idea that the Holy See and the Church should help
and care for people in a material sense. After Msgr. Ratti
came carloads of foodstuffs, clothing and medicine. Ratti's
main concern in the distribution of this material help was to
care for the children and for the aged.

Wherever he went on his travels, over the muddy and war-
torn roads of Poland, the people received him on their knees.
Msgr. Ratti, to whom the forms of rural religiosity were not
alien, since he came from a long line of peasant farmers, was
deeply touched by this extreme self-humiliation of the people.
He urged them not to kneel, but to no avail.

After Czestochowa, he visited Kielce; on September 6,
Wlostow; and on September 8, Sandomierz. No one expected
so much vigor from the Apostolic Visitor who "spent his entire
life" among dusty books. The admiration for him increased
when he continued the same pace and visited Cracow, Lublin, Chelm, Chruslin, Plock, Lomza, Janow and Kalis.

Ratti helped everyone. He liked to walk alone, fearlessly.
If he was asked to bless a marriage, to preside at a religious
ceremony, or to answer questions of historians who wanted
the benefit of his knowledge, he did all these things willingly.
But he acted in exactly the same way with the lowly and
poor. If he met a poor peasant woman, an orthodox Jew crying for his lost relatives, or a little peasant girl who had lost
a cow, Ratti helped. He gave money for another cow, alerted

the authorities to find the Jew's relatives, and comforted the peasant woman, who had believed she was beyond help because her husband and son had been killed before her eyes.

Later, when he became Nuncio (the diplomatic representative of the Holy See in Poland), he continued his visits. Before discussing the official aims of these later visits we must point out that the more difficult the task or situation, the greater was his determination to solve it. In this difficult atmosphere he grew constantly in spiritual stature.

He visited the Ukraine, soaked with the blood of the Uniate Martyrs. Then he spent five days in Vilna. The shrine of Our Lady of Vilna (often called Our Lady of Ostrabrama) is as important as the shrine at Czestochowa. The importance of this Lithuanian shrine cuts across the boundary of Poland and Lithuania because it is revered by Orthodox as well as by Catholics.

On the day that Achille Ratti visited the shrine it was 14° below zero, in one of the most bitter and biting winters Eastern Europe had ever experienced. The Nuncio was not dressed according to the weather, with the felt boots, heavy woolen underwear and fur coat worn by the local population. Yet he did not want to give a bad example, so he remained kneeling in the snow for two hours, with the rest of the pilgrims.

Later, he participated at the Catholic Congress of Poznan. He went to pray at Gniezno, at the tomb of St. Adelbert, apostle and patron of Poland. Everywhere he was received with the same triumphal acclaim. "Now I understand much better who and what the Pope is," he said to his secretary. "I am nothing but a poor librarian, and I see thousands of people prostrate themselves before me, only because the shadow of the Pope follows me."

In his official contacts he was direct with everyone, without being unkind. Since he had a very strict schedule, he assumed that everyone else was anxious to work from early morning until late at night to improve the lot of the people and the

situation of the country. One day he presented himself at
8:30 in the morning to a high official in the Ministry of Foreign Affairs. He was not received, however, because the count
was still sleeping. This did not disturb Ratti. He went down-
stairs to the public park facing the building, sat on a bench
and started to recite his breviary. When Count . . . finally
awakened and was told that the Apostolic Visitor was sitting
on a bench in the park, he was horrified and most apologetic.

Ratti rose every morning at 6:00. Before Mass he meditated for an hour in a small chapel in his apartment. Very often, he repeated this visit to the Holy Eucharist during the
day. After breakfasting at 8:00 he was ready for work and
seated at his desk. From 10:00 to 1:30 he gave audiences.
After a very brief interval for lunch he would take a walk
through the city, stopping en route at several churches. About
4:00 in the afternoon he was again at his desk until dinner
time, around 8:00. After dinner he usually talked with his secretary, Don Pellegrinetti, and then returned to his desk to prepare a report or a coded message to the Vatican. There were
lights in his windows until long after midnight.

When Germany and the Hapsburg monarchy collapsed,
activity was resumed which aimed at the reunification of the
nation dismembered for so many years. In order to enable
Poland to take over those parts of the country which still
were under foreign rule or were being fought over, it was
essential that all provisional regimes be consolidated. This
was made possible by Marshal Pilsudski's return from German internment. He was immediately appointed to command
those troops which gave allegiance to the Provisional Re-
gency Council. A few days later the Council transferred all
its powers to Pilsudski and resigned. The marshal himself
then assumed the title of Chief of State. The Holy See was
one of the first to recognize a fully independent Poland.

Benedict XV had given Ratti jurisdiction over Poland,
Finland, Estonia, Latvia, Ukrainia and Georgia. A few months
after Ratti's arrival in Warsaw, the Pope added a new title

and task. He received jurisdiction over Russia as an Apostolic Visitor. The Pope felt that Ratti was the man who, if necessary, could rise to any occasion that this historic moment might offer. Ratti's reports to the Vatican stressed that the religious feeling was alive in Russia, that the people supported the revolutionaries, but not their atheistic, anti-religious views. But he was so interested in obtaining first-hand and personal reports that he asked Benedict XV for permission to proceed to Russia. This happened after the Bolshevik government had *invited* him. Ratti was ready to go if the Russians accepted his conditions. The Bolshevik government, however, never agreed to the conditions he set. He was ready to proceed to Russia under these conditions: (1) guarantee of free contact and communication with the Catholic bishops of Russia; (2) guarantee of the inviolability of the diplomatic pouch between himself and the Vatican; (3) guarantee of his free travel to and from Russia.

"I think," said Ratti, "that it is not enough to pray to save this immensely great country. More than prayers are needed. The blood of Catholic martyrs and the blood of priests is needed."

Even within Poland, Msgr. Ratti was constantly in touch with the Russian situation. He had seen refugees fleeing the Bolshevik terror, and he interviewed many who escaped from the chaos and nightmare. He became acquainted with the Bolshevik situation as no other churchman could, and he conveyed his information to the Vatican.

Benedict XV and Achille Ratti shared the same purpose. They wanted to relieve the distress of the Russian people, but at the same time they definitely wanted to halt the spread of Bolshevism. On the one hand they wanted to prevent the Poles and other Eastern European nations from falling under the yoke of the Red army. On the other, they were keenly interested in the destiny of the more than 2,500,000 Catholics and in the fate of those Catholic bishops whom the Bolshevik regime arrested and, as it seemed, was preparing to liquidate. They also were interested in the fate of the millions and millions of Russians, non-Catholics, who also were at the mercy of the revolutionists. Benedict XV sent many telegrams to Lenin asking normal treatment for priests of all denominations.

All these aspects of his approach made it imperative that Ratti enter into personal contact with the leaders of the Russian government. It was his hope that a personal contact might bear fruit. He was quite familiar with social problems and revolutionary movements because Milan was a center of Marxist, anarchist, and later, communist activities.

While at the Vatican Library he had worked closely with Cardinal Tisserant and a priest of Russian origin, C. Korolevsky, whom he later sent to the Near East and to the Baltic in search of historical and ecclesiastical books. Korolevsky had written an article for an Italian journal in which he had made several suggestions for the return of Russia to the Catholic Church. Among the means suggested was the formation of a native clergy through the establishment of little and great seminaries for orthodox priests who wanted to become Catholics. He proposed that these seminaries be erected in Russia proper or, temporarily, along the border. He had further suggested that the Oriental Rite be maintained and the Holy See establish a Nuncio in St. Petersburg.

Benedict XV had spent almost all his energies to obtain the cessation of hostilities. He now felt that he had to offer his help to all war-stricken areas of Europe. Archbishop Pacelli, his Nuncio in Munich, helped the Germans, while the Pope was ready to give whatever he had in material aid to the famine-stricken areas of Russia. This offer to help Russia was a genuine one, with no strings attached to it. Nevertheless, Msgr. Ratti felt that much would be gained if he went to St. Petersburg. On October 18, 1918, he sent a telegram to Chicherin, Foreign Commissar of the Bolshevik government, asking that Metropolitan Van der Ropp of Mohilew, Russia, whom the Bolsheviks had transported to Moscow and sentenced to death, be released. In the memorandum, Ratti argued that Van der Ropp was a papal subject and that the Pope was not at war with Russia. The memorandum impressed the Russians and one year later, November 28, 1919, Metropolitan Van der Ropp arrived safely in Warsaw.

While he had expected to be sent momentarily into Russia, the Vatican had other plans. A telegram from Rome read: "Prepare yourself for episcopal consecration. You have been appointed Apostolic Nuncio to Warsaw." It was the new Polish government that had requested the Holy See to send a Nuncio to the capital, specifying that the Poles would welcome the appointment of Msgr. Ratti. Thus, the non-diplomatic appointment of Ratti now became a diplomatic one. On June 6, 1919, Benedict XV appointed him Apostolic Nuncio to Poland. Since all Nuncios have the rank of Archbishop, the Pope made him Archbishop on July 3, appointing him to the titular see of Lepanto.

On July 19, Msgr. Ratti presented his credentials to the President of Poland at Warsaw's Belvedere Palace. Subsequently, on October 28, he was consecrated by Cardinal Kakowski at the cathedral.

Although the Polish state was established, it was none too firm. Nuncio Ratti was in his office in Warsaw when the news broke that the reorganized Russian army, exploiting the temporary lull and the atmosphere of peace that prevailed everywhere, had invaded Poland. Those who were familiar with the conditions in Russia on the one hand and with Bolshevik ideology on the other immediately recognized that the real aim was not recapture of Poland, but the invasion and conquest of Central Europe, and Germany, too. Austria was no longer a major power. The new Hungarian state struggled with major economic difficulties and was flooded with hundreds of thousands of refugees. Newly created Czechoslovakia was attempting to organize its administration. Germany had no army at all.

The time was propitious for Trotsky to launch an offensive.

Inside Russia there was nothing but misery and chaos. The great famine that eventually took at least ten million victims was just beginning. The regime needed an international victory to allay the doubts, discontent and disenchantment at home.

Despite the five peace treaties signed at various places in the Paris region, the conference of 1919–1920 had left much business unfinished. It was the Russian problem, however, which made the whole question of a peace settlement something incomplete and problematic. As a matter of fact, the war lasted in Eastern Europe for two more years after the armistice in the West. And it was not over before the series of peace treaties which the border states, liberated from Russian rule, signed with the new Russian government.

The Bolsheviks denounced the Brest-Litovsk treaty immediately after the collapse of Germany, on November 13, 1918, and invited all peoples of Central Europe to "join a union of Soviet republics."

The Soviet's call was successful only in the case of Hungary, where the weak regime of the liberal idealist, Count Karolyi, was followed by the Bolshevik regime of Bela Kun. This lasted from March to the end of August 1919. Nevertheless, the Bolshevik invitation was a real challenge—though Russia was weak and the revolution not yet victorious. Many White Russian counter-revolutionary armies were still fighting; the mere names of Kolchak, Wrangel, Denikin, all anti-Bolshevik generals, generated hopes that their armies might eventually defeat the Bolsheviks.

This is how Virginia Cowles has summarized the period in her book:[1]

"The gigantic country was in an appalling state of disintegration . . . in the Spring of 1918 they had signed a separate peace with the Kaiser which had allowed Germany to release a million more men to fight the Allies on the Western front. Britain had sent troops to Archangel, the Caucasus and Si-

[1] *Winston Churchill: The Era and the Man*, Harper & Bros., New York, 1953.

beria to prevent oil supplies and Allied materials from falling into the enemy's hands. In the meantime White Russian counter-revolutionary forces, many hundreds of miles apart —those in the south under the leadership of General Denikin, and those in the east under Admiral Kolchak—had remained faithful to their commitments and continued the war as best they could. Now these forces were fighting the Bolsheviks and desperately begging England for help. Lord Milner, Winston's [Churchill] predecessor at the War Office, had more or less promised aid. Was Britain to abandon them? All Winston's chivalrous instincts bade him send assistance. Besides this, looking at the picture objectively, it would not be in Britain's interest to allow Bolshevik leaders who believed in organized terror and who were preaching world-wide revolution to gain the final power. Germany lay prostrate. What would prevent Russia from overrunning the whole of Europe?"

It was one of the most dramatic, and yet one of the obscure, enigmatic periods of modern European history. Here was a statesman like Churchill who saw the essential threat clearly, yet he was unable to carry out his will. Nevertheless Churchill kept trying. Miss Cowles' book continues:

"The next month Winston alluded to 'the foul baboonery of Bolshevism' and came out openly in favour of sending arms and supplies to their adversaries. But there was no action he could take without the approval of the Supreme Council, a body which sat in Paris and represented the five leading Allied powers. He went to France in February and talked to President Wilson who told him affably that he did not pretend to know the solution to the Russian problem. There were the gravest objections to every course, and yet some course must be taken—sooner or later."

But the Allies pursued a vacillating policy. Churchill continued his one-man crusade at home and abroad. At last in May the Supreme Council in Paris offered arms and support to Kolchak, one of the anti-Bolshevik generals. The Allied offer was vague and uncertain yet it enabled Churchill to act. He sent a flow of ammunition and matériel to Russia, and laid plans for the evacuation of British forces. Simultaneously he launched a campaign for a volunteer army to cover this evacuation. Public opinion in Britain, recalling Churchill's catastrophic adventures in Antwerp and the Dardanelles, was mistrustful and hostile. In addition, the English believed that the Russians should be allowed to solve their own problems. With respect to Bolshevism, the country, like all Europe, had its Leftists and Rightists. As was to be expected the working classes in England, influenced by the socialist-oriented Labour Party, sympathized with the aims if not the methods of the Soviet regime. This attitude was also shared by liberals.

Lloyd George was in no sense a Socialist. But in his view the Czarist oppression and tyranny had been the causes of the revolution. Therefore the Russian people could not be blamed. It was important, he thought, that England trade with the Soviets, indeed recognize them, as was also the view of President Wilson. Above all Lloyd George resented Churchill's shrill anti-Sovietism. In his *Memories of the Peace Conference*, he wrote:

"The most formidable and irresponsible protagonist of an anti-Bolshevik war was Mr. Winston Churchill. He had no doubt a genuine dislike for Communism . . . His ducal blood revolted against the wholesale elimination of Grand Dukes in Russia."

In the meantime, however, the Red army pushed ceaselessly toward the West. Thanks to the false sense of security generated by the Armistice, the Bolsheviks had sufficient time to consolidate their power. For the West and most of its statesmen and politicians, only the interests of the moment were of import. They did not perceive the Bolshevik threat in its true implications.

Churchill aided the anti-Bolshevik armies to the last moment. He even supported Poland when that country rather foolishly attacked Russia in 1920. The Russians not only drove the Poles out but marched into Poland themselves. Churchill panicked and urged Lloyd George to put Germany on its feet quickly as a bulwark against Russia. Churchill's words sound prophetic today:

"Since the Armistice," he wrote, "my policy would have been *Peace with the German People, war on the Bolshevik tyranny.* Willingly or unavoidably, you have followed something very near the reverse . . . [But] we are face to face with the results. They are terrible. We may well be within measurable distance of universal collapse and anarchy throughout Europe and Asia. Russia has gone into ruin. *What is left of her is in the power of these deadly snakes.* [Italics added.]

"But Germany may perhaps still be saved . . . You ought to tell France that we will make a defensive alliance with her against Germany if, and only if, she entirely alters her treatment of Germany and loyally accepts a British policy of help and friendship toward Germany."[2]

While Churchill fought a losing battle in the West, another great, but still unknown, statesman was tackling the Russian problem in a different manner in the East. Achille Ratti was no less an adversary of the Bolshevik than Churchill. But because of the difference in their status, he could not campaign for ammunitions, armies and violent solutions. True to the mission of the papacy and the Church, he was interested in the welfare of souls. Nevertheless he was quite aware that spiritual welfare is also linked to material welfare.

The Western powers could not agree, and only the French acted. They sent one of their greatest military geniuses, General Weygand, and some matériel. One night Weygand told the Nuncio: "We must win, Your Excellency. The Poles are fighting. I represent France and you represent the Vicar of Christ. We have done what we could. Nothing else remains but to solicit your prayers."

The ill-equipped and partially untrained Polish militia was unable to hold, and in August 1920, the Bolsheviks arrived

2 *The World Crisis:* Winston S. Churchill.

at the banks of the Vistula River, at the gate of Warsaw. The
occupation of the Polish capital seemed to be a matter of days.
People in office fled. The government transferred its seat
to Cracow, followed by the diplomatic corps. One foreign
representation remained in Warsaw, the Apostolic Nuncio
Achille Ratti and his secretary. They did not closet themselves
in their apartment or in the cellar; instead, they walked
boldly through the streets. Archbishop Ratti's appearance
and courage gave new hope to the population. Ratti still remained in the city when the cannons moved closer and
closer, and even when the sound of machine-gun and small-
arms fire could be heard crackling in the streets. He saw hundreds, later thousands, of wounded, some carried and others
walking, through the streets. He also saw the tens of thousands of panicky, fleeing refugees.

The garrison at Warsaw, however, did not retreat. The
battle raged for ten days. Then a sudden silence fell on the
suffering, sad and destroyed city.

On the next day, August 15, General Weygand launched
his counter-offensive, and a few days later the Red army was
definitely defeated. The Red army that had pushed its victory to the very heart of Poland and had stood on the verge
of a conquest and revolutionization of Eastern Europe and
Germany had withdrawn.

Many Poles attributed the sudden Russian withdrawal to
a miracle. They said the Madonna of Czestochowa, their
greatest and most efficient protectress since the eleventh century, had appeared in the clouds over Warsaw and that the
heavenly apparition had paralyzed the Red army into in-
action.

The enthusiasm of the Poles and the people in government
was indescribable. Since they attributed the victory over the
Red army to faith, the person of Achille Ratti became even
more symbolic for them. Remembering that he remained in
the city during those weeks of terror and desperation, he became in their eyes part of Divine Providence. The newspaper

articles and demonstrations praising him and the Pope, whose emissary he was, were boundless in their enthusiasm.

A few months after the liberation of Warsaw, the Pope appointed Ratti as Commissioner of the Holy See for the duration of the plebiscite in the territory of Upper Silesia, claims to which were being contested by both Germany and Poland. Poland was also in difficulties with Lithuania over the city of Vilna, and with Czechoslovakia over Cieszyn (Teschen), as well as with Germany over Poznan and Danzig.

The territory of Upper Silesia, otherwise called Oppeln, after its capital city, was disputed because of its coal mines. After the collapse of Germany this territory was temporarily occupied by Allied forces. The Entente decided that the destiny of Upper Silesia should be determined by a plebiscite. This, of course, required adequate preparation and protection. In the first place, it had to be established what people had the right to vote. For this purpose an Allied Commission was set up in Oppeln. The Allied military force was supposed to guarantee the freedom and impartiality of the campaign and the balloting itself.

There were, however, other delicate problems. The territory of Oppeln belonged to the German archdiocese of Breslau, under Cardinal Bertram. Religious services in the Catholic churches were conducted in German or in Polish, according to the nationality majority of the parish. There were a number of Polish priests who belonged to the Breslau archdiocese, but who sympathized with the Polish cause. The Holy See sent Msgr. Ratti as Apostolic Commissioner for the duration of the plebiscite, with the sole task of ensuring that the hierarchy and clergy would not become involved in partisanship.

Several names had been proposed to the Secretariat of State at the Vatican before the Pope decided that Ratti was the man for this task. The appointment of a Polish or German prelate would have antagonized one or another section of the population. Nevertheless, the Vatican felt that it should be

someone connected with Polish affairs in order to counter-
balance the fact that the territory was under a German archbishop. Thus, the solution seemed obvious: Although the
Nuncio in Warsaw was an Italian, he was accredited to the
Warsaw government and the Poles liked him.

The Poles thought that the territory of Oppeln should be
temporarily detached from the jurisdiction of the German
Archbishop. Such an action was inconceivable, first from an
administrative point of view, and again because it would have
meant an implicit mistrust of the objectivity of Cardinal
Bertram. The Archbishop declared again and again in the
most solemn form that nobody should try to violate the freedom of the plebiscite. He asked the clergy of Oppeln to refrain from political campaigning and to treat the faithful
among the Poles and Germans with equal love and charity.
He let it be understood, however, that it would certainly be
wrong if he, the shepherd of this territory, cooperated in the
detachment of this land from the mother country.

Monsignor Ratti arrived in Oppeln with no bias whatsoever. He wanted to listen to Germans and Poles alike. The
Polish press, however, hailed the decision of the Holy See in
such a manner that the Germans were strengthened in their
belief that the appointment indicated a prejudice against
them. Such a belief was completely erroneous and without
foundation. The Nuncio in Germany at that time was Archbishop Pacelli, who later became Pope Pius XII. Even the
most chauvinistic Germans had to admit that the Holy See,
through Pacelli, had a great affection for Germany. They had,
of course, forgotten that the Church had the same love and
affection for every nation and helped in the measure as it was
needed. The German people, however, defeated in their
hopes, as well as on the battlefield, overwhelmed by economic
disaster, and facing even further humiliation, were more sen-
sitive than ever. Everything seemed to be against them.

After the appointment of Ratti and after editorials and reports in the Polish press, certain German circles in Oppeln

began to shun the Apostolic Commissioner. He wanted to learn the true situation, but was blocked. Therefore, he obtained most of his information from the Poles.

In the meantime, the situation became more and more serious. Many members of the clergy asked Cardinal Bertram to intervene energetically and immediately and block the participation of priests from foreign dioceses in a village or a city without the specific consent of the local pastor. Therefore Cardinal Bertram forbade any activity of alien priests and at the same time threatened ecclesiastical sanctions. The purpose of the Archbishop's order was to prevent the Polish and German priests from battling each other publicly. According to the Germans the Archbishop's order was clear and unbiased. The point of contention of the Poles, including the clergy, was that the Archbishop acted with intent to hurt their interests. Cardinal Bertram's decree created great excitement in Poland.

Then the Allied Plebiscite Commission refused to give permission to Cardinal Bertram to visit the territory which was part of his diocese. The German press and German circles thereupon became almost hysterical, and accused Ratti of having influenced the Allied Commission. The truth is that he was not even asked for an opinion, because he was not a member of the Allied Commission and it was not part of his mission to interfere in such questions. Ratti managed to get in touch with German circles. Then the Polish press in turn started to have doubts about his sympathies. After a conference Msgr. Ratti had with German bishops and the Nuncio for Germany, Polish public opinion was aroused against him. More and more voices asked: "How is it possible that Archbishop Ratti, a friend of Poland, did not come out more openly or outright for the Polish cause?" This, of course, would have been entirely contrary to his mission as conceived by the Vatican.

Less than six months after his appointment as Apostolic Commissioner for the plebiscite, Achille Ratti had become

quite unpopular in Poland. The same press which a few
months before had eulogized and praised him to the skies now
accused him in an indignant and outraged manner, reporting
allegedly specific instances of his constant hostility toward
the Poles. If Msgr. Ratti had not been the level-headed and
balanced person that he was, he would have been hurt to the
quick. Instead, he smiled indulgently, and did his best according to his conscience.

With respect to the plebiscite in Oppeln, meanwhile, the
Holy See felt it advisable to send another representative
there, one who would reside permanently in this controversial
territory. Thus it was hoped to avoid the semblance of favoring either side. Msgr. Ratti then returned to Warsaw. Legally
he remained Apostolic Commissioner for the duration of the
plebiscite, but *de facto* his rights were exercised by Msgr.
Giovanni Ognoserra.

Achille Ratti spent thirty months in Eastern Europe, primarily as Apostolic Visitor and Nuncio in Warsaw. He returned to Rome on December 2, 1920, where he made his
final reports; then he returned to Warsaw to inform the Polish government that his mission in Poland had come to an
end. Ratti's departure from Warsaw was hastened by a
telegram from Rome on May 19, 1921, urging his immediate
return.

For his part Msgr. Ratti could leave Poland in good conscience. The Pope, and other Vatican officials, knew that
Achille Ratti had performed an excellent job with an objectivity worthy of a papal emissary. Some Polish newspapers,
however, were of another opinion; they demanded that the
Polish government occupy the contested plebiscite area and
that Achille Ratti be expelled from Poland.

Polish officials, headed by President Pilsudski, members of
the cabinet, and Cardinal Kakowski, attended the official fare-
well banquet tendered to the departing Nuncio. Nevertheless,
the atmosphere surrounding the affair was not cordial. Msgr.
Ratti left Poland on June 4, 1921.

In a letter written to a friend, Achille Ratti said that he would have been ready to continue his work in Poland, and quoted St. Martin: *"non recuso laborem"*—work I do not shun. Further, he said that he was leaving Poland in obedience to the order of Pope Benedict XV, who had assigned him to Milan as head of the diocese and shepherd of beloved people to which he himself belonged.

The plain people of Poland, Lithuania and other East European countries expected a prelate who would convey to them the spiritual message of the Pope. Monsignor Ratti had satisfied their expectations.

In the thorough manner so typical of him he had become acquainted with the problems at hand in all their complexities. Because of these very complexities he had decided to consider all the problems from a supernational angle; otherwise, he would have been completely lost in the maelstrom of violent and conflicting nationalism. His motto was: "There are certain situations which cannot be resolved short of sanctity." And he gave them saintly example.

Monsignor Ratti increased the prestige of the Holy See in that crucial area by actually settling most of the problems confronting it there. Many members of the new Polish government and of the political parties were inclined to grant the state a preponderant role in matters ecclesiastical. This problem was a highly important one from the point of view of Church property. The Polish government wanted Church property problems to be handled by a government commission. Ratti approved this idea and succeeded in bringing about an agreement according to which a commission headed by bishops and representatives of religious orders was charged with the problem. He was also successful in reactivating five dormant episcopal seats; he took great pains to see that able, deserving priests were appointed as bishops to these seats and other vacancies. He advised peasants and clergy constantly. He also reorganized the religious orders. In territories which had formerly belonged to Germany and

Russia, many convents and monasteries had been closed;
others lived in a manner incompatible with their regulations.
In several monasteries, the law of cloister was not enforced,
and in others, members of religious orders lived privately in
apartment houses.

One of Ratti's most important contributions to the revival
of a strong unified Church was the founding of the Catholic
University of Lublin. The decision to establish the university
had been made on July 27, 1918, during a conference of Polish bishops, over which he presided, just two months after his
arrival in Warsaw.

He acted just as promptly with respect to other problems.
Ratti was fully aware of the tension existing between Poles
and Ukrainians. When extreme Polish nationalists clashed
with Ukrainian Catholics of the Oriental Rite, he came out
openly for the latter. He visited Metropolitan Szepticky, the
great and venerable leader of Ukrainian Catholics in Lvow,
as a gesture of moral support. Achille Ratti remained a friend
and sponsor of Ukrainian Catholics until his death. He did
his best to mediate between Poles and Ukrainians in order
to attenuate their centuries-old controversies. In the same
way, he also tried to mediate between Poland and Lithuania.
The territory around Vilna was a contested area, both Poland
and Lithuania claiming it on historical grounds. He visited
Vilna and Kaunas, the capital of the new Lithuania, a country
with overwhelming Catholic population and tradition, and
tried to prepare the ground for a future concordat with the
new state which, together with Latvia and Estonia, rose from
the ruins of the Tsarist empire. Latvia had only a small per-
centage of Catholics; nevertheless, Ratti, true to his mission
as Apostolic Visitor to all the Baltic countries (as well as Finland and Russia), wanted to report on the religious situation
and prepare the first steps to be taken for the safeguard of
religious liberties. In Riga, capital of Latvia, he met the local
bishop, Msgr. O'Rourke, and discussed with him the outlines
of a future concordat.

In the plebiscite question he was as successful as in all other matters, even if it looked as though he had been forced to withdraw. The truth of the matter was that Benedict XV had absolute confidence in his Nuncio and would not think of recalling him if he had not had the intention of making Ratti a Cardinal.

As far as Soviet Russia was concerned, Ratti's mission was also successful. Though the Soviet government did not permit him entry to St. Petersburg, Ratti's telegrams and memoranda to Chicherin did establish between the Holy See and the Soviet a contact that was very important in view of future negotiations and plans.

Men of the stamp of Achille Ratti are not frightened by the magnitude of a task. The very existence of such a task, so difficult of solution, automatically arouses their interest and determination to come to terms with it. The effect of the mission in Central and Eastern Europe had a great effect upon Ratti, though it might be expected that a man over sixty, accustomed to act *sub specie aeternitatis,* would approach new ideas and problems with a kind of tired resignation. But here Ratti proved again to be a faithful disciple of his beloved Manzoni: "There is no need to flee or deny the world. The strong person creates harmony around himself without giving up his principles and ideas. Such a person never forgets that individuals as personalities transcend abstract ideas. Such a view automatically excludes a view rooted in defeat and resignation."

This feeling ever came through in the reports Ratti sent to the Holy See. Ratti wrote all his reports from Warsaw in longhand, by ordinary pen; he never used a fountain pen. His handwriting was a clear classical calligraphy, narrow and upright in form. The reports themselves revealed and characterized the scholar. First he described a given situation, factually and meticulously; then he enlarged upon the salient points, with comments expressing his own points of view and evaluation of the data and the persons concerned. None of his reports was a dry enumeration of facts.

While Ratti brought comfort to millions of frightened and hopeless people on the great plains of Eastern Europe, he was stricken by an irreparable loss himself. His mother died at the age of eighty-one. She had lived in Milan with her daughter Camilla and watched with loving care the events in the life of her son. When Pope Benedict XV decided to send Msgr. Ratti to Poland he dedicated a photograph of himself to the mother of Achille Ratti with the inscription: "To our beloved daughter Teresa Galli . . . we send our Apostolic Benediction as an exchange for her son who entered the service of the Holy See."

Benedict XV knew how close was the mother to Achille Ratti's heart, and the Pope said to Ratti: "You can be sure that we will take care of your mother. We will think of her all the time while you are abroad."

Teresa Ratti died September 29, 1918. Her son could not even come to her funeral, and when he returned to Italy his dear Milan was somehow empty.

CHAPTER FIVE

Toward the Summit

BENEDICT XV had only one reason in urging Achille Ratti to return to Rome: the Pope planned a secret consistory on June 13, 1921, to create new cardinals. Achille Ratti was to be one of them. He was elevated to the rank of cardinal-priest and his titular church was San Martino ai Monti; the appointment of Ratti to the See of Milan was also announced officially.

Cardinal Ratti received the red hat that day from Benedict XV in a private audience, together with Cardinals Laurenti and Tacci. The Italian papers at that time reported that Benedict XV ended his brief address to the three new Cardinals with the following words: "We gave you the red robe of a Cardinal . . . very soon, however, one of you will wear the white robe."

Some people attributed a prophetic and mysterious significance to these words of Benedict XV. In the light of historical research it is quite clear that Benedict XV, who sensed his end drawing near, thought of nobody else but Ratti as his successor. Of course, the Pope does not designate his successor, and his personal wishes, in this respect, carry no weight. It merely proves Benedict's profound esteem for Ratti. Many biographers overlook the importance of the fact that the Pope had sent Ratti to Eastern Europe charged with missions to accomplish that usually were given only to experienced diplomats.

Cardinal Ratti's inauguration as Archbishop of Milan was scheduled for September 8. Since the Archdiocese of Milan is of such importance, it was decided that Archbishop Ratti would lead the Italian national pilgrimage to Lourdes before his entrance to his diocese. After the consistory in which he was created Cardinal, he remained in Rome for a while, then left for the famous Benedictine Abbey of Monte Cassino. He remained there for an entire month, completely secluded from the world, immersed in prayer and study.

The Italian national pilgrimage to Lourdes departed from Rome on August 26. These were hard times for Italy. Though Italy was on the side of the victors, there were many signs of impending social revolution, particularly in the north, and this left deep marks on the attitude of the pilgrims. Cardinal Ratti was constantly with them.

He returned to Italy with the pilgrims early in September, and on his way to Milan stopped in Alassio on the Italian Riviera to spend two days in meditation. Msgr. Confalonieri relates that he proceeded from Alassio on September 6, by auto, toward Milan and when he passed through the bridge of the small Ticino River, which marks the boundaries of the Milan archdiocese, Archbishop Ratti stopped his car, descended and, visibly moved by great emotion, imparted his blessing to the land that now became his spiritual responsibility. Then he told his driver to proceed to his native town, Desio.

On September 8, the Feast of the Nativity of the Blessed Virgin, he entered Milan. After the Pontifical Mass in the cathedral he formally received the secular and ecclesiastical authorities. He then took time to lay the cornerstone of a charity center sponsored by his predecessor, and to inspect the progress of work on the projected Catholic University.

Msgr. Confalonieri has recorded the reaction to the occupation of the bishopric of Milan: "The appointment of Achille Ratti as Archbishop of Milan met with the general satisfaction of the clergy of the archdioceses. Nevertheless, there were certain discordant voices who spread the fear that this appointment would become advantageous for certain liberal trends because the ex-prefect of the Ambrosiana was on good

terms with certain elements of the nobility and the bourgeoisie who had been of great help to him when he decided
to repair and renew the old edifice of the Ambrosiana. Such
fears were, of course, unfounded. The echo of such doubts
arrived in Rome to the very ears of the new shepherd, and
he suffered in his heart but was very careful not to say a
word; he received everybody with equal cordiality—indeed,
one could say, with a greater cordiality—even those who were
not among his most enthusiastic supporters. Shortly after he
formally assumed occupancy of his diocese he took every opportunity to go where the reserve toward him was the strongest. He overcame the embarrassment of the lukewarm priests
with a generous, overflowing politeness, and knew how to
open their souls for a sincere confidence."

As an Apostolic Visitor and Nuncio in Poland, he had already had an opportunity to act independently. But now, as
an Archbishop, many more opportunities to do so presented
themselves. The few months he spent as Archbishop in the
diocese of Milan are still remembered. No other Archbishop
had done so much in such a short time. At the end of the
long reign of the ailing, saintly Archbishop Ferrari, who died
of cancer, there was a tendency in certain villages and cities
to take things easy.

First, Archbishop Ratti immediately began his canonical
visits. Typical was the one he made on the first Sunday of
Advent, 1921, in Seveso, fourteen miles from Milan. He arrived at 6:00 in the morning, to say Mass, preach and give
Communion to about 1,000 persons. Seveso was particularly
dear to him because, in 1867, as a ten-year-old boy, he had
entered the seminary there. From Seveso he went to the township of Neda in the Brianza and blessed the flag of the Catholic Girls' Association there. At 10:00 he returned to Seveso
for similar brief services and talks. Then he presided at the
high Mass in the local church. Around noon he had a quick
lunch and then rushed to Pavia, forty miles distant, to participate in the closing ceremony of the diocesan Eucharistic
Congress. He gave a sermon in the Pavia cathedral and car-

ried the Sacrament in the long outdoor procession that followed. In the afternoon he returned to Milan. Around 6:00
he was already in the cathedral to give the Advent sermon
after Vespers. This pace was typical with Achille Ratti. He
knew how to make the fullest use of time.

A few days after his arrival in Milan, Achille Ratti visited
the prison of San Vittore, where he celebrated Mass for the
inmates. During the sermon he spoke in his usual simple manner, and deeply moved the prisoners. And after Mass he
talked with everyone who wanted to see him. About 350 of
the inmates expressed the wish to have a word with him. The
director of the prison never forgot this visit and each year he
wrote to the Pope to thank him, on behalf of the prisoners.
In turn, Pius XI each year sent a gift of money to the prison
and asked the warden to use it for the improvement of the
holiday meals.

The prisoners never forgot their eminent visitor and they
took literally his suggestion to turn to him when necessary.
This was not just a gesture on Ratti's part. The first former
prisoner who availed himself of the opportunity was a young
man who wrote to the Pope at Christmas in 1922, thanking
him. The Pope acknowledged his letter immediately and sent
him his autographed picture. A year later, another young
prisoner asked for help. The Pope never forgot these juvenile
offenders. Every year he would ask about their well being and
send them money and gifts. And whenever one of them got
into a situation where it was impossible to get a job, the Pope
would write a letter to the prospective recalcitrant employer,
suggesting that he show a more charitable attitude toward
the offender, who had already paid his debt to society.

Cardinal Ratti also played a great part in the realization of
Fr. Gemelli's plan to create a Catholic University in Milan.

Such a university had been the desired goal of the Catholics
of Italy for a long time. The project had first been discussed
at the Catholic Congress in Venice in 1873. The plan was
never lost sight of by Italian Catholic lay leaders, but its re-

alization called for a man who would dedicate himself totally to this task. This man was Fr. Agostino Gemelli.

Fr. Gemelli found spiritual and material backing in Cardinal Ferrari, in Prof. Toniolo, and in Count Lombardo, a Milanese industrialist. With financial help from the latter, an abandoned monastery was purchased close to the church of St. Ambrose. In April 1919 detailed plans were ready, and a few weeks later Pope Benedict XV and the congregation for universities and seminaries in Rome enthusiastically approved the project. Besides Count Lombardo, a number of others made generous financial gifts to the university. In a relatively short time, within two and a half years, the university opened its doors—in December 1921. At that time it had only two faculties—of philosophy and of the social sciences. The founders dedicated the university to the Sacred Heart of Jesus and the coat of arms bore the following inscription: "*In religione scientia, in scientia religio.*" This meant that the university would be a place for study and research, where the scientist would not lose his religious conviction, and where religious research would be conducted with scientific methods.

The Catholic University and this inscription remarkably expressed the ideas of Achille Ratti. Fr. Gemelli did not get these ideas from Ratti, nor did Ratti get them from Gemelli. It was a meeting of two geniuses which blossomed into a friendship that lasted until the death of Pius XI. Ratti evidenced a great interest in the university even when he was abroad. In March 1921, he wrote to Gemelli from Warsaw:

"The creation of the Catholic University expresses the reality of the marriage of faith and science . . . It seems to me a happy and much promising sign that its creation coincides with the centenary festivals of Dante, a poet whose faith was enlightened by philosophy and theology. The best place for such a university is Milan, the city of Manzoni in whose personality genius and faith met in such a fortunate way . . . Only such an institute can serve for a Christian rebirth of society which sets the highest scientific aims for itself; an in-

stitute in which the god of science and the science of God
complement each other in a way designated by Dante and
Manzoni. Only such an institute can create the necessary elements of action and reaction for the renewal of society. Such
an institute will educate laymen to become scientists and
Catholics, and both in the most profound sense of the word."

It is significant that when Ratti became Archbishop of
Milan he visited the university on the very same day of his
enthronement. From this time on he discussed with Fr. Gemelli all the problems of the university, including appointments to the faculty.

His speech at the opening festival on December 8, 1921,
again revealed his conviction of the need to reconcile faith
and science. December 7 is the Feast day of St. Ambrose,
patron of Milan, and December 8 the Feast of the Immaculate
Conception. Ratti referred to both occasions in his speech.
His remarks on St. Ambrose had a ring of sadness: "This truly
learned scientist among the saints; this saint among the
learned; this last voice of the dying classical latinitas: St.
Ambrose! He preserved the light of knowledge of the entire
ancient world and the beauty of the classical world for those
who might want to find it after the destruction of the barbaric
migrations."

Achille Ratti had been a Cardinal for only seven months
when Pope Benedict XV died suddenly. He received the news
with deep regret, because of the affection and affinity of views
on many questions between him and the Pope.

Before Cardinal Ratti left for the conclave in Rome, he celebrated a requiem Mass. At the end of the service he asked
the congregation to pray with him that God provide a worthy
successor as the new Pope. On the same evening he took the
train for Rome. Upon arriving in Rome, he took up his quarters in the Lombard Seminary, the institution where he had
spent three years during his youth.

Until this time Achille Ratti had been a very balanced,
good-humored person, who never exhibited any moodiness.
Now, though he remained as balanced and good-humored as

ever, his friends and those who met him discovered with surprise that he was now prone to sudden periods of melancholy and depression. In the midst of a conversation, he would suddenly stop, gaze into the distance and sigh. Then, as if awakening from a dream, his eyes would again become lively and he would pick up the thread of conversation where it had dropped. There is no doubt that he was fully aware of the possibility that stood before him, namely, to become Pope. It was but a premonition. Ratti had no vaulting ambition to become the leader of the universal Church.

Now a premonition told him that "something might happen." And these premonitions were based on some real information. That he had an inkling of the fate in store for him is shown by a letter he wrote on January 28, 1922, from Rome, to Signor Colombo, head of diocesan Catholic Action in Milan. In this letter he asked Colombo for prayers for the Church and for him. "I am unable to express my feelings towards my duty as a participant in the election of a Pope." Such a letter was prompted certainly by something beyond just the sense of responsibility incumbent upon a Cardinal. In the Lombard College he constantly asked his students for their prayers. On February 2, 1922, when he entered the conclave, he said good-bye to the seminarians by asking again for their prayers, and left them with the words: "*Fiat voluntas tua*"—Thy will be done. To the rector of the Lombard College, however, he turned and said, jokingly, in Milanese dialect: "*Ed ora vamus en gabbia*"—And now we are going to enter the cage. Cardinal Ratti was again himself: balanced, serious and humorous.

He did not like any talk about his being "*papabile*," but he never became angry when people talked about it or let him sense what they thought. He knew that guessing and speculation is a favorite pastime in any country, particularly in Italy where current events are always discussed with great fervor. Some Milanese friends gave a dinner to honor Cardinal Ratti before he entered the conclave. At the dinner they presented him with a bouquet of white roses and asked him to take it into the conclave. Cardinal Ratti made no reply; neither did he smile. The white bouquet was an expression of their desire to see him on the throne of St. Peter's. Cardinal Ratti took the bouquet, and when he arrived at his quarters at the Lombard College he personally placed it before the statue of the Madonna.

Cardinal Mercier, the renowned Belgian prelate, was an ardent admirer of Ratti and made no secret of his intention to campaign and vote for Cardinal Ratti. While passing through Milan en route to Rome from Belgium he was greeted at the railway station by Milanese Catholics. There somebody said to Mercier that the Milanese wanted their Cardinal back, because they liked him so much. Mercier waited a second before replying, then said with a smile, "I am afraid this will be difficult." It was Mercier again who at a meeting of cardinals whispered in Ratti's ear the words *"Raptim transit,"* the motto that Ratti had inscribed on his episcopal coat of arms, a motto he kept as his upon being elected Pope. Mercier whispered the words several times in Ratti's ear, but they were audible to everybody and were even printed in the newspapers. The Italian press listed Ratti prominently among the most likely *"papabili."*

An interesting incident related to Achille Ratti's mission in Poland illustrates his status before the conclave. When the cardinals were summoned to Rome to elect a new Pope, Cardinal Bertram of Breslau stopped for a day in Munich on his way to Rome to be briefed by Nuncio Pacelli. The two prelates talked about the papal election, too. Who were the cardinals who would have a chance? Who among them were *"papabilii,"* as the Italians put it? To Cardinal Bertram's great surprise, Pacelli, who was usually well informed, told him that Ratti was one of them. Bertram regretfully told Pacelli: "And I antagonized him! How will he feel about me should he be elected?" Pacelli, who knew Ratti well, assured Bertram that Ratti would be the last man to hold anything against anyone. After the papal election Ratti was extremely cordial to Bertram, but during his seventeen-year reign he never once mentioned the plebiscite at Oppeln.

The election of a new Pope is a tremendous event, imposing the heaviest responsibility upon the cardinals from among whom one is to be selected. The cardinals gather, representing the churches of Rome, to elect the Bishop of Rome. This is the time-honored custom. In the past, the clergy of the city (and, for a while, the people as well) directly elected their Bishop, whose absolute supremacy was always accepted and never questioned. Since 1349, only cardinals have been authorized to take part in the election of a Pope.

At the time of the death of Benedict XV, the apostolic constitution of Pius X regulated all details. In accordance with its rules, a conclave was to begin on the eleventh day, at the latest, after the death of a Pope.

During their meetings, the cardinals appoint those ecclesiastics and laymen who will be admitted to the conclave. These are: the governor of the conclave, a high-ranking prelate; two masters of ceremonies; physicians, surgeons, pharmacists, and others. In addition, each Cardinal has the right to take his secretary and his valet with him.

In 1922 the conclave was held in a restricted area of the Vatican Palace. Each Cardinal was assigned three rooms: one for himself and two for his secretary and valet.

The balloting itself is held in the Sistine Chapel. There are four ballots every day; two in the morning and two in the afternoon. At the end of a balloting the ballots are immediately burned in a stove, the chimney of which faces St. Peter's Square. When the new Pope has been finally elected, wet straw is added to the ballots that are to be burned and this produces the famous white smoke that traditionally conveys to the outside world the news that a new Pontiff sits on the throne of St. Peter.

In 1922, a two-thirds majority was needed and the balloting was elaborately controlled to avoid the possibility that a Cardinal might vote for himself.[1]

The election of a Pope involves many ceremonies in which every action or gesture has an ancient liturgical or symbolic meaning. When the cardinals in a solemn procession finally proceed to the conclave, they first ask the help of the Holy Spirit. Then they identify each other's secretaries and aides, whereupon the governor of the conclave, a prelate, and the marshal of the conclave, a layman, cry out *"extra omnes,"* ordering everybody not authorized to be there to leave the area. When it has been determined that the room has been cleared of all such persons, the marshal locks the entrance door with his own key. From this moment on it is his flag that flies over the Vatican, because he is responsible for the safety, the freedom and the integrity of the elections.

Participating in the election of 1922 were Cardinals Vanu-etelli, De Lai, Vico, Belmonte, Pompili, Cagliero, Logue, Bontife, Richelmy, Bacilieri, Merry del Val, Cagiano, Maffi, Lualdi, Mercier, Gasparri, Lucon, Andrieu, Bello, Bourne, Van Rossum, Csernoch, Piffl, Mistrangelo, Frühwirth, Sca-pinelli, La Fontaine, Ranuzzi, Sbarretti, Dubois, Boggiani, Ascalesi, Maurin, Bertram, Silj, Soldevila, Valfre, Kakowski, Dalbor, Ragonesi, Faulhaber, Benlloch, Asis, Schulte, Tacci, Ratti, Bisleti, Billot, Lega, Gasquet, Marini, Giorgi, and Laurenti.

They were divided according to nationality thus: 31 Italians, 5 French, 4 Spanish, 4 German, 3 British, 2 Polish, 1 Austrian, 1 Hungarian, 1 Belgian, and 1 Dutch.

The College of Cardinals, when full, has seventy members. At the death of Benedict XV there were sixty; of these, fifty-three participated in the election.

From the diary of the election kept by Confalonieri, Cardinal Ratti's secretary, it appears that the first three days were uneventful. Toward evening of the third day, February 5,

[1] Pius XII, in his apostolic constitution of December 1945, decreed that for the election of a new Pope two-thirds plus one vote must be cast, thereby avoiding the necessity of so elaborate a control.

1922, according to Archbishop Confalonieri: "one could notice a more intense coming and going and more frequent visits on the part of the Cardinals to the Cardinal of Milan."

Descriptions of the proceedings of conclaves have very often been published by participants, yet certain aspects of the proceedings of a conclave are secret, and any Cardinal who reveals them would be breaking his oath. There are, however, certain aspects of a papal election which are not secret and if revealed do not harm the Church.

Most of the published accounts agree that Achille Ratti was elected on the fourteenth ballot on February 6. Cardinal Mercier, who was one of the electors, issued a pastoral letter to his diocesan faithful, telling them about the conclave.

Schmidlin, the renowned German church historian, accepts the account of the conclave as reported in *Nuova Antologia* for December 16, 1935. According to this report, the voting went as follows:

	Balloting of													
	Feb. 3				Feb. 4				Feb. 5				Feb. 6	
Belmonte	–	–	–	–	–	–	–	–	–	8	–	–	–	–
Bisleti	3	1	4	4	2	2	1	1	–	–	–	–	–	–
De Lai	2	2	1	1	1	–	–	–	–	–	–	–	1	–
Gasparri	8	10	11	12	21	24	24	24	19	16	2	1	–	–
Giorgi	–	–	–	–	–	–	–	–	–	1	–	–	–	–
La Fontaine	4	9	2	1	7	13	22	21	18	8	23	22	18	9
Laurenti	2	4	3	2	2	2	1	1	3	5	4	3	4	2
Lega	–	–	–	1	–	–	–	–	–	–	–	–	–	–
Maffi	10	10	10	9	1	–	–	–	–	–	–	–	–	–
Mercier	1	–	1	–	–	–	–	–	–	–	–	–	–	–
Merry del Val	12	11	14	17	13	7	1	–	–	–	–	–	–	–
Pompili	2	1	1	1	1	1	–	1	1	–	–	–	–	–
Ratti	5	5	6	5	5	4	4	5	11	14	24	27	30	42
Sbarretti	–	–	–	–	–	–	–	–	1	1	–	–	–	–
Van Rossum	4	–	–	–	–	–	–	–	–	–	–	–	–	–
	53	53	53	53	53	53	53	53	53	53	53	53	53	53

It is quite evident that Cardinal Maffi was the first to withdraw. Then Cardinal Merry del Val recognized that he had no chance. The same happened to Cardinal Gasparri and finally to Cardinal La Fontaine. These, of course, are conjectures.

Cardinal Ratti accepted the election and was immediately vested in the traditional white robes. He chose Pius XI as his new name, because, as he said, he had been born into the Catholic Church during the pontificate of Pius IX, and it was Pius X who had called him to Rome. Furthermore, Pius is a name expressing peace; his predecessor Benedict XV dedicated himself to peace and he, Ratti, wanted to devote himself to the pacification of the world.

After a moment of silence, he lifted his voice. As he pronounced the words of acceptance, he was humble though firm. But then his voice became the voice of the Pope making his first pronouncement, declaring that he would defend all the prerogatives and rights of the Holy See. And he told the assembled cardinals that he would make an appearance on the outer balcony of St. Peter's because he wanted to give a sign of his good will to Italy and to the entire world, something no Pope had done for the last fifty years.

CHAPTER SIX

Ruler and Father

ALTHOUGH the people of Milan used to say of Achille Ratti that he was a born Pope, he had quite a different opinion about his office and about himself. Above all, he felt the tremendous, frightening responsibility attached to the papacy, but in his heart he hoped that with the help of God he would be able to master it. Further, he realized sadly that henceforth he would become virtually a prisoner, his movements restricted, and that the only natural scenery and landscape he would enjoy would be the hills surrounding the Vatican. And what were the hills of Rome to Achille Ratti, who had climbed remote Alpine peaks and Mont Blanc? In addition there was also the fact that he knew less about many aspects of the administration of the Church than the other cardinals.

There were moments during the first days and weeks of his papacy when he was overcome by nostalgia for his former life. He knew from history that when a man is elected to be the Vicar of Christ on earth he changes his name and ceases to exist to the world. But he knew, too, that one cannot dehumanize oneself, or strip oneself completely of one's essential being. The world may think that the Pope is a semi-supernatural being. This, however, is not so.

These moments of sadness and nostalgia would come over him whenever he looked at the horizon from the Vatican Palace. And he would say at such times that one of the most difficult things for a human being is to remain inwardly free when his physical freedom is a thing of the past. Another time, as Archbishop Confalonieri has reported, he wrote a letter to a former student of whom he was particularly fond. This letter was very personal; Pius XI never employed the customary "we" that is used by the Popes when speaking of themselves. Thus Pius XI, in February 1922, addressed his young friend as *"Carissimo."* "This is the first letter that I write after having been elected," he told him. And he terminated it with the words: "Come and see Peter in your old teacher who always loved you and wanted the best for you."

After his election there were some misgivings and fears in the Vatican, because Achille Ratti had the reputation of being stern and authoritarian. Msgr. Mella, who had served Pius X and Benedict XV, relates that for one reason or another it was believed that Pius XI was not going to keep him in office.

Actually, Pius XI summoned Mella and confirmed him in his post as his master of ceremonies. Then he let Mella escort him through a tour of the living quarters which were now to be his. At the end, Pius XI asked Msgr. Mella to select any object for himself that he might want to keep as a souvenir. Mella, after a brief reflection, took a paperweight. Pius XI smilingly consented, but he then took a particularly precious and beautiful golden watch that had belonged to Benedict XV and gave it to the astonished Monsignor, saying: "This is given to you by Pope Benedict XV through the hands of Pius XI as a token of his appreciation." And when Mella protested, Pius XI told him: "No, it is not too much for you. You have been as important to him as his own hand."

The enthronement of Pius XI was not followed by "a sweeping reorganization and rolling of heads." He kept most of the advisers, secretaries and chamberlains of Benedict XV. Outwardly, nothing changed; but, in another sense, one of the greatest changes had come over the Vatican. After the death of Pius XI, Prof. Schmidlin wrote: "Leo XIII impressed one by the loftiness of his spirit, Pius X through his pastoral en-

deavors, Benedict XV by his superior wisdom and diplomacy;
but Pius XI united in himself all these characteristics in a
harmonious unity, and in addition he was also a great
scholar."

His first actions were deeply marked by just these attri-
butes of his character. Yet a word of caution is necessary at
this point. Given the nature of the papacy, every deed, every
action is attributed to a Pope; overlooked is the fact that the
Curia in Rome is the real source of many papal projects,
ideas, and recommendations. These, when put into effect,
are generally attributed to the Pope and not to the Cardinal
or lesser official who might have originated the idea or action.
Pius XI, however, was very anxious not to appear as the author or originator of ideas, moves or actions that were not his
own. Since a Pope requires the collaboration of many advisers, he needed them, too, but he always found a way to
reward his collaborators or to point out the contributions of
others. If this is borne in mind, one is astonished by the success achieved by Pius XI, during the first years of his papacy,
in learning "how to become a Pope."

His first actions were those of generosity and justice. He
appointed a number of domestic prelates and bishops all over
the world whose appointment had been pending during the
previous reign. He also made a number of awards. Then, on
March 1, 1922, he changed the constitution regulating the
conclave. According to the old constitution, it had to begin
the eleventh day after the death of a Pope. Because of this,
the American cardinals had not been able to participate; Cardinal Dougherty arrived on February 6, after Pius XI had
already been elected, and Cardinal O'Connell arrived only in
time for the coronation. Now, Pius XI decreed that the conclave should start no earlier than the fifteenth and no later
than the eighteenth day after the death of a Pope. And as a
sign of his regret and generosity, he accorded the conclavists
(the secretaries and valets) of the American cardinals the

same religious privileges, gifts and awards that were due
only to those who actually were inside the conclave.

Then he turned his attention toward the international
scene. The world situation had not changed since he had left
Eastern Europe. The Bolshevik armies had been repulsed
from Poland, but the Soviet regime in Russia was still quite
firmly in the saddle. In Italy, socialists, anarchists and fascists
fought one another in the streets, and revolution of the extreme left was in the realm of possibility. Germany was in the
grip of total exhaustion; inflation was ruining her industries,
banks, and wiping out the middle classes. France was in the
hands of Clemenceau, a man heavily motivated by hatred
and revenge. The British were withdrawing from Europe to
take care of their own imperial problems. The United States,
though many of its leaders were instrumental in preparing
the blueprint of the postwar world, was not yet ready to
take over world leadership, and its attendant responsibilities.

This was the atmosphere in which the Conference of
Genoa opened during the first week of April. It was for the
first time since the war that victors and vanquished now sat
down together to discuss problems, mostly economic, whose
solution would insure peace and welfare. Two main problems
still dominated the conference: the German and the Russian
problems. Whether the Western powers should place their
confidence and trust in Germany was one question, and
whether the Western powers would recognize Soviet Russia
and trade with her was the other. Both questions were of
capital importance, because the German problem was connected with the payment of reparations. The Russian problem was not generally felt to be a danger; the possibility of
establishing commercial relations with the Soviets appealed
to the imagination of the Western powers.

Pius XI recognized a historical opportunity and acted
accordingly. On April 7, 1922, in a letter addressed to Archbishop Signori of Genoa, he called the attention of the delegates to the sad world situation and, after warning them of

its dangers, pointed out that the alleviation of burdens of the vanquished would help the victors, too. He criticized the entire concept of reparations and implored the delegates to forget their hatreds and to act in the spirit of love and friendship. For this letter Pius XI used the draft of a declaration prepared by Benedict XV for the participants of the conference.

But Pius XI went further. On April 29, in a letter addressed to his Secretary of State, Cardinal Gasparri, the Pope reiterated his conviction that peace cannot be re-established merely by silencing guns. A real reconciliation should be brought about. In this letter he declared that he was following the Conference of Genoa with the deepest concern and anxiety. A favorable termination of the conference, he said, would be a victory for Christian civilization. At the end of his letter the Pope repeated his warnings and suggestions.

The world press accorded a sympathetic treatment to the papal message. The French reaction, however, was more important than that of the rest of the world. The attitude of the press and government of France can be summarized in one sentence: If the Pope had been aware of the French fear of Germany, he would have spoken differently. *Osservatore Romano* replied by declaring that the words of the Pope were directed not only to France, but to the entire world. Once again the world did not want to understand that the Pope and the Church have no favorites among nations. If a Pope is to remain true to his mission, he must be a guardian of justice, love and truth, not of national interests.

On May 5, Pius XI sent his emissary, Msgr. Pizzardo, the second highest ranking official of the Secretariat of State, to Genoa with a memorandum to be delivered to the delegates. Very few documents of modern Popes achieved such an importance in the light of subsequent events than this memorandum. The Pope asked the civilized world and the Christian powers to help the starving Russian people and the other peoples of Eastern Europe, and at the same time he asked their help in putting a halt to religious persecution. It is significant to note that the Pope spoke about the persecution of all religions, not only the Catholic.

He also asked that Soviet Russia should immediately grant the following: freedom of conscience, both for Russian and foreign citizens residing in Russia; the exercise of religious freedom, and the freedom to hold divine services both in private and in public; freedom for religious bodies to acquire property for their clergy.

The Pope asked that Russia should provide guarantees that it would observe the above-mentioned points. Further, he requested that no country should recognize the Soviet government until the Soviets signed such an agreement.

Msgr. Pizzardo delivered the memorandum personally to Chicherin, the Russian Foreign Minister, and orally explained its contents. Pizzardo, on behalf of Pius XI, also urged Chicherin to have his government free the head of the Russian Orthodox Church, Patriarch Tychon, and other priests. Further, Pius XI made an offer to the Soviet government to purchase the liturgical vestments and holy vessels belonging to the Orthodox Church that had been confiscated by the Soviet government. Pius XI said that he wanted to leave these vestments and holy vessels in Russia, and preserve them until the religious persecutions were over and then to return them to their rightful owners.

Pius XI acted quickly, but never in an impulsive, haphazard way. He concentrated his efforts upon saving the Russian people; simultaneously, he initiated two other moves. He sent a welfare mission to Soviet Russia, under the leadership of the American Jesuit, Fr. Edmund Walsh, of Georgetown University. He also established formal contact between Chicherin and Msgr. Pacelli, whom Pius XI retained as his Nuncio for Germany. Negotiations were thus begun for a concordat with Russia.

The negotiations between Nuncio Pacelli and the Russian government took place while the mission under Fr. Edmund

Walsh, S.J., was inside Russia. The initiative did not come from the Holy See, but from the Soviet government. The Holy See, however, did not refuse to explore the situation and kept in contact with the Russians. But it turned out that the Bolshevik government was in bad faith. Chicherin and Lenin told foreign diplomats that they were about to conclude an agreement with the Holy See. The purpose of their maneuver was to lure other countries into negotiations for diplomatic recognition.

The conditions for recognition of the Russian government set by Pius XI included in the memorandum given to the delegates at the Conference of Genoa also contained an additional stipulation with respect to the education of youth. The Soviet government seemed to show, at least outwardly, to negotiate the points of the Genoa memorandum. But it refused even to consider the question of the education of youth. Moscow told the Vatican that no compromise was possible with respect to the education of youth. The negotiations thereupon were broken off. No report was ever issued about these negotiations, which were kept secret. (The Soviet government, it may be added, made repeated attempts to start new negotiations with the Holy See during the last thirty-five years, but all of them failed.) A few months later *Pravda* published an article accusing Pius XI of imperialistic aims and expressed the opinion that the Pope was guilty of oppression. Further, the article declared that the Pope deserved capital punishment.

Pius XI was not discouraged because of the meager results of the Genoa Conference. But from then on he avoided, when possible, any direct contact with international conferences, preferring to deal with each nation separately.

While Pius XI had to deal immediately with burning international problems, he did not allow himself to forget spiritual requirements. In May 1922, on the occasion of the twenty-fifth International Eucharistic Congress, held in Rome, he received 200 bishops. The speech he made to them radiated optimism. He had every reason to be optimistic, because, for the first time in decades, a procession comprising several hundreds of thousands of the faithful had wended its way through the streets of Rome to the basilicas, to the catacombs, and other holy places. Rome was reasserting its Christian primacy.

But the new Pope had not yet presented a program. This was twice as important in the case of Ratti, whose ideas and intentions were unknown. Such a program was adumbrated in his first encyclical letter, *Ubi Arcano,* issued December 23, 1922, which dealt with "The Peace of Christ in the Kingdom of Christ." This encyclical is a singular document, written by the Pope himself. It was an outcry against violence and a plea for sincere reconciliation. He made mention of the excessive nationalism abroad in the world, of the inner strife of nations, class warfare, terrorism, profit-hunger, and all the ills of a postwar society. But he did not stop at the enumeration of the ills; he outlined the basic causes of these evils. And in the third part of his encyclical he suggested the remedies. He stated, among other things:

"There exists an institution able to safeguard the sanctity of the law of nations. This institution is a part of every nation; at the same time it is above all nations. She enjoys, too, the highest authority, the fullness of the teaching power of the Apostles. Such an institution is the Church of Christ. She alone is adapted to do this great work, for she is not only divinely commissioned to lead mankind, but moreover, because of her very make-up and the constitution which she possesses, by reason of her age-old traditions and her great prestige, which has not been lessened but has been greatly increased since the close of the war, cannot but succeed in such a venture where others assuredly will fail. . . .

"The Church does not desire, neither ought she to desire, to mix without just cause in the direction of purely civil affairs. On the other hand, she cannot permit or tolerate that the state use the pretext of certain laws or unjust regulations to do injury to the rights of an order superior to that of the state, to interfere with the constitution given the Church by Christ, or to violate the rights of God Himself over civil society."

Those who had thought Pius XI was only a dry historian were surprised to discover that the passionate tone of the encyclical revealed the heart of a true father of peoples, a priest, a human being, full of feeling and love for all mankind.

All his life Pius XI was a methodical administrator. He had a program for each day, and that program was written down.

He awakened at 5:30 in the morning, at the sound of an alarm clock. He shaved himself, then meditated and recited the breviary until 7:30. He celebrated Mass in his private chapel, assisted by his two secretaries. And after Mass he had breakfast, which usually consisted of coffee and milk and one slice of bread. During the winter months he added butter and honey for his bread. While he breakfasted, his secretaries opened his correspondence and informed him of its contents. At 9:00 he was already in his private library, and the audiences began immediately. Private, special and general audiences lasted sometimes until 2:00 or 2:30 P.M. He received visitors every day, even when he was ill.

A private audience with Pius XI was a great experience, because he listened carefully. Then he would speak, and encourage his visitor to answer. He was a great conversationalist in the best sense of the word. He discussed every detail of a subject with great interest. Pius XI possessed an exceptional memory. Everything he learned he retained; he remembered poems from his childhood as well as details of mathematics and geology. Sometimes his private audiences were protracted and other people on the list had to wait, but the Pope would not be aware of this until he was reminded that others were outside waiting.

The general audiences would have been a tiring experience for anyone. But Pius XI drew strength from them. It is known

that Pius XI was an acute observer of the entire scene around
him—of men and of situations. He responded quickly to unusual and sudden exigencies that might arise. During one of
his general audiences, while he was passing before a long
row of kneeling pilgrims, each of whom was to kiss the papal
ring, he suddenly noticed that one pilgrim who had grasped
his hand was unable to find the ring. He immediately realized
that the man was blind. The Pope bent down and said: "We
all are blind my friend. We *all* are blind."

He never interrupted a general audience for lunch. Only
after the audience was finished did he retire for lunch. For
lunch he usually had risotto with saffron, Milanese style, or
a thick Italian soup with vegetables, and a piece of meat with
cooked vegetables, and fruit. Pius XI always drank half a
glass of wine during lunch, and a great quantity of water.
He did not care what kind of wine it was, though he constantly received the best wines in the world from admirers.
All were given to charity, and very little kept in his own
household.

While he lunched, his secretaries stood beside him and continued to report on his correspondence. Several weeks after
his election the secretaries felt that this system would become very hard on them, but they dared not mention this to
the Pope. Finally they decided on "a maneuver." Two small
and narrow stools were brought into the room and placed
against the wall. Next day the secretaries, after having reported, sat down on their stools. The Pope looked up and did
not say a word. The new system was accepted.

After lunch Pius XI would retire for half an hour, and
then stroll in the Vatican gardens, accompanied by one of his
secretaries or by whomever he had invited to walk with him.
At first, Pius XI rode in a horse-drawn carriage to the Lourdes
Grotto. The horses were matched black Arabians. During the
fall of 1922, however, he received as a gift an automobile of
Italian make from the Association of Italian Women, and the
beautiful horses were sold in an auction. Later, in 1925, the

Automobile Club of Milan gave him an Isotta Fraschini. Subsequently, Pius XI rode in a Bianchi, in a Fiat, in a French
Citroën, a German Mercedes, and an American Page. The
cars always stopped at the Lourdes Grotto of the Vatican gardens and waited there. After the Pope prayed there a few
minutes, he began his stroll. During his stroll the Pope would
discuss with his companions various literary, philosophical
and other problems, and recite from Dante, Manzoni or Zanella—his favorites. Then he would ask his companions for
their opinions, because he tested his own ideas and tastes
against theirs.

After this exercise the Pope would take a cup of coffee,
or lemonade, or just a glass of water. Msgr. Mella relates that
once the Pope's chamberlain offered him a cup, too. (The
Pope drank his coffee in his study—alone.) Arborio Mella said
that the coffee was exceptionally bitter. He put two heaping
teaspoons of sugar in it. Its aroma was the finest, but the
bitterness alarmed him until he remembered Talleyrand's
words: "Coffee must be pure as an angel, black as the devil,
and hot as hell." This cup of coffee, however, kept Msgr. Mella
awake all night. The next day, since he had become alarmed
about the Pope's health, he found an opportunity to call the
Pope's attention to it: "I enjoyed the coffee, but there were
moments when I thought I was going to die." The Pope
just nodded. Two days later, when Mella asked the chamberlain what was on the tray, the chamberlain answered:
"*Camomile.*" Pius XI had accepted the warning that too much
coffee might be harmful.

During his strolls in the Vatican gardens Pius XI often went
to a small aviary and fed the birds. He was particularly fond
of a parakeet.

After his stroll in the afternoon he would retire for an hour
of prayer, then go to his private library, where he received
officials of the Vatican until about 8:00, sometimes even later.
Then, with his secretaries and other close officials of the papal
family, he would recite the Rosary in the chapel.

Dinner consisted of a cup of soup or milk, an egg, and some fruit. Around 10:00 the Pope retired again to his private library to work. Generally, he was in bed and asleep by midnight, sleeping, as a rule, soundly and deeply. He would often say that he was able to switch off all the problems of the day from his mind the moment his head rested upon the pillow. But in the morning he would always awaken refreshed, ready for the problems the next day would bring.[1]

Pius XI was a realist. Christian realism includes the recognition both of the realities of the world and the realities of the supernatural. In his daily life he remained true to his ancestors; he esteemed the value of human effort and therefore he was careful in making judgments. He did not like people to use superlatives, nor did he like people when they tried to hide the truth behind superfluous verbiage. He used to say: "Get to the essentials!"

Pius XI was not prejudiced against anybody, but he definitely disliked the atmosphere of a court and he did his best to discourage it. Gossip and intrigue did not reach his ears. If they did, the person who dared gossip or say ill about anybody left in a mood of shame and penitence. Pius XI did not scold; the look that came over his face was enough.

Pius XI also was displeased by loud and authoritarian voices. Once, one of the high ranking prelates in his personal service left the Pope's studio and the moment he found himself outside the door he shouted orders peremptorily to the ushers and the service personnel. The Pope at once rang his bell, summoned the prelate, and in a calm but firm voice told him that he should not shout and that if he wanted to be understood he should talk softly but firmly.

All this belonged to his methodical way of life, a characteristic that he extended to the handling of finances. The administration of the Holy See has an adequate accounting

[1] The time of his meals actually depended on his duties. Sometimes he did not eat dinner before 11 P.M., because he was busy with work. His household, the Franciscan Tertiaries, were alert at all hours.

service, to be sure, but the Pope personally receives gifts from all over the world and these are kept in his private safe.[2]

Pius XI made his accounting every day before he went to bed. On one side of the ledger were the receipts and on the other side were the gifts he had made. He would allow no one else to do this for him. As he expressed it, he wanted to leave a clean house for his successor. But he omitted one thing. He would never add the totals, lest there would not be enough. And he was right. He often received requests for money for the most worthy purposes. And just as often promised to comply, despite the fact that at the moment he had no money at all. But in each case, on the deadline, in some miraculous way, he managed to have the necessary sum. He requested the same accuracy from his subordinates. At the beginning of the month he gave a certain sum that was needed for food and for other personal needs of the household, including the wages of the household staff. At the end of the month his private secretary had to account for every expense in detail.

Pius XI had three rooms. The first was a kind of salon, with gifts and souvenirs placed in showcases with glass sides. The second was his bedroom, no different from the bedroom of an ordinary village priest. The Pope slept in a simple brass-frame bed that can be seen in the poorest parishes in Italy. There was an old-fashioned chest of drawers decked with a white tablecloth, a gift from his brother. On the walls hung photographs of his father, mother, brother, and other relatives. The third room was the library, the walls lined with row after row of books. It had three windows; the Pope's desk faced the third window.

Only since Pius XI has this studio been called the private library. Cardinal Tisserant has explained why: "Pius XI was Pope, but he was librarian, too, and he began his pontificate

---

[2] When Benedict XV died, his safe was totally empty. He always gave away whatever he received, and even spent much of his own personal family fortune for relief work.

with the creation of a new library—a special library for the Pope. Assuredly, his predecessors had possessed books, but at their deaths these volumes were removed from the papal apartments; the library of Pius IX was transferred to St. Apollinaris University (Seminario Pio); that of Leo XIII was distributed to seminaries. Pius XI judged it expedient that a collection of reference books that would be useful to the Pope should remain permanently in the papal apartments. Since he was an excellent bibliographer, he purchased the best books available—mostly through the Vatican Library."

Only such persons were allowed to enter his apartment on the third floor whom he had specifically invited. The secretaries and other prelates who reported to him during mealtimes constituted, of course, an exception.

His household consisted of his personal valet, Signor Malvestiti, whom he had brought with him from Milan, and Signora Teodolinda Banfi, an elderly woman who had been his housekeeper when he was at the Ambrosiana. She was chosen at that time by his mother. On December 1, 1926, the Pope reorganized his household and gave it over to the care of the Franciscan Tertiaries of the Holy Cross, a German religious community whose members are laymen, highly competent and totally dedicated to their tasks. Thereby Pius XI introduced a great and permanent innovation at the Vatican, for since the middle ages the Pope's household had remained a private affair, of which the Popes personally were in charge.

Pius XI first fell ill in December 1936, but later he recovered. Fr. Gemelli, rector and founder of the University of Milan, whom the Pope often asked for advice, came to visit the ailing Pope. He was admitted before noon. The Pope was in a bad mood because of his great pain, and when Gemelli asked about his food, the Pope said, with a faint smile: "The food is very monastic . . ." Gemelli then, after a moment of hesitation, asked in Milanese dialect: "Do you want me to prepare something for you, Holy Father?" The Pope's eyes

lit up. Gemelli, a doctor, was also an excellent cook. He left
the room and after a half hour or so returned with a *risotto
à la Milanese*, made with saffron and cooked "*al dente*." The
Pope consumed the risotto with gusto, sighed and said: "The
best is still that which comes from home."

He felt lonely in Rome and in the Vatican—not as a Pope,
of course, but as a human being. The Roman atmosphere was
not completely his world. From that moment in 1922 when
he was elected, he became aware of the walls that separated
the Vatican from the surrounding streets, and this made him
homesick. He said to a friend in 1922, while pointing to the
walls: "You see those walls? I want to cross over them."

His nostalgia for home, however, was not excessive and it
was completely under control. This was revealed particularly
in his relations with his own family. Upon being elected
Pope, he sent the first benediction by wire to his brother,
Fermo Ratti. Later, loving as he was, he kept his family at a
respectful distance. At the time of his elevation to the papacy
his brother Fermo and his sister Camilla were alive. Achille
Ratti was very close to his immediate family, but he was not
clannish. He expressed his love by caring for them before he
became Pope; he gave them his affection, but never for a
moment did he forget that he was a priest who has a much
larger family than his own. This had been his attitude even
in Milan, where he kept contact only with his closest relatives.

From the time he became Pope his relatives, even in
private, addressed him as Holy Father, or Your Holiness.
Whenever they wanted an audience, they had to go through
regular channels. He did not send Vatican vehicles for them
and they waited in the antechamber like anyone else. He discouraged their frequent visits and made it clear that they
were forbidden to recommend anyone to him as Pope. Not
even his brother and his sister were taken into the private
apartment of Pius XI and, when they participated at the Mass
celebrated by the Pope in his private chapel adjoining the

private apartment, they were admitted through the outer salon. He did not receive them there, but in the library on the
second floor.

When his brother's daughter married, it was the Pope who
performed the marriage service in the consistory hall of the
Vatican. There was no fanfare. It was a simple service. After
the ceremony there was a reception in the adjoining halls—
but without the Pope. His wedding present to the bride was
typical: a library of one hundred volumes, carefully selected
by a prominent Roman matron under the direction of the
Pope.

His nephew, Franco Ratti, a civil engineer, performed several tasks, important ones, for the Vatican. But he was never
paid for them. The Pope accepted his contribution on the
condition that he should remain on the payroll of the Banca
Commerciale Italiana (his employer for many years).

Pius XI possessed a small sum of money of his own. He
helped his sister Camilla out of this personal fund. He left
enough in his last will to assure the same monthly payment
for the sister, provided, however, that after her death the
remaining sum should be used for a specified charitable
purpose.

This was the pattern of his days during the seventeen years
of his pontificate.

In 1922, Pius XI was about five feet nine inches in height,
erect, vigorous, and agile. His bearing was imposing. His
shoulders were square and broad, his forehead was unlined,
his oval face harmonious, and the dark eyes behind the gold-
rimmed spectacles were friendly and alert. There was no
tenseness in his attitude. People who spoke to him immediately recognized that fundamentally he remained the same
person he had been during his stay at the Ambrosiana. In
his expression one saw goodness and kindness, and gracious-
ness in his behavior. But there was an unmistakable melan-
cholia, although restrained and controlled, about the Pope.
This was most evident in his conversation which in the first

stages was characterized by curt phrases and sentences; subsequently, he would warm up, to the delight and pleasure of
his friends.

He was formal, first of all because his office required it,
and because it was a means of self-protection against unwar-
ranted intrusions. Fundamentally, he was very emotional and
he responded quickly to love, affection and friendship. The
characteristics of the "little old man" remained, visible
enough to color the total context of his personality.

Of the fact that he was Pope there was never any doubt.
Before Pius XI would ever pronounce a word, his visitors
and secretaries sensed his authority. There is a great difference between being authoritarian and radiating authority
that is accepted and welcome. Pius XI did not tolerate any
contrariness for its own sake, but he encouraged free speech.
He wanted his advisers to speak freely and even critically.
And they did.

CHAPTER SEVEN

The Fascist Challenge

WHEN, on February 6, 1922, Cardinal Bisleti appeared on the balcony of St. Peter's Church facing the piazza, a sudden silence fell upon the hundreds of thousands gathered in the historic square. They knew that the new Pope had been elected because they had seen the traditional white smoke, but they did not yet know his name. The Cardinal then lifted his right hand slowly to indicate that he would speak to the multitudes.

"*Annuntio vobis gaudium magnum . . .*" "I announce to you a great joy; we have a new Pope . . . His Eminence Most Reverend Lord Cardinal Achille Ratti, who has chosen the name of Pius XI."

His last words were drowned by the cheers of the throng. Then everybody started to push toward the entrance of St. Peter's Church, because the Popes no longer appeared on the outer balcony of St. Peter's but on the inner one, from which they would impart their first apostolic benediction to the people gathered there. This was done in protest, ever since 1870 when the Popes became voluntary prisoners of the Vatican, and no longer set foot on Italian soil, not even appearing on the outer balcony of St. Peter's.

Suddenly, however, great confusion arose because papal ushers in uniform appeared on the outer balcony and started to hang a red carpet from the balcony.

The festive, cheering throng outside did not know of the incident that had occurred inside the Sistine Chapel where

Achille Ratti had just pronounced the Latin word *Accepto,* meaning that he bowed to the decision of the College of the Cardinals that had elected him. The new Pope was vested in his white robe, while the sacristan, a bishop, and two of the cardinals placed the mantle upon his shoulders. Then Pius XI suddenly turned to them and said: "I will impart the apostolic benediction from the balcony facing the piazza."

This gesture meant a break with a fifty-year custom; those who knew the mind of Achille Ratti were aware that this meant the beginning of a new era.

It was one of the greatest days in the history of post-World War I Italy, because no one had expected so symbolic and promising a gesture. Italian officials and the people knew, of course, that his predecessor, Benedict XV, had been ready to negotiate to end the self-imposed captivity and settle "the Roman question." Yet everybody thought no Pope would "compromise" and evidence a public sign of good will. The "intransigents" in the Catholic camp secretly hoped that the Italian government would apologize before the Pope would do anything in the way of reconciliation.

Achille Ratti's education in the climate of the Italian Risorgimento and his absolute distaste for power politics, his clear vision about the role of the Church in the temporal order, were not known to the mass of the people.

The Italian people did not know that the new Pope did not belong to either the intransigents or the compromisers, nor did they know that he was imbued with the ideas of harmony between Church and state derived from Manzoni, or that the former librarian of the Vatican was an admirer of Thomas More (whom he later canonized), who had given his life for his principles.

By his appearance in public the new Pope gave overt, eloquent sign of his generosity and magnanimity toward the Italian state and the Italian people.

In Achille Ratti's mind the Roman question was not purely an Italian question, as many writers, politicians and even statesmen were accustomed to present it. He felt no resentment toward the Italian state, or toward the history preceding its formation. The ghosts of Garibaldi, Mazzini and the rest of the anti-Church revolutionaries and super-enthusiasts did not trouble him, because he was firmly set on something positive. He did not want to argue over questions in which he was in agreement, even with the Italian ultra-liberals; the Holy See has no need of a large territory to express and assert sovereignty. But the Holy See did require a minimal allotment of territory, regardless of how small it might be, because the Church—though its aims are supernatural—lives partly in the temporal order. And the head of the Church, who is a sovereign, cannot depend upon the benevolence of the Italian, or any other secular, government. The see of the Pope must be firmly established within the temporal order, accepted by other states and assured immunity and continuity by international agreements.

Thus, Pius XI, despite the public blessing he imparted on the occasion of his election to the papacy, was just as firm as his predecessors in insisting upon the claims of papal sovereignty and absolute freedom of action. This was expressed in statements of his predecessor Benedict XV and after Ratti's election in an inspired article in *Osservatore Romano*.

This is proved by his restatement of them in his first encyclical of 1922. There he asserted that the divine origin of papal rule, as well as the rights of all Christianity, demanded that the Vicar of Christ be free and independent, that he be subject to no foreign power; that as a matter of duty he, too, repeated the demands of the Popes who had preceded him. Further, that he, too, had to deplore such a situation. He expressed the hope, however, that God would bring a day of peace and reconciliation in the interests of Italy and the entire world.

Pius repeated these statements often, in particular during the secret transfer (in order to avoid anti-clerical incidents) of the remains of Leo XIII to the Lateran, and again when he declined to take part in the consecration of an important religious institution in Rome. And again in 1925—during the Holy Year—Pius XI regretfully stated that, unlike the pilgrims, he could not cross the threshold of the Vatican. Finally, in 1927, he deplored the fact that he could not be present at the opening of the Lateran Museum.

His whole program was broadly outlined in his statements. The only question was: Would he be able to solve the immense task that loomed ahead?

The Bolshevik problem was far from being settled and it was evident that the Western powers were eventually going to trade with Soviet Russia, thereby strengthening the regime.

Pius XI, who knew the East as well as the West, foresaw the coming of a Hitler. It was obvious to him that the German people would not tolerate the oppressive Treaty of Versailles. He foresaw the violent outbreaks of German nationalism because he was familiar with both the material and spiritual ingredients that led to such outbreak. As a librarian in Milan he had read Nietzsche and other philosophers who glorified instinct and irrationalism.

The Pope also knew that the situation in France might cause the Holy See more trouble. He read *L'Action Française,* and, being a true intellectual, was well informed about the attitude of the French hierarchy and clergy. This gave him cause for grave concern.

Through his contacts with foreign diplomats and his historical studies he also was familiar with the situation in Spain. He knew that the organization of the Church there was outmoded, that social conditions were beyond imagination, that the state and the wealthy were identified with the Church in the eyes of the Spanish working classes and peasantry. He was fully aware that the Spanish ills had a contagious effect upon Latin American countries, and, furthermore, that the primitive religiosity of the peoples in Latin America was often the outcome of ignorance rather than an expression of true religious awareness and sensibility.

Wherever he looked he saw signs of alarm and crises. But he was prepared and determined to act.

The tremendous program he set for himself could have been carried out only by a man who deeply understood the main spiritual and ideological currents of his time, and his own relationship to them, and was able to act decisively.

At home, the situation in Italy was not too promising for a settlement of Church-state tensions. The new fascist regime bitterly fought the Partito Popolare (People's Party) for which the Vatican was held responsible, despite the statements of the papal Secretary of State and *Osservatore Romano* that the papacy sought to refrain from any interference in Italian politics, or from influencing the Partito Popolare.

On August 6 and October 22, 1922, the Pope sent two letters to the Italian episcopate, urging them to be true to their mission of loving their neighbors in the name of Christian brotherhood. He also expressed his concern over the outbreak of violence and discord, and pointed to the harm this would cause Italy at home and abroad. Further he called for a return to God, and observance of the law as a remedy for discord, calling upon the bishops to take the lead in pacifying their fellow citizens.

Tension became more acute in October 1922 when Mussolini marched on Rome at the head of his Blackshirts. Later, he split with the Partito Popolare, from which Don Luigi Sturzo resigned as leader. At this time the Centro Nazionale was formed, a party of rich, aristocratic Catholics who openly supported fascism. But the papal press refused support and collaboration.

A series of state-sponsored actions caused the Pope great concern. In the spring of 1924, just before parliamentary elections, attacks on religious orders and organizations increased. In his consistorial speech of May 24 the Pope deplored the situation, but instructed religious authorities and priests not to interfere in politics or use their organizations for political purposes. At the same time, he protested against unpunished acts of crime and violence, as did *Osservatore Romano* time and time again.

Despite these tensions, an increasing number of signs indicated that an understanding could be reached between the Church and the government. Mussolini, for his part, let no opportunity go by without publicly insisting upon his respect for religion, the papacy, and the inherent Catholicism of the Italian people. He restored Catholic primary schools and made religious instruction obligatory at all school levels; later, he acknowledged recognizing the indissolubility of marriage, abolished anti-clerical legislation, and exempted the clergy from compulsory military service. These acts were properly appreciated and praised by the Pope in his consistorial speech of March 24, 1924. Further, the fascist regime broke the spell of the past, purged certain patriotic celebrations of their traditional anti-clerical themes and flavor (particularly the celebration of September 20, marking the fall of Rome), and returned the Chigi Library to the Pope as a gift. The University of the Sacred Heart in Milan was recognized and houses of religious orders were restored.

Despite these friendly gestures, the Pope's allocution of December 14, 1925, bitterly denounced fascist excesses. However, a clue was offered for negotiations. The initiative came from Mussolini, who wanted to buttress his reputation by restoring religious peace to Italy. After obtaining the unanimous approval of the College of Cardinals, Pius XI authorized the holding of meetings of Italian and Vatican officials in private to prepare for official negotiations.

There is no doubt that Achille Ratti always wanted a reconciliation with Italy. Upon becoming librarian of the Vatican he met Benedict XV and Cardinal Gasparri often. Both Church dignitaries were in favor of a settlement. Benedict XV, indeed, made several statements to this effect. On the

other hand, the Italian government and parliament, since
1915, were not as anti-Catholic as before, despite the fact that
certain laws remained in effect—on paper. Pius XI started the
work of reconciliation *before* Mussolini became prime minister; all statements on the Italian side that the reconciliation
was totally the work of Mussolini belong to the realm of
imagination or ignorance.

Pius XI was aware, and often expressed it as his opinion,
that Mussolini, an astute politician, was in need of peace with
the Church. Knowing the ideology of fascism better than anyone else, Pius XI was aware of the fact that Mussolini would
try to dominate and use the Church for his political purposes.
The Pope hoped that Mussolini as an Italian and nominal
Catholic, despite his ideology and lust for power, would refrain from committing an irreparable act against the papacy.

Pius XI had no more sympathy for fascism than the Italian
masses who accepted it as a political fact. Furthermore,
he had grown up in a political atmosphere in which he
had shared its humanitarian aspects, but none of the anti-
religious biases that accompanied it. This is the ever-recur-
ring question that Catholics have to face when confronted
with the dogmatic and hierarchical structure of their religion that *seems* to be opposed to human freedom. Pius XI
was determined to settle the Roman question and he would
have worked for it whether Mussolini or a democratic prime
minister happened to have been head of the Italian government.

The negotiations to restore papal sovereignty and to establish a concordat with the Italian state—two different tasks, yet
closely connected, because the Pope considered a concordat
a *sine qua non* to the negotiations relative to papal sovereignty—began during the summer of 1926. The contacts
were typical of the century-old Vatican diplomacy. The negotiations were secret, responsibility for them being placed entirely in the hands of Domenico Barone, representing the
Italian government, and Francesco Pacelli, a brother of Eu-

genio (the future Pius XII), representing the Vatican. The Pope made one condition: if it were revealed that the negotiations were going on, "I will shelve the project!"

Thus began the 200 meetings in which the problem was studied. Francesco Pacelli made it clear at the first meeting that the Pope would insist on two conditions: that in some way or other the Pope's temporal sovereignty be re-established; and that religious marriage ceremony be put on a par with civil marriage ceremony.

Since Barone agreed, this became the basis for the preliminary negotiations during which the territorial limits of the Vatican state were agreed upon. It was also agreed that a concordat would follow the agreement, and that the state would adjust its marriage laws to those of the Church. On his part, the Holy Father renounced any guarantees from any other powers. In 1926, the negotiators had 110 conferences and 129 audiences with the Pope (often lasting from three to four hours). On November 24, 1926, the first drafts were ready.

In the last months of 1926 and thereafter, negotiations on behalf of the papacy were carried on by Msgr. Borgongini-Duca at Cardinal Belmonte's villa. They often lasted from 10:00 in the morning until 7:00 at night. On September 5, 1928, when the whole question was almost settled between the two parties, it was announced that negotiations could begin *officially*. On November 22, 1928, the king formally authorized Barone, and the Pope authorized Cardinal Gasparri, to sign any agreements that were reached. Barone fell ill, and his place was taken by Mussolini himself.

After January 21, 1929, the treaty and the concordat were discussed point by point, so that Francesco Pacelli could report to the Pope every morning. There was, of course, an army of jurists, specialists, protocolists, and others involved. On February 7, 1929, Cardinal Gasparri, Secretary of State of the Vatican, called together the heads of the diplomatic missions accredited to the Holy See to his official chambers.

There he announced that the seemingly insoluble Roman question had been peacefully solved, and that the Vatican and Italy were working on a concordat to regulate their mutual relations. At noon on February 11, 1929, Cardinal Gasparri, representing Pius XI, received Mussolini, who was representing King Victor Emmanuel, in the Lateran Palace. Both were accompanied by their entourages and both signed the documents that had been prepared.

On the next day the Pope celebrated the seventh anniversary of his coronation in the festively adorned St. Peter's Church. He was acclaimed by cheering thousands. Among the honored guests were high Italian army officials, three government ministers, and King Gustav of Sweden. From the loggia he imparted blessings to 200,000 persons in the square. Rome was gaily illumined that night, public buildings decked with flags of the papacy and the Italian kingdom. Crowds gathered respectfully before the residence of the king and queen, a *Te Deum* was celebrated, and the Nuncio held a reception. On March 9 the diplomatic corps (twenty-seven ambassadors and ministers) was festively received in the Vatican.

Pius XI was exposed to criticism by some anti-fascists because of the speech he delivered on the day after the signing of the Lateran Treaty. In this speech it was said he called Mussolini *"l'uomo della providenza"*—the man of providence. The critics asserted that, despite the joy that the Church felt over the reconciliation, it was not necessary to express papal approbation of Mussolini's character. This criticism later gave birth to the myth that Pius XI was personally, as well as in his policy, an authoritarian who did not tolerate criticism, and that therefore he was psychologically more disposed toward dictators than toward democratic statesmen. Even books that claim merit from a historical point of view contain the same error, primarily because they failed to evaluate the personality of Achille Ratti. They seemed to have forgotten that he was sixty-five years old when he was elected to the papacy, and they dealt with the person of the Pope as if

the weight and experience of those sixty-five years had left
no mark upon him. It can be safely said that Achille Ratti,
Pius XI, had no more sympathy for fascism than for Voltairian
liberalism. This is evident from his life.

His famous statement about the "man of providence"
sounds quite different in the light of fact. When the negotiations for the Lateran Treaty were ended and the text of both
the treaty and the concordat were ready and the date for the
signatures set, Pius XI decided to give a speech that would
fit the occasion. It was an event of world importance which
affected the papacy much more than it did the kingdom of
Italy. He was, however, very careful and wanted to avoid any
undue solemnity. Therefore, he asked the rector of the Catholic University of Milan that a pilgrimage, composed of professors and students, be organized and appear before him on
February 12, one day after the signature, because he wanted
to incorporate his remarks on the reconciliation into a speech
delivered to a non-political academic educational body. That
he chose a Milan institution is of secondary importance, but
not exactly accidental. He felt at home with the Milanese
and wanted to talk as if to his immediate family. He pondered
his decision well. Ever conscious of his authority as a Pope,
he knew that he could have planned his speech in a different
way, by holding a consistory or issuing a brief or an encyclical
letter to the Italian episcopate. This would have been more
solemn. He chose, however, a more casual way. The fact that
he talked to educators and students underlined the keynote
of his talk, and projected the problem into the future, thereby
foreshadowing the possible causes of conflict. For nothing
stood so close to his heart as the Catholic education of youth,
and this right and duty he considered to be pillars of basic
freedom. One could, therefore, explain his speech and the circumstances in which it was held as a friendly warning to the
totalitarian pretensions of any state.

In this speech Pius XI declared: "We must say that we
have been nobly seconded by the other side. And perhaps it

was also necessary to have such a man whom Providence
arranged that we should meet; a man who did not have the
preoccupations of the liberal school; for those men (who belonged to the liberal school) all those laws, orders or, better
said, disorders, all those laws and rules were fetishes, and because they were fetishes they were the more untouchable
and venerated the uglier they were."

And in the same speech the Pope stressed the importance
of those points which were *sine qua non* of the concordat;
points which were basically anti-fascist in their ideological
context.

The expression "a man whom Providence" is reduced to
proper proportion because Pius XI used it in relation to other
statesmen, too, and when he mentioned the "liberal school"
he meant those who under this name enslaved the Church
in Italy, Germany and France. He used the word "Providence" because he was a priest, a believer in God; other people might have used the word "destiny."

The importance of the education and formation of youth,
a basic freedom in the eyes of the Church, was very soon
questioned by the fascist government. It interpreted the freedom of Catholic Action in a way quite different from that
envisioned by the Pope. For the sake of the reconciliation,
both parties, Pius XI and Mussolini, had made certain com-
promises; after the ratification of the treaty no compromise
was possible. The good will of Pius XI went very far, made
evident by the following episode.

Though Mussolini did not need a parliament, he maintained the appearance of legislative discussion and instituted a fascist chamber of deputies and a senate. There were
elections held from time to time to send deputies to the fascist
chamber. The right to vote was the prerogative of the few.
In 1929, the year in which the Lateran Treaty was signed,
Mussolini prepared "elections" for the chamber. He knew that
he was going to "win" anyhow, but he was not unaware of
the limits of his real popularity. Therefore, he felt that the
peace with the Pope would increase his popularity.

On March 10, 1929, Mussolini delivered his most important electoral campaign speech, and praised the Church, and the Pope. Being a good politician, he exploited to the utmost the signature of the treaty. The elections took place on March 24, and, as expected, the national list of the fascist party received an overwhelming majority (8,500,000 votes to 136,000). The opening speech of King Victor Emmanuel III, inaugurating the fascist chamber, also hailed the reconciliation between the Holy See and Italy. The first sign of how Mussolini might interpret the treaty came from Mussolini himself in his speech of May 13, when the Lateran Treaty came up for formal ratification in the fascist chamber. Mussolini minimized Italy's concession and presented the treaty as a victory of the Italian government, that is, a victory of the lay state over the Church. The fascist chamber passed the ratification unanimously. In the senate, 293 voted for the treaty and 10 against it. Benedetto Croce, the philosopher of liberalism, whom Mussolini esteemed highly and kept as a member of the senate, spoke against the treaty. The opposing votes were those of Croce's followers.

Mussolini's speech could not have been left unanswered by the Holy See, because, whatever his reasons, they did not correspond to the truth. The Pope wrote a letter to his Secretary of State, Cardinal Gasparri, pointing out the errors in Mussolini's speech. This was published in *Osservatore Romano* on May 30, 1929. It was unlikely that a major debate would ensue that might have jeopardized the treaty. Nevertheless, Mussolini's reply was awaited with considerable tension. Mussolini, however, remained silent. Contemporary politicians and some historians considered his restraint a sign of political wisdom. From his own point of view, it was wisdom indeed. It would have been unwise to give any further indication of his bad faith, and thereby signal to the country the violations of the most important stipulations of the treaty and the concordat.

Mussolini had no intention of letting the Catholic youth movement and Catholic education and freedom of the Church be interpreted and carried out as it was stipulated by the letter and spirit of the treaty. The Lateran Treaty became effective June 7, 1929, but toward the end of the year the controversy was already in full swing.

The Italian government and the fascist party insisted that every youth become a member of the fascist youth organization. Catholic Action was not allowed to hold public meetings and the freedom of its press was hampered. Tension between the Vatican and the fascists had reached the breaking point by 1931. The government ordered the dispersion of the entire organization of Catholic Action at local and national levels. Fascist police ransacked the archives and the files of Catholic Action in each city and in most villages. It was a police action on a grand scale, with the apparent purpose of finding some compromising documents in order to prove that Catholic Action, under the direction of the Pope, conspired against the fascist government.

We now know that Mussolini did not want to undo the Lateran Treaty, but, as a man whose teachers were Nietzsche and Georges Sorel, the philosopher of violence, he always thought in terms of power politics and wanted to secure advantageous strategic positions for future attacks or defense. Real or fake documents about papal conspiracy could have placed him in the position of playing the role of the injured party, hoping that this might reinforce his position of strength in order to carry out his own ideological dreams.

Yet no such documents were found. Italy, however, was shaken again by a deep political crisis and on the verge of a possible civil war. About 3,000 Catholics were murdered by black-shirted fascist gangs during those two years. Local leaders of Catholic Action and the faithful stood firm and were ready to fight. Certain circles of Italian society, however, were most anxious to yield to Mussolini, because at that time they saw in him the rising star of Italy's imperialistic rebirth.

Everything depended upon the Pope and his intentions. He expressed his views in the already quoted utterances; but these were declarations of principles, not of immediate purpose.

At the height of the tension Pius XI called one of his main advisers, a friend in Lombardy, to Rome. This friend enjoyed the respect of the Vatican court and men of political life, because it was known that the Pope very often asked his advice and followed it. When he arrived in the Vatican Palace, he was led to the antechamber to be received by the Pope at once. Several high dignitaries of the Vatican, some of them instrumental in the preparation of the Lateran Treaty, were there waiting for him. They urged the man whom the Pope had summoned to use all his influence and eloquence to convince Pius XI not to act and not to do anything that might jeopardize the treaty. They told him that the Pope should refrain from issuing an encyclical against fascism.

Then the doors of the Pope's study opened and the invited adviser was ushered inside. When the friend was inside the following conversation ensued:

The Pope asked, smiling: "With whom did you speak in the antechamber, and what did they tell you?"

"Holy Father," answered the friend, "you asked me, so I must answer. This way it is not a denunciation, for originally I did not want to tell you anything . . . You have ordered me to do so, however." And then he related the scene that had occurred outside.

"I have known that they think this way. But I was awake all night; I prayed and I prepared everything. Though I am going to defend the work of reconciliation I have decided that I will issue the encyclical, whatever its consequences might be. Here it is." And he showed the final draft of the encyclical, "*Non Abbiamo Bisogno.*"

When the government did not give in and went a step farther against Catholics, requesting a new kind of oath from all civil servants, many Catholics thought they should not take the oath because it might harm the Church. When Pius XI heard about this problem which struck hundreds of thousands of small people whose jobs might have been taken away by the government, he decided to issue a statement in which he declared that those who took the oath were not obliged to consider it as binding. He wanted to help these hundreds of thousands of little people.

The agreement with Italy known as the Lateran Treaty was an international treaty of greatest importance, and it cannot be dealt with exclusively as if it were a domestic affair between Italy and the Holy See. The Lateran Treaty which assured freedom and sovereignty for the Holy See is one thing and the concordat with Italy another. Mussolini and some fascist leaders thought that if they observed the international provisos of the Lateran Treaty, that is, leaving inviolate the sovereignty of the Pope, fascism would thereby be free to suppress the freedom of Italian Catholics, those very freedoms which were guaranteed in the concordat. This was a great mistake and, as has been said, Pius XI was ready to undo the entire work of reconciliation if need be in order to prevent this, despite the fact that he once said that he was ready to negotiate with the devil if the salvation of the faithful were at stake. Later on, he often expressed the view that he was ready to make agreements after a good fight. But this never meant that he was ready to sacrifice his principles or those of the Church. This was a declaration that he made immediately after his election.

After the stormy years of 1930 and 1931 the fascist attacks were called off, and a cordial relationship developed between the Holy See and the Italian government, as well as with the House of Savoy. The king and queen of Italy paid an official visit to the Pope, and it seemed that a relative state of calm had at last descended upon the country. There were not lacking, however, a number of hotheads who were of the opinion that because fascist Italy had signed the Lateran Treaty the Vatican should become a sort of exponent of the imperial Roman government. This obviously was absolutely impossible. Individual Italians, clerical or lay, were free to express any opinion; the papacy itself remained impartial. While the entire press of the Italian peninsula was under a rigorous censorship, *Osservatore Romano,* edited and printed in Vatican City, published news forbidden to the Italian press. This greatly irritated some of the fascist leaders. Outwardly, for appearance's sake, the peace was kept. But behind the scenes the fascist government fought the Vatican's influence.

It was announced as a great moral achievement that Italian censors did not allow the publication of books in which a suicide occurred, and it was said that the Holy See was particularly grateful because masonic lodges were forbidden in Italy. The Holy See did not express a specific opinion on such moves, but it expressed general opinions that were applicable to these fascist measures. The fascist regime became particularly alarmed when it noticed that the relationship between the House of Savoy—to which the Italian army was loyal—and the Holy See was growing more and more cordial. It just happened that Mussolini's first steps in the direction of an alliance with Hitler were taking place at that time. In fascist thinking the leaders of the Italian army, including such figures as Marshal Badoglio and the House of Savoy, were linked with freemasonry, generally anti-Catholic. Such an alliance between the Church, the dynasty, the army and freemasonry could present a mortal danger to fascist aims. The years from 1935 should be evaluated from this point of view. As a matter of fact, the tension behind the scenes increased. Pius XI sent warning after warning to Mussolini, who did not heed them.

Pius XI was occasionally criticized because of alleged profascist statements and particularly about utterances—allegedly—favoring Mussolini's war against Abyssinia. With due respect for Italy's genuine liberals, one has to emphasize that certain Italian anti-clericals considered the papacy even in our twentieth century as if it were a domestic Italian institution. No wonder, since the papal state for more than a thousand years had participated in the power politics of the Italian peninsula.

During the stormy decades of the reign of Pius IX many

anti-clericals wanted the Pope to become the king of Italy because, for a brief historical moment, it seemed that Pius IX, though Pope, would serve their ideology. Less than a hundred years later Pius XI was disliked by the heirs of the same ideological trend because he did not lead the anti-fascists to the barricades. They were forgetting again that the Pope as head of the Catholic Church cannot pursue Italian (or any other) politics. Whenever Pius XI seemed to be satisfied with the papacy's relationship to the Italian state, these circles resented it, overlooking the fact that Pius XI had not made a treaty with the fascist party but with the Italian state. If the anti-fascists wanted a change of government it was their job to make it, not the Pope's.

During Mussolini's war against Abyssinia, it was even said that the Pope blessed Italian arms that were dispatched to that war. Pope Pius XI never blessed any arms or weapons. He blessed individual soldiers or sent his benediction to groups for purely spiritual purposes. There was no reason why soldiers should be excluded from the papal benediction: a soldier sent into battle is closer to death than anybody else.

Pius XI never favored Mussolini's war against Abyssinia, nor has such a statement ever been substantiated. Even the Abyssinians never believed it, as is proved by their acceptance of an Apostolic Delegate with a special high-ranking status in Addis Ababa. Obviously the emperor would never have consented to receive and tolerate such an envoy of the Vatican if he believed the Holy See had favored Italy. After all, the emperor is aware that the "right-hand man" of Pius XI in 1936 is now Pope himself.

Pius XI made many speeches before, during, and after the Abyssinian war. Many of these speeches were extemporaneous, and Pius XI did not check the texts before they were printed, often in a summarized form, in the *Osservatore Romano*. One of his speeches in August 1936 was addressed to nurses, male and female, who served with the Italian Army fighting in Abyssinia. It was one of those paternal, warm-hearted, spiritual, and humanitarian admonitions so peculiar to Achille Ratti, and it was extemporaneous. There was a touch of emotion in it, and since he spoke to Italians it was Italian emotion.

This speech was edited by a Vatican official who thought there should be some note of Italian patriotism in it, otherwise it would seem hostile to Italy. The editing he did was not authorized by the Pope, and when Pius XI heard of it he made public the fact the changes were unauthorized.

Pope Pius XI did not make an issue of this incident, because he felt that both Italian and world public opinion could not be misled into believing that the Pope (who had warned Mussolini against the Abyssinian campaign) would condone the action of the Italian dictator. Indeed, Abyssinian seminarians in Rome were the only ones whose *Collegio* (Papal Educational Institute) is located on the territory of Vatican City proper.

The Lateran Treaty provided, among other things, for the establishment of Vatican City, with everything that belongs to a modern state: boundaries, a telephone, postal and telegraph system, a railway station, a courthouse; even a jail. The little territory became a sovereign country with its formal citizen population, passports and border control. Not only did Vatican City proper become the domain of the Popes, but also the villa and huge park at Castel Gandolfo in the Alban Hills, as well as several important edifices within the city of Rome. Originally, Pius XI wanted to extend the boundaries to the Tiber, which would have permitted the construction of an airstrip. But the negotiators decided otherwise.

Pius XI participated personally in the construction of Vatican City, involving himself in the smallest details, whether they concerned the erection of the broadcasting station or the appearance of the walls at the palace of the governor of the new city. This was not done out of lack of confidence in the man whom he had selected to supervise the construction job —the Milanese contractor and architect-engineer, Leone Ca-

stelli—but because of his genuine pleasure and interest in this
kind of constructive participation in the tasks to be done. It
was akin to the industry and zeal with which he had reorganized the Ambrosiana Library in Milan, where two new
wings had been built under his supervision, and to his interest
in the building of the Catholic Universities of Lublin and of
Milan. His prudence in these matters, combined with his native sense of business in the best sense of the word, enabled
him to continue to act in the tradition of the great Popes,
whose spiritual greatness was matched by their sense of
beauty and respect for all the arts and sciences.

So involved did Pius XI become in the construction work
that he almost became a bricklayer himself. Leone Castelli,
director of technical services of the small state, who died in
1956, could tell anecdotes by the hour about the building interest of the Pope.

Castelli came from a family of small contractors in Lombardy. Pius XI liked him because of his frank, honest, un-
compromising nature that complemented his architectural
talents. The relationship between Pius XI and Castelli was
somewhat like that between a Renaissance Pope and his art-
ists. When Castelli died in 1956, he left an enormous amount
of scribbled notes, plans, drafts, projects, letters—small pieces
of paper and large sheets—of Pius XI's suggestions to him.
This material fills twelve large binding folders. It indicates
that much of the new construction and many of the renova-
tions in Vatican City, including archaeological projects, were
initiated by Pius XI. He had found an eager collaborator in
Castelli, to whom he sent all these projects for approval and
study. Pius XI's notes, projects and letters to Castelli are full
of wit and irony. One day he sent Castelli a piece of string
glued to a white piece of paper. The Pope had found the string
in the bread he had had for breakfast, and since Castelli was
responsible for everything, including the bakery, the Pope
sent him this friendly "warning." Pius XI exempted Castelli
from any courtly formalities; he gave orders that whenever

Castelli was summoned he should be admitted immediately, "even if his shoes are dirty with plaster."

Once Pius XI asked Castelli to give him back the first draft of the delimitations of Vatican City, made also by the Pope himself. This was a historical document and Castelli wanted to keep it. He avoided a direct answer each time the Pope asked for it. Finally, the Pope said to him: "Well, I understand now, we won't find it any more." He understood that he should not ask for the return of something that he had once given away.

Pius XI wanted Vatican City to have the most modern equipment. He had new presses installed for *Osservatore Romano* and for the Vatican Polyglot Press. The Vatican radio station was installed under the supervision of Guglielmo Marconi himself. The famous observatory was transferred from its inadequate location in the Vatican Gardens to Castel Gandolfo, and also remodernized. An automatic switchboard was installed by the United States Bell Telephone Company. Yet Pius XI himself never once used the telephone. The Pope of progress who recited Zanella, even during his strolls in the Vatican Gardens, the Pope who modernized the entire papacy as an institution and brought the Vatican's administrative and technical facilities up to date, felt that he never could be in so great a hurry that he had no time to ring the rope bell that would summon his secretary waiting in the anteroom.

Pius XI was often compared to Sixtus V (1520–1590), a Pontiff of great energy and tenacity of purpose, as well as of great piety, simplicity and generosity. Sixtus V was one of the greatest builders of Rome. It was he who founded the Vatican Polyglot Press, and the churches and other buildings that he constructed were many indeed.

It would involve too much detail to list all the construction sponsored by Pius XI in Rome, in Italy, and throughout the world. We will mention only that which he personally initiated and financed.

In Rome he partially restored the ancient baptistry of the
Lateran Basilica and rebuilt the patriarchal palace at the
Lateran. In the church of Santa Maria Maggiore the basilica
was completely restored to its most ancient form, its mosaics
repaired, and a modern lighting system installed. The Can-
celleria, one of Rome's beautiful Renaissance buildings, was
completely restored; the Palace of Convertendi of the Sacred
Congregation of Oriental Rites and for the Apostolic Penitentiary was restored. So were the Palace of the Holy Office,
St. Paul's Basilica, and many other structures—their ancient
forms, hidden through the centuries, again brought to light.

St. Peter's Basilica, seemingly ever in need of repair, underwent a major restoration, beginning with the dome of Mi-
chelangelo. It also received new flooring, and many of its
pillars were covered with new marble. Pius XI installed elec-
trically operated bells and restored the Vatican grottoes, except for excavation work around the tomb of St. Peter.

Also in Rome were built: the Oriental Institute, the Institute of Christian Archaeology, the Russian College, the Abbey of San Gerolamo (for the Benedictine monks who worked
on the Vulgate edition of the Bible), and the Ateneo Later-
anense, one of the great papal universities. In addition, he
completed a building for Catholic Action headquarters and
several universities and institutes for the education of the
clergy from all nations, one of the most important of which
was the Ruthenian College on the Janiculum Hill.

Most of the catacombs were reinforced and new excavations were dug, resulting in significant archaeological find-
ings. New finds also were made as a result of excavations
under the Lateran Basilica. During his seventeen-year reign
Pius XI was responsible for the building of twenty new
churches.

His most important contribution in the field of construction
was a highly practical one. Before Pius XI, the Roman congregations had been housed and scattered in many buildings;
now most of them are in the great complex palaces known as

San Callisto in Trastevere that he started in May 1936. They are modern office buildings in every sense of the word and contribute largely to the efficiency of the congregations.

All the planning for the new buildings in Vatican City was done under his personal supervision. He enlarged the Casina di Pio and gave it to the Pontifical Academy of Sciences. In the Porta Angelica section he installed an industrial and technical center for the small state; garages, workshops, a new thermoelectric center for central heating, a new power station. An entire street of shops came into existence, cold storage warehouses, electric bakeries, post office, telephone and telegraph buildings, a modern pharmacy, and a medical dispensary. The entire underground of Vatican City Territory is perforated by sixty miles of tubes, for the existing wiring systems and for new ones as needed.

In the center of this mass of buildings Pius XI made the unused Torrione di Nicolo V available for the offices of the Opera di Religione, the Vatican bank. The consistorial hall received marble flooring, and the offices of the Secretariat of State were improved and enlarged. Construction works best known to the public are his complete modernization of the Vatican Library and Vatican museums, and the construction of the beautiful Pinacoteque.

It was Pius XI who built a hydraulic center, an enormous subterranean cistern to be used for ordinary irrigation work in the Vatican Gardens, and a sprinkler system. He also completely transformed and reorganized the immense Vatican Gardens. Pius XI was very fond of gardening; he planted trees, created tree-lined walks, provided evergreen plants, and decorated walks with objects of archaeological interest.

Pius XI built about thirty seminaries in Italy, which were badly needed. One of the greatest monuments to his memory outside of Rome and Italy is the Catholic University in Peiping, later taken over by the communists.

Pius XI often declared that he was working for his successors. Thus, he thought they would be free from any material preoccupations and could dedicate themselves completely to their spiritual tasks.

Eight months after his death, his prophetic words became reality. World War II proved the importance of an independent and free Vatican City. For about nine months nazi paratroopers stood guard on the border between the Italian state and the Vatican. Three bombs actually fell on Vatican territory. Once, while the successor of Pius XI was speaking to the people of Rome, his words were drowned by the sound of cannon and the drone of airplanes. Nevertheless, the Holy See remained inviolate. The Pope received ambassadors and his ambassadors traveled unmolested through belligerent territories. International law guaranteed the temporal sovereignty of the Popes. And the wise and practical technical organization of Vatican City, sponsored by Pius XI, permitted the Vatican to remain materially independent, and to help the stricken populations of Italy and the rest of Europe.

But this was only one part of Pius XI's activity. Few Popes have been as active in so many fields. Archbishop Confalonieri relates that, when certain works on St. Paul's Basilica were finished, the usual commemorative plaque was prepared and its text submitted to Pius XI. The plaque bore the following text in Italian: "*Sedente Pio Papa Undecimo*"—"while Pius XI was sitting" [on the throne]. When the Pope saw this text, he exclaimed: "Sitting indeed! No! No! Always on the move, always on the move!"

CHAPTER EIGHT

The Man of the Spirit

ON SEVERAL OCCASIONS Pius XI said that he felt himself to be the common father of *all* Christianity. As the spiritual head of the Catholic Church, he meant this in the broadest sense.

In 1927, Bishop Nikolaus Bares, Bishop of Berlin, went to Rome to make his customary report. Before he left Berlin he received many letters and telegrams from his parishioners wishing him Godspeed. These communications continued to pour in even after Bishop Bares arrived in Rome. He told Pius XI about these letters and the Pope asked him to show him the most recent. Bares had one on his person and, pulling it out of his pocket, gave it to the Pope to read. As he read it, the eyes of Pius XI began to twinkle with amusement, and at the end he laughed so heartily that tears ran down his cheeks. The letter, written in a childish scrawl, read as follows: "Dear Herr Bischof: I wish you the very, very best. Particularly that you should remain always a good Catholic." Pius XI said that the child who had written this letter had given expression to a profound admonition. "This is the best greeting for us bishops. Troubles always begin when the bishop is not a fearless, unerring, loving Catholic."

"You should defend the truth and through that you defend the Catholic Church," Pius XI once said to members of the Pontifical Academy of Sciences.

Only the grace of God can give so much faith and strength to individual Catholics, but only prayer and a Christian way of life can preserve the faith. Achille Ratti, as has been seen, was lovingly educated in things religious by his family and his first teachers. He perfected his faith through daily spiritual exercises.

On the other hand, as a scholar, diplomat, archbishop and Pope, Achille Ratti had always been an extremely active man. But the word activity here requires some qualification. Pius XI knew quite well that the late nineteenth and early twentieth centuries indulged in what might be called the heresy of excessive or exaggerated activity. The centuries before had sinned with the heresy of relative inactivity. In this regard he agreed with the great Czech Dominican, Fr. Reginald Dacik: "It is true that where there is life there must be activity, but we should not forget that there are two kinds of activities: exterior and interior. Exterior activity should not be allowed to become preponderant over interior. The feverish activity of the world has a tremendous attraction. Nevertheless, one should not forget that a Carmelite nun, who lives secluded from the world and prays, can do more for the Church of God with her prayers than ten members of any parliament. Many Catholic initiatives have failed because they had greater confidence in human effort than in supernatural help."

When Pius XI described life as action, he had in mind this special kind of activity in which human effort and prayer are in perfect harmony. To be sure, he drew his physical strength from his healthy and well-trained physique, but his extraordinary spiritual strength had deep roots in Christianity.

The spiritual development of Achille Ratti would have attained the same heights even if he had not become Pope. Such a development was inherent in his personality, character and inner life. From early childhood he felt a vocation to serve God and he followed the call, perfecting himself constantly and living the inner life of those who find their nourishment and inspiration in contact with God, whether this be established through the intimacy of meditation and contemplation or by loving contact with one's fellow man seen as an image of God. Pius XI, as those who knew him attest, lived constantly in union with God.

The Vicar of Christ is a human being like the rest of mankind: mortal, subject to all the challenges and attractions of the world, and capable of the greatest sins. His responsibilities are tremendous. If a person is not spiritually alert, he tends to panic over or shirk these responsibilities. People, Popes included, often do not attribute importance to their responsibilities in this sense.

A Pope cannot avoid being aware throughout the day that he is the leader of the 400,000,000 Catholics in the world who look up to him for guidance and inspiration. To be sure, a Pope must be equally aware that half the world is friendly and the other half unfriendly, even hostile, toward him. To cope with the expectations of the former and the machinations of the latter requires divine assistance.

Pius XI sought this assistance through union with God in the Holy Eucharist. On important occasions he would go to the Chapel of the Blessed Sacrament in the Basilica of St. Peter and sometimes remain there more than an hour on his knees—even when he was well over seventy. Pius XI would visit the tabernacle in his private chapel three times a day: before and after his audiences, and before retiring at the end of the day.

Although he drew inspiration from all the sources of the Catholic Church, he had special devotion to St. Ambrose, the great Bishop of Milan, to St. Charles Borromeo, one of his predecessors as Archbishop of Milan, and to St. Ignatius Loyola, particularly because of his practical method of religious exercises. Among his favorite saints he was particularly dedicated to St. Thérèse of Lisieux. It was he who beatified and canonized her. In his allocution at the canonization ceremony in 1925 he pointed out that St. Thérèse was an *omen novum* on the horizon of the Church, a new sign that should be followed. He put his entire pontificate under her protection, and particularly declared her to be protectress of missions and dedicated to her his two major projects, the Oriental Institute and the Russian Seminary.

Thérèse Martin, who was born in 1873 and died in 1897, was a contemporary of Achille Ratti. It probably was her genuine simplicity which appealed to him. His secretaries and intimates have described him as one who never looked for the extraordinary. He was somewhat impatient with people who pushed themselves into the limelight or who claimed extraordinary graces; he would advise them to be more restrained and to withdraw into solitude. Very often such a warning had the effect of a cold shower on people whose interest in the religious was sensationalist or superstitious.

Archbishop Confalonieri quite properly has said this about Pius XI: "He attached importance to and appreciated the fulfillment of ordinary duties, such duties as life calls forth in the natural course of the day. Spiritually, the days of Pius XI did not differ from one another; if one knows one day, one knows all the days of his pontificate. Those who are looking for something new and rare will not find anything 'great' in their research. Nevertheless, such uniformity was not a boring uniformity, because it always contained a note of freshness."

A more illuminating light is thrown upon his spiritual life if Pius XI's comment on St. Thérèse is read: "A saint is a work of God come alive. This is how God works: He speaks with His own works, He manifests Himself through them . . . It is evident that God loves and appreciates the great deeds as much as He does the quotidian ones, the small ones . . . It was the simplicity, the sincere humility of heart, that He liked in St. Thérèse; the complete devotion to the duties of her own status, her incessant prayers, and her generous disposition toward any sacrifice; the continuous slow burning of the lamp of her faith; the abandonment to God and the complete confidence in God, giving oneself to Him that He should do whatever He wants with ourselves; and above all the exercise of true charity, devoid of competition with others." With these words Pius XI, it can be said, was unconsciously describing himself.

It is significant that another favorite saint whose example he wanted to follow was St. John Vianney, the Curé of Ars. Vianney was a most humble person, whom his superiors once considered too inept a student to become a priest; in fact, he was unable to deliver a sermon, after settling in the village of Ars, until he finally abandoned himself to the mercy of God. John Vianney died in 1875. The Curé of Ars became the symbol of the good parish priest. Again, it was Pius XI who canonized him. After the canonization Pius XI received the saint's rosary, which he used until the end of his life and which was buried with him.

It is also of significance that it was Pius XI who canonized Catherine Labouré, to whom the Blessed Virgin appeared in 1831 in Paris, and who became the heroine of silence. She died at a very advanced age, but she spoke to no one about her "experience" except her confessor and the bishop. She lived and worked in humility, simplicity and obscurity.

We also owe to Pius XI the canonization of St. Bernadette Soubirous, the girl of Lourdes whose person was chosen for the most spectacular and challenging miraculous events of modern times. Yet she knew that she was but an instrument of Providence. When she herself fell seriously ill and was in great pain, she refused to go to Lourdes, saying: "The well is not for me."

Achille Ratti lived like these saints. By this we are not presuming to say that he was a saint. We say only that his life was similar to theirs. Upon becoming Pope he felt that he should convey the message of these saints to the world. At the canonization of Bernadette Soubirous, he declared: "The life and sanctity of Bernadette is a miraculous and mature fruit of the work of salvation. The new saint shows us something that the world refuses and despises: the hidden life, the humble life, renunciation and dedication, which is one of the greatest lessons given to us by the Saviour. 'Take my example because I am soft and of humble heart,' said Christ. The gospel can be summed up in this one sentence, in this essential lesson. This is the goal of a Christian life and the sense of the teachings of the Saviour. The sense of humility that He brought into the world was entirely unknown in the pagan era . . . After nineteen centuries St. Bernadette shows the same great example and lesson to a world ruled by pride that despises humility."

More could be quoted from his speeches, allocutions and encyclicals to illustrate his spiritual views, but these by themselves would not be enough without the knowledge that he lived in a principled manner according to these very views. Those who saw him only once or twice during his pontificate might have received the impression that he was a stern authoritarian. This was indeed the impression obtained by persons who never heard him speak, but who just observed his bearing as he passed by before the multitudes of pilgrims. He knew how to command and this attribute made him appear sterner than he really was, in the usually easy-going indulgent atmosphere of Rome, where people often preferred those who postponed decisions or those whose decisions could be circumvented. As Pius XI remarked about St. Thérèse of Lisieux: "The important thing is to perform the duties belonging to one's status." His status was to be a good Pope, and the Pope is a supreme ruler. No other ruler in the world has to make so many decisions as does the Roman Pontiff. Therefore, a man who knew how to make decisions quickly and who then checked to see that his orders were being carried out might at first sight appear to be sternly authoritarian.

The sources of strength of Pius XI were, then, the most ordinary sources, available to everyone. His spirituality started with his morning prayers, reading of his breviary, and the celebration of Mass. Before and after holding the audiences, there would be the adoration of the most Holy Sacrament, and in the afternoon the recital of the Rosary. In addition, he had private devotions to which he was bound by vows since his early youth.

From this schedule an uninformed person might assume that such a life certainly must have made him grim and severe in character. That this was certainly not the case is evident from all that we have seen of his life. He kept his fine sense of humor and understanding of human foibles until the end of his life. Once, the eighty-year-old Bishop of Foligno came to him and asked to be relieved of his episcopal duties because the years weighed too heavily on his shoulders. The good bishop had forgotten that the Pope was the same age. Pope Ratti was quick with his response: "We don't feel it. We don't at all!"

There was no grimness in his spiritual life because he did not force his own way of life upon anyone. Whatever he did he felt would be good for others in the Catholic Church. He merely recommended this type of spirituality in apostolic letters or in allocutions. He followed the Ignatian pattern of retreats until his health precluded this practice. He meditated every day, almost in each free moment. And he liked to set down subjects for meditation, usually from the Psalms, returning to them during the day whenever time permitted. On his seventieth birthday he wrote from memory twenty quotations from the Psalms to meditate upon during that particular day.

The story of his spiritual life would not be complete if no mention was made of his great devotion to the Madonna. Since 1875 he had been a member of the Confraternity of the Sacred and Immaculate Heart of Mary for the Conversion of Sinners, a pious association connected with the shrine of Loreto. Later, he was equally devoted to our Lady of Lourdes and to our Lady of Czestochowa, in addition to the Madonnina of Milan.

His desk held several pictures of the Madonna, the most important a reproduction of the Madonna by Crivelli, the great pre-Renaissance painter.

This life of piety and his small sacrifices were dedicated to the salvation of others. At least three times a day, for instance, he prayed for the dying. As far as he was concerned, he told one of his aides that he would like to die a sudden death. Surprised, the prelate reminded the Pope: "The Church has a prayer to save us from unexpected death." Whereupon Pius XI told him: "That does not refer to priests, because they should live a life in which death would never find them unprepared."

CHAPTER NINE

Man of Action

I T W A S the aim of the cardinals who elected Achille Ratti to choose from among themselves a man with the unquestioned will and ability to assure the continuation and further development of the established policy of the Holy See. By the continuation of established policy was meant that the papacy would pursue the following aims: the establishment of friendly relations with all the nations of the world whether or not they were in diplomatic relations with the Holy See; non-interference in the domestic affairs of the states, but at the same time the strongest insistence, and if necessary struggle, for the basic freedoms of the individual and of the Church; strengthening the organization of the Church; extension of missionary activity; greater emphasis on the education of youth.

Obviously, any Pope would have needed an army of able collaborators to carry out such a program. Equally evident was the fact that, unless the new Pope were a "revolutionary," he would more or less employ the same methods of realizing these aims as did his predecessors.

Pius XI was far from being revolutionary, but this does not mean that he was not a man of original ideas. As he had explained to one of his former secretaries, who had come to visit him after his election, Achille Ratti felt that first he had to "learn" how to become a Pope. He confirmed in office most of the associates of Benedict XV, and he kept Cardinal Gasparri as his Secretary of State. This was a step of major wisdom, because Gasparri's person, his knowledge and dedication, assured the smooth transition between the two papal administrations. A great and talented man himself, he liked talented, able people and he was not afraid to appoint them to high office. Archbishop Pacelli, Cardinal Merry del Val and Cardinal Gasparri had been appointed by Pius X. Pius XI recognized Pacelli's great abilities and furthered his career by appointing him in 1932 to succeed Cardinal Gasparri as Secretary of State. During the seventeen years of his pontificate he created new cardinals almost every year. He elevated to the dignity of cardinal the Jesuit Franz Ehrle, a great historian and the former librarian of the Vatican, and Luigi Sincero, one of the great Church jurists of the twentieth century; in 1924 he bestowed the red hats upon George William Mundelein, Archbishop of Chicago, and Patrick Joseph Hayes of New York; in 1929, upon Ildefonso Schuster, the saintly Benedictine monk who later became Archbishop of Milan; Eugenio Pacelli, the present Pius XII; Jean Verdier, Archbishop of Paris, whose name is identified with the beginning of the French Catholic renaissance; in 1930, Achille Lienart, Bishop of Lille, a former soldier and intrepid defender of labor's rights; in 1935, Federigo Tedeschini, one of the most brilliant Church diplomats, and former Nuncio to Spain; Nicola Canali, whose manifold and great talents were instrumental in saving Rome from destruction in World War II; Celestin Suhard, Bishop of Rheims, later a most worthy successor to Cardinal Verdier; Ignatius Gabriel Tappouni, Patriarch of Antioch, a Russian who had lived under the Soviet regime and who was an expert in Oriental problems; Henri Marie Alfred Baudrillart, the great French scholar, head of the French Catholic Institute; and in 1936, Giovanni Mercati and Eugene Tisserant, former prefects of the Vatican Library.

Pius XI took great care to appoint as bishops churchmen who were not involved in the domestic politics of their native countries, and who were not strongly associated with political direction. He generally preferred to assign scholars or priests with extensive pastoral experience or Church diplomatic background to bishopric sees. Since no one is free from error in judging people, some of the appointees of Pius XI did not come up to his expectations. But this accentuates even more the Pope's good faith in them. Pius XI was always particularly anxious to provide missionary lands with native priests and native bishops. Because of his great efforts in this direction, Pius XI has been called the Pope of the Missions.

Pius XI approached and posed the problem to be resolved by making use of the same media as were employed by his predecessors. He outlined his general programs in encyclical letters, or in other papal utterances, always stressing the importance of the issue at hand. He issued thirty encyclicals, including twenty-three letters and several shorter ones designated as epistles. He never issued a statement because of an occasion *per se*. But he used an occasion if he felt that something important that he wished to say could be related to it. It is of interest, therefore, to see how the encyclicals were specific responses to the questions or challenges that rose during his pontificate.

It was to be expected that his first encyclical would outline his general program; the second, *Rerum Omnium,* issued in January 1923, commemorated the three-hundredth anniversary of the death of St. Francis de Sales. Pius XI felt that it was both fitting and important to recall his memory to the world, because the times during which the saint lived were as chaotic and violence-ridden as our own. In this encyclical he especially recommended St. Francis de Sales to writers, authors and journalists. He called their attention to the responsibility and sanctity of the written word that has so often been used for evil purposes.

During the same year, on June 29, 1923, the Catholic world celebrated the six-hundredth anniversary of the canonization of St. Thomas Aquinas. There was no special need to issue an encyclical for such an anniversary, but Pius XI did so because he was deeply convinced that Catholic higher education should be imbued with Thomism; also, because he was convinced that Aquinas had a message for the confused and bewildered statesmen of Europe. This encyclical, entitled *Studiorum Ducem,* contained the following two paragraphs:

"In the second part of the *Summa Theologica,* those teachings are famous which regard the paternal or domestic rule, the legal rule of state or nation, the law of peoples, peace, war, justice and dominion, laws and their observance, the duty of providing for private necessity as for public prosperity, and all this as well in the natural as in the supernatural order. Because, if privately and publicly and in the mutual relations of nation with nation, these precepts are preserved holily and inviolately, nothing else is required for that conciliating 'Peace of Christ in the Reign of Christ' which the whole world so much desires.

"It is, therefore, to be hoped that the doctrines of Aquinas, concerning the ruling of peoples and the laws which establish their relations with one another, may be better known, since they contain the true foundations of that which is termed the 'League of Nations'."

In view of Pius XI's interest in Thomism, it was no surprise that he should have issued an encyclical on the Angelic Doctor early in his pontificate. As has been seen, the former teachers of Achille Ratti had "created" and spread neo-Thomism. The greatest impulse in modern times in this direction, however, was reserved to the contemporaries of Pius XI and to himself. It was during his pontificate that neo-Thomism, particularly through Jacques Maritain, Cardinal Mercier, Etienne Gilson and others, became an active, all-embracing movement, influencing individuals and educational institutions, Catholic and non-Catholic as well.

It remains yet to be seen how certain acute social problems were approached in France, Spain, Italy, Germany and in many African and Asiatic countries. But it can already be said that the impulse came from Pius XI. It was he who put the official stamp of approval on movements in Catholic and non-Catholic countries which, while adhering to the strictest orthodoxy in faith and morals, created movements that brought Christian and non-Christian nearer and closer to the *anima ecclesiae,* demonstrating before the entire world that the Catholic Church was a defender of human dignity, truth and freedom.

The encyclical *Quas Primas,* issued during the Holy Year of 1925, is important because it constituted a further step in the realization of the Pope's program expressed in *Ubi Arcano Dei.* Published on the Feast of Christ the King, *Quas Primas* gave the Pope an opportunity to expound the duality of the nature of Christ, the fact of His resurrection, and the vicissitudes of Christianity. In it the Pope declared that the royal power of Christ rests in the union of His human and divine nature. This is why all creatures, angels and men, have to obey Him and belong to Him. His rule is based upon His birthright of being God and man at the same time, as well as upon His sacrifice, the work of salvation. As King, He holds the key position between God and the world, both in creation and salvation. Pius XI clearly pointed out that the world has always fought against this kingdom of Christ, in our time as socialism, communism, Bolshevism and the "plague of our times and society, namely, godless and frivolous laicism." And the Pope put his finger on the heart of the matter by pointing out that the ills of any society can always be traced to the falling away of peoples from God.

In 1926, Pius XI issued three great encyclicals. One was on missions, *Rerum Ecclesiae.* The second was *Rite Expiatis,* on the occasion of the seventh centenary of the death of St. Francis of Assisi. It is a singular document because it so well reveals the uniqueness of the personality of Achille Ratti. He himself was a Franciscan tertiary and had great reverence for the Franciscan way of life. His aim here was to call the attention of all peoples to the original form of sanctity, based upon fundamental—almost primitive in their simplicity—pronouncements of the Gospel. Excellent historian that he was,

Pius XI re-created the times of St. Francis of Assisi. He explained the great significance of the phenomenon of Francis and did not shy from admitting some harsh truths about the great failures of individuals, society and the clergy, high and low, before the times of St. Francis. The third encyclical issued in 1926, *Iniquis Afflictisque,* deals with the persecution of the Church in Mexico. It was a flaming denunciation of the crude and violent anti-clericalism of the regime. He described the anti-Church legislation as worthy of Diocletian and quoted examples of heroism exhibited by thousands of martyrs in Mexico. This encyclical letter can be considered as a prototype of his later protests against persecution: characterized by a lofty dignity, and moderation, denunciatory where necessary, but devoid of hysteria and lamentation.

All three encyclicals were of greatest importance with respect to the events of 1928. Here it should also be pointed out that Pius XI gave many speeches, radio broadcasts, and many other utterances. Often, he would give talks extemporaneously. In these he never touched upon any other issues but the religious, ever indicating a desirable direction, as befits the Vicar of Christ. He went into specific detail only when his office required an ultimate decision with respect to a question.

In 1928 there were ecumenical congresses in Stockholm and Lausanne for the purpose of attempting to bridge the disunity of the Christian churches. Pius XI never doubted the good faith of those non-Catholic Christians who laboriously tried to reach a formula for Christian unity. Yet he abhorred superficial and opportunistic solutions, based on compromise for its own sake. In his view, what good could come from a unity in which neither of the parties is really convinced? Pius XI was sharply criticized because of the remarks his encyclical contained about prominent proponents of Christian unity, like the Protestant bishop, Soderblom. His critics overlooked, however, that Pius XI in no wise doubted their good will, or offended their sensibilities. But he did point out the essential conditions for unity on the part of the Catholic Church which are also *sine qua non* of its existence: belief in its divine foundation; belief in its dogmatic structure; belief in a central teaching authority which preserves the purity and clarity of the doctrine. This encyclical, nevertheless, was an invitation to unity. The solution of the problem would, however, lie not in the proposition that each Christian denomination give up something of its patrimony. It was an invitation to study those points outlined in his encyclical.

The encyclical *Rerum Orientalium* was also concerned with the question of religious unity, and dealt with the unity of the Eastern churches. In it Pius XI enumerated briefly the achievements of other Popes in the Christianization of the Orient and on behalf of unity among schismatic groups. He quoted Pope Hadrian II, who had canonized the apostles among the Slavonic peoples; Gregory X, who had sent Franciscans and Dominicans to the Far East in the thirteenth century; John XXII, who had instituted the Oriental College in Paris; Clement V, who had instituted chairs dealing with the Oriental churches; Gregory XVI, who had been a student of Russian history; Pius IX, who had sponsored the publication of many documents pertaining to religions of the East; Leo XIII, who had confirmed the foundation of the Assumptionist Order, dedicated to the schismatics; Pius X, who had fostered the teaching of Oriental languages at the Pontifical Biblical Institute; and, finally, Benedict XV, who had founded a congregation and a college dealing with the problems of the Oriental churches. Pius XI also made one of the greatest contributions toward the union of Christian churches by his reorganization of the Oriental Institute. He entrusted its direction to the Society of Jesus and provided it with a new and adequate palace and a great library.

In the same year he issued the encyclical *Miserentissimus Redemptor*, which called upon the faithful to make reparation to the Sacred Heart of Jesus. This encyclical was very dear to him because of his life-long membership in pious associations honoring the Sacred Heart.

In 1928, *Osservatore Romano* published an article entitled "The Screen." The article was signed only by the letter "P" and the identity of the author has never been disclosed. It has been conjectured that the "P" meant Pacelli, but it is not written in Pacelli's style at all. Besides, Pacelli hardly ever wrote for the press. Well-informed people have concluded that the author might have been Pius XI himself, or Pacelli writing under the instructions of the Pontiff. The article, which was quite long, made reference to a cartoon entitled "The Screen" that had appeared in *Bezbozhnik*, an organ of Bolshevik atheists, published in Moscow. Christ is depicted as a mysterious super-Rasputin and shown with His left hand raised aloft as if to calm a mob of emaciated, sick, hungry, dirty proletarians. The implication of His gesture is "Be quiet; you will get your reward in heaven." Behind the caricature stands a fat bourgeois whom the proletarians do not see. His face is bloated, fingers padded with fat and studded with rings; his eyes gleam avariciously. Christ, according to this cartoon, acts as a screen for this fat exploiter who commands a group of people with a rope tied around their necks.

The article, to be sure, condemned the false and sacrilegious nature of the cartoon. It went on to say, however, that it was not enough to be indignant over communist effrontery; it was also necessary to think it over humbly, and to search one's own conscience for the reasons why so many people believed the idea so crudely expressed by the cartoon. Further, the article declared that it should be admitted openly that among the people who declared themselves followers of Christ's teaching—"there are many of them today, too—who betrayed Christ." Then the article went on to say that "a prayer whose fruit is not charity and love of one's neighbor is a lie. Love of God and love of the neighbor is one." It is very important, continued the writer of the article, to be clear as to what we understand by charity. If our neighbor does not have the necessities that are due him, these needs have first to be satisfied. Only afterward can we give him gifts. But to give gifts in the name of charity without satisfying the neighbor's primal needs is an act against God. "The working man has a right to a wage that enables him to maintain his family decently; he has a right to health, life, family and to the pleasures of life . . . The working man has a right to receive a sufficient income and it is his duty to fight for the realization of his right. He should not accept alms from the purse of charitable people. It is his duty to refuse . . . We should not forget the words of St. Thomas Aquinas that a certain amount of material goods is indispensable for the exercise of virtue."

If we do not act accordingly, the article concluded, we deserve the anathema of Christ: "O you hypocritical pharisees who devour the houses of the widows behind the screens of your long prayers!"

In 1929 Pope Pius XI celebrated the fiftieth anniversary of his ordination. His encyclical *Quinquagesimo Ante* was a joyful document, for 1929 was also the year of the Lateran Treaty. In this encyclical Pius XI reviewed the events of that year, and praised God for his long life and all the spiritual gifts received.

The second encyclical of this year was *Mens Nostra,* the subject of which was the necessity of spiritual exercises. Here the Pope recalled the day when he celebrated his first Mass. Now that he was celebrating his fiftieth anniversary, he wrote, he would like to make a gift to the clergy, religious and secular, and to the laity, by pointing out the blessings of spiritual retreats and exercises. Such exercises, he said, not only perfect the spiritual sensibility of individuals, but they also are a great help in developing intellectual abilities. He traced the history of spiritual exercises and called attention to the system of St. Ignatius Loyola and St. Charles Borromeo. It was in this encyclical that he announced his plans to organize spiritual exercises inside the Vatican for members of the curia, then for Bishops, for secular priests and members of religious orders, and for groups and collaborators of Catholic Action, as well as for members of all professions and occupations. In conclusion, the Pope recommended a withdrawal from the world, lasting for several days up to one month, and as a basis for spiritual discipline and meditation he suggested the methods of St. Ignatius.

The third encyclical of 1929 concerned the Christian education of youth and was addressed to the Italian episcopate. *Rappresentanti in Terra* is one of the most beautifully written encyclicals of Pius XI, and one in which he stressed the importance of the Christian family and criticized naturalism and autonomy in education. What gives this encyclical its special flavor is the fact that in it Pius XI distilled the essence of his own experience with his family and of his years with Don Giuseppe Volontieri and his other teachers, who helped to form a solid and sound Christian world-view and a harmonious, well-rounded secular knowledge. Pius XI also took this opportunity to reassert the right of the Church to educate youth and to explain that this right did not conflict with the right of the family and the right of the state to have their share in the education of youth.

The year 1930 saw two papal encyclicals: one, *Ad Salutem*, in April, on the occasion of the fifteenth centenary of St. Augustine, and *Casti Connubii*. *Ad Salutem* was a hymn of praise to St. Augustine, and an evaluation of his teachings. Not one aspect of St. Augustine's life was left untouched. It was clear that Pius XI was more interested in the great example that the life of St. Augustine presented than in his system as against Thomism. Augustine, it will be remembered, had lived in Milan, was baptized by its Bishop Ambrose, and is buried near Pavia. This may explain the special affection for him so evident in the encyclical written by the former Archbishop of Milan.

The encyclical on Christian marriage, *Casti Connubii*, remains to this day a fundamental document of Christian doctrine on marriage, married life, and responsibilities of society toward married people. In this encyclical Pius XI strongly attacked the idea of sterilization and it was here that he used the word *neo-paganism* for the first time. Among other things, this encyclical stated:

"Mutual familiar intercourse between the spouses themselves, if the blessing of conjugal faith is to shine with becoming splendor, must be distinguished by chastity so that husband and wife bear themselves in all things with the law of God and of nature, and endeavor always to follow the will of their most wise and holy Creator with the greatest reverence towards the work of God.

"This conjugal faith, however, which is most aptly called by St. Augustine the 'faith of chastity,' blooms more freely, more beautifully and more nobly, when it is rooted in that more excellent soil, the love of husband and wife which pervades all the duties of married life and holds pride of place in Christian marriage. For matrimonial faith demands that husband and wife be joined in an especially holy and pure love, not as adulterers love each other, but as Christ loved the Church. This precept the Apostle laid down when he said: 'Husbands, love your wives as Christ loved the Church,' that Church which of a truth He embraced with a boundless love not for the sake of His own advantage, but seeking only the good of His Spouse. The love, then, of which We are speaking is not that based on the passing lust of the moment nor does it consist in pleasing words only, but in the deep attachment of the heart which is expressed in action, since love is proved by deeds. This outward expression of love in the home demands not only mutual help, but must go further; must have as its primary purpose that man and wife help each other day by day in forming and perfecting themselves in the interior life, so that through their partnership in life they may advance ever more and more in virtue, and above all that they may grow in true love towards God and their neighbor, on which indeed 'dependeth the whole Law and the Proph-

ets.' For all men of every condition, in whatever honorable
walk of life they may be, can and ought to imitate that most
perfect example of holiness placed before man by God,
namely, Christ our Lord, and by God's grace to arrive at the
summit of perfection, as is proved by the example set us of
many saints."

The year 1931 was the most eventful and fruitful in doc-
trinal teaching. All the four encyclicals Pius XI issued in this
year are of great importance. *Quadragesimo Anno*, published
to commemorate the fortieth anniversary of the appearance
of *Rerum Novarum*, the social encyclical of Leo XIII, was
published on May 15, 1931. Before issuing this encyclical
Pius XI sent one of his close collaborators, Fr. Gemelli, and
others to Europe and to the United States to talk with social
scientists, economists, businessmen, and labor leaders. "You
are my windows on the world," he told them. He could not
be satisfied with expert opinion, regardless of the stature of
the experts, which was derived only from books. Pius XI understood the principles involved quite well. What he wanted
to know was how they would stand up in practice. In this
sense he felt his isolation in the Vatican keenly. Once he complained: "I am an isolated monk here." This is the reason why
he made constant efforts to get in touch with more and more
people and to solicit more and more opinions and to gather
more facts about a problem under scrutiny. Strangely enough,
he assigned such tasks to people he knew were already over-
loaded with work, because he felt that their great capacity
for work would enable them to discharge such tasks well.

Quadragesimo Anno was elaborated and complemented by
another encyclical issued in October 1932, *Caritate Christi
Compulsi*. This dealt with the economic depression, unem-
ployment and with increasing armaments. A counterpart to
these two encyclicals, *Divini Redemptoris*, denouncing atheistic communism, was issued in March 1937.

Many of the ideas of Pius XI about Catholic Action and
Catholic social theory found expression in his allocutions, par-

ticularly that of May 12, 1936, delivered at the opening of the International Catholic Press Exhibition in Rome, as well as his speech of September 27 at Castel Gandolfo to the delegates of the Press Congress in which twenty-eight nations participated. One of the Pope's encyclicals, *Vigilanti Cura,* warned against the effects of certain motion pictures as inimical to the aims that Catholic Action sets for itself in community and private life.

The second encyclical issued in 1931, entitled *Non Abbiamo Bisogno,* had a twofold importance: First, it clearly established the thesis that no Catholic can be a fascist; secondly, it defined Catholic Action as this was conceived by Pius XI. According to the Pope, Catholic Action is the participation of the laity in the apostolate of the Church; an active participation, that is, amounting to collaboration and cooperation with the priesthood. The Pope used the latter expressions as synonyms for participation.

True Catholic Action, he elaborated, is the participation of lay people in the apostolate for the defense of religious and moral principles, for the development of a healthy and beneficial social action under the leadership of Church hierarchy outside of and above political parties for the purpose of restoring Catholic principles to family life and to society. Pius XI stressed the importance in the Catholic Action of young men and women, hailing them as "the apple of our eye." The encyclical expounded no rigid set of ideas on Catholic Action, pointing out, instead, that it should vary in form according to particular situations in different countries. One of the best programs of Catholic Action was carried out in Spain, but it lasted, unfortunately, only for a few years. The Spanish program was under the leadership of *Accion Popular,* founded by Fr. Ayala, S.J., and later led by Angel Herrera, a young jurist who edited *El Debate,* one of the best Catholic newspapers in the world. Herrera and his associate, Gil Robles, set themselves the task of liberating from social enslavement and left-wing influences those Spanish peasant and

worker masses, mostly the *braceros* (day laborers), who more
and more were becoming the targets of anarchist and communist agitation. Pius XI encouraged the work of *Accion
Popular*.[1]

Catholic Action as conceived by Pius XI, because it tran-
scends politics, is applicable to democratic, authoritarian or
even totalitarian regimes. Nevertheless, it is well known that
the Pope's program met the greatest difficulties in Italy and
Germany. Catholic Action was successful in Austria, Hungary, Czechoslovakia and in other countries, however, where
it helped to create and foster renewals of Catholic principles
in all spheres of life, patterned after the French Catholic renaissance joyfully welcomed and blessed by Pius XI. The Pope
realized that there was no need for a new organization to be
established in the United States, where the National Catholic
Welfare Conference already flourished.

Only after a distance of more than a quarter of a century
can the importance and significance of his redefinition of the
role of the laity in the Catholic Church, officially termed Catholic Action, be fully grasped and understood. By launching
Catholic Action programs Pius XI actually became one of the
great reformers of the Church. Catholic Action as a term and
as a program grew out of the need of Italian Catholics to defend themselves against those oppressions and vexations to
which they were subjected by the anti-clericalism of the old
liberal regimes and, later, the totalitarian pretensions of fascism. Pius XI himself had always moved and had his being
in the atmosphere of an active, intense Catholic life, despite
the fact that it might seem as though he were quite detached
from the world while sitting at his desk in the Ambrosiana
Library and teaching in the seminary. In reality, Achille Ratti
as prefect and doctor of the Ambrosiana had important and
continuous contacts with the best Italian scholars. He used

[1] After the Spanish Civil War Herrera became a priest; he is now Bishop
of Malaga. Gil Robles collaborated, as did Herrera, with the non-communist
republican regime. Then he fled to Portugal, where he now lives in exile.

to say that the contact with these lay people was a means by which a priest could introduce them to the Catholic Church and make her understood and loved.

On Christmas Day, 1931, the Pope issued a commemorative for the fifteenth centenary of the Council of Ephesus. This was the encyclical *Lux Veritatis*, in which he hailed the victorious stand of the Church against all the great heresies of history. In this encyclical he also discussed the importance of the hypostatic union, the union of Christ's divine and human nature in one person, and he emphasized the importance and beauty of the veneration of the Blessed Virgin.

In 1932, his first encyclical was the already cited *Caritate Christi Compulsi;* the second, *Acerba Animi,* dealing with the persecution of the Church in Mexico. He protested with equally strong words against the persecution of the Church in Spain in *Dilectissima Nobis,* issued in 1933. Pius XI issued no encyclicals in 1934. In 1935 there was only one, *Ad Catholici Sacerdoti,* which was a counterpart to other encyclicals, constitutions and decrees on the Catholic priesthood. It is most significant that, out of thirty of the encyclicals of Pius XI, ten dealt directly and indirectly with the importance of the Catholic priesthood. The apostolic constitution issued in 1931, *Deus Scientiarum Dominus,* and the encyclicals dealing with education, however, were those which Pius XI himself considered the most important.

Vigilanti Cura was the only encyclical to appear in 1936. That year the Pope fell ill, but after recuperating he set out with his former vigor and energy and determination to give expression to his views. The year 1937 brought four great encyclicals from his pen. On March 14 *Mit Brennender Sorge,* directed against nazism, was issued; on March 19, *Divini Redemptoris,* denouncing atheistic communism; on March 28, *Firmissimam Constantiam,* deploring the conditions in Mexico. More will be said about these encyclicals later.

His last encyclical, *Ingravescentibus Malis,* issued on Sep-

tember 29, 1937, was on the Rosary. The first three expressed his great concern about the freedom of the Church.
The Pope was jealous of freedom; his own, that of his fellow
man, and that of the Church. Though they dealt with burning
problems of world history, and were marked by revelations
of his anxiety over impending storms, they were not the documents of a fretful or angry man. These were papal documents
in the great tradition, rooted in a sense of fatherhood, affection and respect for all the peoples of the world. The last
encyclical reveals a characteristic of Pius XI described by
many of his friends as *dolcezza*—difficult to translate, because
"sweetness" does little justice to the character of Pius XI,
one of the most vigorous Popes who ever sat on the throne
of St. Peter. This last encyclical was a gentle request to Catholics to pray to the Blessed Mother, protectress against the
dangers of daily life, and perennial favorite and inspiration
of those striving for the realization of faith, hope and charity
in the world.

During the pontificate of Pius XI there were two Holy
Years: one in 1925, and another in 1933. These and other festive celebrations were used by Pius XI as occasions to assert
his pontifical policy. The Eucharistic Congresses also were of
particular importance to him. As is known, he always stressed
the importance of the continuous adoration of the Holy Eucharist and frequent reception of the sacrament. The 26th
Eucharistic Congress was held in Rome in May 1922. Subsequently, international Eucharistic Congresses were held in
Amsterdam, Chicago, Sidney, Carthage, Dublin, Buenos
Aires, Manila and Budapest. This last one took place shortly
before the outbreak of World War II, in the summer of 1938.
In addition to such congresses, Pius XI encouraged national
and regional Eucharistic Congresses all over the world that
brought great spiritual benefits to the faithful.

The extraordinary Holy Year of 1933, to commemorate the
nine-hundredth anniversary of the Redemption, was the first
such celebration in the history of the Church. Its closing fes-

Pius XI inspects the Vatican's Palatine Guard after a parade in the Vatican Gardens in 1926.

Guglielmo Marconi explains to Pius XI the short-wave station of the Vatican Radio. April 26, 1932.

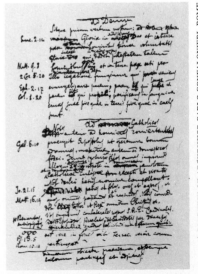

Handwriting of Pius XI. His own draft for the allocution at the inauguration of the Vatican Radio.

Pius XI at a ceremony held in the Lateran Basilica, November 3, 1937.

Pius XI arrives for the inauguration of the Pontifical Academy of Science, January 30, 1938, held in a building of the Vatican Gardens. The Franciscan standing on the left is Father Agostino Gemelli, president of the Academy and an adviser of the Pope.

Pius XI shortly after the signing of the Lateran Treaties with Italy.

Pius XI listens attentively during the inauguration of the Pontifical Academy of Science, January 30, 1938.

Pius XI at the inauguration of the new building of the Vatican's Mosaic Workshop. On the right of the Pope is Marchese Serafini, the first governor of Vatican City, 1933.

The last photograph of Pius XI, February 3, 1939.

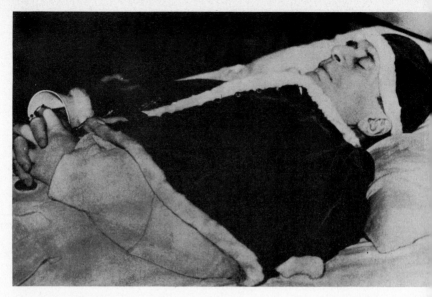

Pius XI immediately after his death, February 10, 1939.

Pius XI on the catafalque in Saint Peter's Basilica, February 12, 1922.

Pius XI's body is transported from the Vatican to Saint Peter's Basilica. The picture was taken at the bottom of the Scala Regia. In the first row, extreme right, is a Swiss Guardist in gala uniform, behind him a mace-bearer. Second from right is a high-ranking officer of the noble guard, and next to him is a privy chamberlain in sixteenth-century court uniform.

ius XI's statue on the tomb.

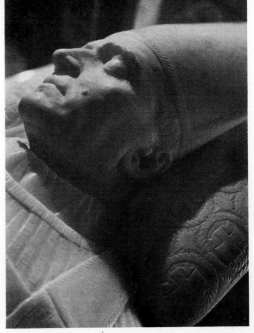

Pius XI's tomb in the
Grotto of Saint
Peter's Basilica. The
mosaic on the right
represents Saint
Thérèse, the Little
Flower, canonized
by Pius XI in 1925.
He put his pontificate
under the protection
of this saint.

tivities took place in Lourdes, however, and not in Rome. This was the specific desire of the Pope, and he sent as his legate to Lourdes Cardinal Pacelli, the Secretary of State.

The following feast days were added to the universal Church calendar by Pius XI: Christus Rex for the last Sunday of October; the Maternity of Mary for October 11; St. Gabriel dell'Addolorata, February 27; St. Peter Canisius, April 27; St. Robert Bellarmine, May 13; St. John Vianney, August 9; St. John Eudes, August 19; St. Thérèse of Lisieux, October 3; St. Margaret Mary Alacoque, October 17; St. Albertus Magnus, November 15; and St. John Bosco, January 31. He elevated the feast days of the Most Sacred Heart of Jesus and that of the Most Precious Blood to feast days of first class. During his pontificate there were thirty-three canonizations and nearly 500 beatifications.

In the case of Albertus Magnus he participated in the process from the beginning to the end, because he wanted the great Dominican set before the world as the example of a true and worthy scholar.

The first person to be beatified was Theresa Eustochio Verzeri, on April 2, 1922. The beatification decree, written by the Pope himself, expresses perfectly his own personality, background and even his policy: "Not all are called to perform miracles through which God wishes to glorify His faithful servants by a magnificent manifestation of His goodness and power. But we all are called upon to exercise Christian virtues. It is not said that all who are thus called upon are to exercise them in a heroic manner. It is indeed true that the hero of the virtues is not the one who walks the common, easy and plain walks of life, but those who are not frightened by obstacles and difficulties and who are ready to face the steep and difficult paths that lead to heaven. But is not the Christian life similar to a militia? Does it not present us every day with a war that is to be waged and a battle to be fought? Now, it is a law that in times of warfare there is no other alternative but the choice between heroism and treason; the glory of a heroic enterprise or the ignominy of the defeat and of the surrender."

At an audience granted in 1923 to students and friends of the Catholic University of Milan, Pius XI said: "There is something great in science; not in pure and simple science but in that science that is allied with faith." It was the constant concern of Pius XI to bring science and faith together. And he did not limit himself to talking about this wistfully or hopefully. In fact, he did more than any other modern Pope. On May 24, 1931, Pius XI promulgated the apostolic constitution *Deus Scientiarum Dominus,* with which he gave a new direction both to scientific research and education of theologians in the seminaries. The Pope always considered himself to be on solid ground in this respect because he had consistently stressed the importance of St. Thomas Aquinas in Catholic higher education. In his August 1922 letter to Cardinal Bisleti, secretary of the Sacred Congregation of Seminaries and Universities, Pius XI already had hailed the Angelic Doctor as an inexhaustible source of learning and scholarly discipline. In his encyclical *Studiorum Ducem,* on the occasion of the sixth centenary of the canonization of St. Thomas Aquinas, he set St. Thomas as an example of Catholic doctrine and life before teachers and theologians. On March 18, 1923, Cardinal Bisleti paid a call on Pius XI to thank him for his efforts on behalf of the Pontifical Academy of St. Thomas Aquinas and for promoting Thomist philosophy and studies.

Pius XI modestly passed over the praise that was showered upon him on this occasion. He took pains to point out that the merit was not his, for he had only followed his predilection and love for St. Thomas Aquinas, acquired during his youth thanks to efforts of his first teachers for whom he expressed his eternal gratitude. At this point the Pontiff graciously revealed that one of them was present at this audience, Fr. Talamo. The latter, three years older than the Pope, had been a brilliant Thomist during the 1870's and 1880's when young Achille Ratti was implementing his studies in Rome.

When we bear in mind this Thomism of Pius XI, the apostolic constitution of 1931 dealing with the unification and integration of Catholic higher teaching around the *Summa* assumes special significance. It must also be borne in mind that before 1931 there was no general plan for ecclesiastical higher institutions. In his essay on the subject Fr. Gemelli has pointed out that in the middle ages each university enjoyed the greatest autonomy and freedom in choosing its curriculum.

The agreement that existed was due to their common tradition stemming from scholastic philosophy. In modern times, an exaggerated nationalism encouraged and influenced the universities to acquire real or imagined national characteristics. Pius XI recognized that such a state of affairs was not a healthy one; it was not his intention to limit the freedom of the universities and institutes of higher learning but to give them a unified direction. To prepare the way for this reform Pius XI established a commission of eminent educators to study the situation thoroughly. His aim was to introduce an analytical study of theological problems in addition to the synthetic treatment of them then current in the Catholic institutions of higher learning. If only the synthetic studies of theology were available, education would be too generic, he maintained.

The apostolic constitution, a result of the researches of the commission, aimed to train young theologians on the basis of a more systematic, rigorous and exacting pedagogy, stressing the particular as well as the general. Reading the apostolic constitution and the reports of the commission brings to mind the ideals of young Ratti in the seminary and, later, as a teacher of theology and sacred eloquence. In this apostolic constitution he again drew upon his own experience and genius for the benefit of others. Fr. Gemelli has described the reform of the departments of theology and in general theological studies, a historic encounter between theology and the profane studies. Lay people attending secular universities where analytical teaching methods were current were not too impressed by the generalities of their professors of theology. Such students appreciated theology only if its single problems were explained in terms of a more rigorous and scientific method. Pius XI advised the members of the commission to bear this in mind in their recommendations for the reform of higher ecclesiastical studies. It was his aim that theologians should possess sufficient knowledge and appreciation of profane studies to deepen their own knowledge of religious problems. He believed that the distance between profane scholars and scholars of the sacred science had to be bridged in the interests of both.

The reform was carried through and had a most important effect in the Catholic academic world. The Catholic University of Milan was organized on the basis of the ideas contained in the reform proposal. So were the University of Louvain in Belgium, the Catholic University of America in Washington, D. C., and the Institute of Higher Education in Santiago, Chile, opened in 1930. The apostolic constitution prescribed the curricula and the teaching methods to be followed. This program was carried out under the control and supervision of the Congregation of Universities and Seminaries.

Other achievements of Pius XI in the fostering of both profane and sacred science were the following:

In 1928 he sponsored the construction of the new three-story wing attached to the Vatican Library. This project was completed with the help of the Carnegie Foundation. This wing of the Vatican Library was equipped, again with American help, with modern steel filing cabinets, shelves and equipment, and now houses 250,000 volumes. Pius XI purchased or received as gifts the Chigi, Caprotti, Ferraioli, Caetani and other libraries.

One of the most important and most cherished achievements of Pius XI was the foundation of the Pontifical Academy of Sciences. An association called *Nuovi Lincei* for the study of natural sciences had existed for several centuries in papal Rome. During the last century, however, it had completely lost its importance. Pius XI, with his *motu proprio* of October 28, 1936, made this association into the Pontifical Academy of Sciences and restored it to a new and vigorous life of scientific study and research in all fields of human inquiry.

This was Achille Ratti's way of trying to prove to the world that religion in general, and the Catholic Church in particular, was no foe of science.

When Pius XI discussed the plans for this Pontifical Academy of Sciences, its method of operation and requirements for membership, even his closest collaborators were surprised. Fr. Gemelli, for instance, had suggested at a meeting that only Catholics should be eligible for membership. Pius XI immediately interrupted him to explain that he wanted only those Catholics who were top-level scientists. "As a matter of fact," he declared, "the Academy should have many non-Catholics, non-Christians and Jews. What is important is that they should be scientists of the highest level and men of moral integrity." At the end of one of these discussions, Pius XI returned to the subject of science and religion and said: "We should not use science always for the purpose of defending the Church. One should defend truth. This by itself also helps the Church."

Among the scientists and savants Pius XI appointed to the Pontifical Academy of Sciences were: Professors Armellini, famous astrophysicist of the University of Rome; Niels Bohr of Denmark, world-famous nuclear physicist; F. J. J. Buytendijk, physiologist at the University at Groningen, Holland; Cruz-Coke, professor of physiological chemistry at the University of Santiago, Chile; Peter Debye, former director of the Kaiser Wilhelm Institute for Physics in Germany and later of Cornell University; Edward Adelbert Doisy, professor of

bio-chemistry at the University of St. Louis; Sir Alexander
Fleming, professor of bacteriology at the University of London and discoverer of penicillin; Wilhelmus Hendrikus Kee-
som, professor of physics at the University of Leyden, Holland; Sidney Langfeld, professor of psychology at Princeton
University; Robert Andrews Millikan of California Institute
of Technology; Franco Rasetti, professor of physics at Johns
Hopkins University; Leopold Ruzicka, professor of organic
chemistry and director of the organic chemical laboratory of
the Federal Institute of Technology in Zürich; Erwin Schrö-
dinger, professor of theoretical physics at the University of
Dublin; Hugh Stott Taylor, professor of chemistry at Princeton; Edmund Whittaker, professor of mathematics at the
University of Edinburgh, and others.

The Catholic University of Milan once faced a serious dilemma because there was no Catholic to fill the chair of philology, suddenly become vacant. There were a number of
Catholics who desired the post, but they did not measure up
to the academic standards required by the university. The
question was brought before Pius XI, to whom the rector of
the university expressed regret that he could not engage the
only competent professor, a resident of Padua, because he
was not a Christian. Pius XI replied: "Go to Padua and ask
him in my name whether he would accept the chair of philology at the Catholic University." The professor accepted.

In 1933, Pius XI was asked to help a great German scientist.
The scientist came from a strongly Protestant Lutheran family, and had no connection at all with the Catholic Church.
Nor was he a member of the Pontifical Academy of Sciences.
The Pope listened attentively for a while and then said: "This
man is a genius. Mankind cannot afford that he endure any
hardship because of financial difficulties." Pius XI then con-
tributed a substantial sum of money, enough for the scientist
to maintain his family and pay his debts. The scientist never
knew the identity of his benefactor. The Pope was glad to
assist him because such aid would enable this man to achieve

highly important scientific results which would become part
of the world's patrimony.

At the 1938 session of the Pontifical Academy, Pius XI
asked his advisers to suggest a speech for the occasion. *"Cosa
fare? Cosa fare?"* repeated the Pope, already near death.
The two advisers came up with various suggestions. One was
that he should deliver a speech in which he stated the position
of the Church toward science. Pius XI discarded this suggestion with a brusque motion of his hand. "Such things should
be done in books." Another suggestion was that he select a
great saint, Thomas Aquinas or Albertus Magnus, and talk
about him as a prototype of the scientific mind. Again he rejected the suggestion.

The following day, about an hour before the inauguration,
the Pope appeared to be in an exceptionally good mood. He
turned to one of his advisers and said: "I have found a solution. The real solution. I found it while reading my breviary."
The speech that he did deliver was a religious one, yet not a
sermon. It started with a quotation from the Gospel according to St. John which he said he had read the night before.
It was a simple, unpretentious speech about the greatness of
God, without any reference whatsoever to science. All the scientists who were present, men of stature, Christians and non-
Christians, were deeply touched. Little did they know that
this was the last speech ever to be delivered by Pius XI.

CHAPTER TEN

The Fight with the Giants

THE period between the two world wars, coinciding almost exactly with the pontificate of Pius XI, was a strange period of transition everywhere in the world. It is obvious now that this transition meant something quite different to the European than it did to the American and Asiatic, or to the Russian. Those who fancy that the dream of "one world" is already a reality might give this some thought. For this unity, although desirable, consists merely in the fact that the progress of technology permits politicians and statesmen to synchronize their actions. But the nations and their peoples, as masses or individuals, were and are far from being synchronized. Things that may seem true in London are not always true in Buenos Aires, Brazzaville, Moscow and Washington, and vice versa. Thus, the transition from one period to the other had a different meaning for the different parts of the world. For those who think in terms of power politics the transition was nothing but the passing from one war to the other, or the toying with the possibility of another war, as has been the case since time immemorial.

Between these two world wars the heart of the world was still somewhere in Europe. From here the actions of politicians had effects bearing on the destiny of the whole world. France, eternal as ever, seemed to be "dying" every day. The country was shaken by cabinet crises and the problems of the fluctuating franc. Yet France was still a great power with great colonies and great problems, among which the realists focused on only one: the German danger. Great Britain was still an empire and India was a colony with Gandhi fighting his inevitably victorious war "non-violently." But there was optimism in Britain as elsewhere. Only a few people were aware of the fact that certain British universities had more Marxists among their students than in Russia where Marx was already passé and the Bolsheviks ruled only because of the dead weight of a routine power. Lenin was dead. Trotsky had barely made it to the border. Iosif Dzhugashvili, alias Stalin, became the supreme ruler of the Soviets. Among other things, he had Tuchacevski and his friends executed for their collaboration with the German general staff, a plan to which Lenin had agreed and that Stalin himself helped realize.

The small countries between or on the outskirts of the realms occupied by the German and Russian colossi were frightened, for the little people must be extremely astute and resourceful not to be hurt when a group of big people starts a row. They began to confess their love for one or the other great power, a love that basically remained unreciprocated. This was the case with Poland, Czechoslovakia, Hungary, Rumania, Bulgaria and the rest of the neutrals, either ready to be invaded or to jump in whichever direction prudence dictated. Power always corrupts people and even nations. The small countries between the great powers invite invasion, and the great ones, save for a few exceptions, never hesitate to oblige.

The period between 1922 and 1939 was a period that can be characterized as the fight of the giants. These giants were the statesmen who were conscious of their fantastic power: Lenin, Hitler, Mussolini, Stalin and Franklin Delano Roosevelt. The period began with great hope, based on the thrilling concept of a League of Nations. But the League remained the league of the strong and refrained from dealing with issues that involved the interests of the strong. Nevertheless, this was a great hope everywhere among the peoples. Unfortunately, the hope was based upon two erroneous suppositions: that those who won the war had a prior right to enjoy material welfare; and that no problems except material ones are important. An ill-conceived political realism was the issue. Germany should be helped because then the vanquished nation would be able to pay reparations; Soviet Russia should be included in the family of nations because it offered great possibilities for world trade; the Pope is of interest only because the Vatican is a clearing house of news.

Pius XI questioned the validity of these issues. He fought with these giants and tried to make the transition as easy and as beneficial as possible for mankind; a transition from war to peace, poverty to plenty—even on the purely material level.

At the level of practice, Prof. Oscar Halecki has rightly observed, Pius XI, "like his predecessor, had the same special interest in the most urgent problem of peace. The first encyclical of Pius XI, *Ubi Arcano Dei*, had as its theme the 'Peace of Christ in the Kingdom of Christ,' which Achille Ratti had chosen as his motto. While, however, his predecessor had still hoped that all states united in one league would 'safeguard the order of human society,' the new Pope, on December 22, 1922, was already fully aware of the shortcomings of the League of Nations, and contrasted that human institution with that 'true league of nations,' which, in his opinion, medieval Christendom had been. Disappointed by the successive failures of so many international conferences, in which the Holy See had no part, he concentrated on the more limited but also more concrete task of improving the relations between the Vatican and the individual countries by concordats with as many of them as possible.

"Here, too, it is interesting to note the continuity of papal policy. Benedict XV, in one of his last allocutions, stated on November 21, 1921, had stressed the importance of such concordats, especially with so many new or enlarged states and also with nations whose forms of government had radically changed."

Nevertheless, it would be erroneous to call Pius XI the Pope of the Concordats. He was not a jurist. He signed agreements because he felt that a solemn promise would bind a country or government more than an informal state of affairs. But his range was much wider than concordats. He was not rigid in his policy and was always ready to negotiate, that is, to *believe* in the good faith and honest intentions of others. But he lived and ruled in an age of the Russian Cheka and GPU; of the German Gestapo and SS; of the Italian secret OVRA; in an age when China was in chaos, Japan militantly imperialistic and the United States reluctant to assume world leadership.

One tends to forget that the head of a nation is concerned primarily with his own nation's interest and he is not so obligated to know or care about the interests of other countries and their problems.

But one should not forget that the Pope bears a burden that is almost impossible to bear short of supernatural help. One may have one's reservations about religion and papacy, yet one must grant that the task of a Pope is one of enormous proportions. The Catholic reaches a point at which one must believe in the reality of the Holy Spirit. Pius XI's life and actions, in the international field alone, prove this amply.

In the following pages we present only those great issues through which Pius XI became involved in the fight against the evil of his period.

The attitude of Pius XI toward international affairs was not that of a diplomat or an international jurist, but of a priest who in all circumstances must be available as a priest, even for those who oppose and attack him. In 1922 he took over the leadership of the Catholic Church and the papacy when Europe was still in a leading position in international affairs and the foremost European powers were still holding major colonial empires. Pius XI felt that the issue of the epoch was nationalism as much as the trend toward social revolutions. (At that time Soviet Russia had not the great attraction for

the masses of the world that it had for intellectuals and mis-
guided social reformers.)

This situation prevailed through the reign of Pius XI. In
the circumstances he felt that the Holy See should let its voice
be heard on important issues. That is why he addressed international conferences. He quickly recognized that the governments of the world, with few exceptions, would not welcome the Pope's words at international political conferences,
when he pointed out the mistakes in their attitude. Governments fought for their own interests. The Pope reminded
them of the truth. This was the case at the Genoa Conference,
in which the parties seemed to agree with Pius XI's views on
international reconciliation. But when the French occupied
the Ruhr region and the Pope voiced his opinion, he was vili-
fied by the French press.

The concordats and other agreements tended to assure freedom for the Church and for the individual through bilateral
contracts. We have observed Pius XI's methods in negotiating
with Italy for the concordat that he considered *sine qua non*
for the Lateran Treaty. The Lateran Treaty was an international agreement to re-establish the sovereignty of the Holy
See. The concordat was an agreement—no less valid in international law—that assured the rights of Italian Catholics.
And, since Pius XI was an intrepid defender of the truth, nobody expected conciliation on his part. He was prepared for
"an honest fight" with prospective contractual partners, but
when he discovered that the immutable principles of the
Church were in jeopardy he became a lion in their defense.
And he was most careful to protect the universalism of the
Church, watching closely the behavior of Catholic hierarchy
and clergy in every country, to insure that they did not fall
into grave error.

It is interesting to note that after peace had been established between Italy and the Vatican, Pius XI proceeded to
make peace with France. As he had done with Italy, Pius XI
concluded what might be called an indirect peace with

France. This was made simpler by the friendlier attitude of the republican government toward the Church and religious matters, as a result of the resumption of diplomatic relations with the Holy See and the mitigation of the law of separation of Church and state under the influence of the *union sacré* of World War I. But this law was still carried out more or less vigorously on occasion.

On the other hand, republican-minded prelates and Catholics, in accord with Bishop Chapon of Nice's reconciliation program, warned against too inflexible a policy toward the laws of separation because of the generous spirit with which they were applied in practice in favor of freedom of conscience. Yet, integralist and royalist elements in the French episcopate and among the laity worked against such an approach, still in the spirit of Pius X, thereby maintaining or sharpening the tensions between state and Church, something in which they were interested. This tendency came to the fore at the Bishops' Conference of 1922–1923, where, despite references to *union sacré* and national unity, the voices of the bishops of Rouen and Bordeaux were heard denouncing separation laws as anti-God and anti-Church.

In 1922, Pius XI opened discussions on the French question. Later he was able to publicize the results of his study of the problem in his famous encyclical of January 18, 1924, *Maximam*. In this encyclical he reviewed French-Vatican relations, stressing that he did not agree with the laws of separation and that he did not wish to remove the objection of his predecessors. But he pointed out that things *since* then had changed and a new regulation was possible. He said that, of the two conditions proposed as a basis for understanding in 1922, one had been met, namely that the statutes of the welfare organizations had been harmonized to accord with the Church laws; the second condition, that the Holy See be assured of security against expropriations by any anti-Church regimes, had not yet been completely fulfilled but a basis for negotiations had been offered. This *rapprochement* be-

tween the French state and the Vatican was celebrated with
a *Te Deum* on February 12, 1924, in Notre Dame Cathedral,
and a brilliant reception was held for the French elite by the
Nuncio. On March 24 it was also celebrated in the Pope's
consistorial speech.

In connection with the approaching elections, however, opposition within the Church in France again came to the
fore. At a gathering of French cardinals and bishops on February 6, 1924, a reference to Pius X, who had dealt very
firmly with Gallicanism, and some unfriendly remarks about
candidates sympathetic to secularism had to be expunged, on
orders from Rome, by Cardinal Lucon. On March 10, a resolution was proposed urging a struggle to the bitter end
against this laicism. A "Catholic Action" committee declared
itself in solidarity with this resolution on March 20, 1924, and
urged a political campaign against the godless regime. Finally, on March 28, the Nuncio was recalled.

The French voters answered these moves by voting in a
leftist majority in both houses, under the leadership of Herriot, thereby enkindling a new war of laws against the
Church, going so far as to propose that the papal ambassador
be sent back, a proposal which passed the lower chamber but
not the senate.

Herriot's regime was followed by the ministry of Painleve-
Briand, which put an end to the Jacobin policy and the drive
to break off relations with the Vatican. All in all, the Pope
felt that his hope for increasing tolerance as a basis for future
relations had been fulfilled.

The new Nuncio, Maglione, worked out an agreement with
Briand on December 4, 1926, according to which representatives of the French government in its colonies were to be paid
special liturgical honors on Christmas, Easter and during
Pentecost. This was symbolical of the new friendship and tolerance developing between the state and the Church. And
this state of affairs was not even disturbed by the effort of
the education minister, Herriot, to establish a unified, totally

secular school system or by the threat in the social security law of 1928 against Church possessions. On the contrary, the financial laws of 1929 again opened the doors of France to many religious congregations, confirmed by the visit of Foreign Minister Laval to the Vatican in the beginning of 1935.

Meanwhile *Action Française* raised another storm. Its political nationalism had drawn a large proportion of the French episcopacy, clergy and Catholic population to it, despite the fact that its leaders, Maurras and Daudet, actually represented anti-Christian ideas which the Pope himself examined carefully in the pages of their newspaper, *L'Action Française*, before he attacked them as agnostic, atheistic and representing a rebirth of paganism, thus supporting similar criticism made a month earlier by Cardinal Andrieu of Bordeaux. He repeated these general charges in a speech before French Franciscan tertiaries on September 25. A letter Maurras sent to the Pope on October 12 went unanswered. And when the lay leaders attempted to persuade French theologians and some bishops to support their stand and views, Pius XI found these efforts to be objectionable. In his consistorial speech of December 20 he made precise his objection. Soon thereafter, in a decree dated January 5, 1927, he condemned Maurras' work and his newspaper.

Maurras and his followers raised a storm of protest, claiming that they would not betray their country by following a papal political program, not without a torrent of abuse and vilification. These charges were answered by Nuncio Maglione on January 7, 1927. Many bishops were still reluctant. Cardinal Dubourg of Rennes expressed his hope that Catholic monarchists would enjoy political freedom, and Archbishop Villerable published the Pope's orders from Rome without commentary, in violation of specific papal instructions. Moreover, Izart of Bourges postponed its publication because it was too painful a task for him. Finally, Bishop Marty of Montauban asserted that he had learned from irreproachable sources that the Pope did not wish to forbid membership in the League (*Action Française*) or the reading of its organ, something that the Nuncio and *Osservatore Romano* promptly denied.

Nevertheless, the French episcopacy sent the Pope a letter of submission, prepared by a commission headed by Archbishop Lucon of Rheims. A brief statement was made first on March 2, 1927, and signed summarily by 104 bishops. Quite a number had refused to sign. This was followed later by a long declaration, containing 119 names, among them *not* the names of Bishop Marty, the coadjutor Llobet of Avignon and Archbishop Penon. Later, Llobet and Marty expressed their regret over the Pope's sorrow because of their insubordination, as well as over the resignation of Bishop Quilliet as a result of the papal directive.

Among the theologians who "submitted" to the Pope was the Dominican Pegues, who, as a highly esteemed master of theology, had advised the ladies belonging to the *Action Française* to continue to read its magazine, that Rome would see its error and would eventually bless them for their steadfastness.

Fr. Le Floch, C. S. Sp., rector of the French Seminary in Rome, was removed after two visits by an Apostolic Visitor because he had suppressed the declaration against Maurras and indoctrinated seminarians with the rebellious spirit of the integralists, so that, in his audience granted to teachers on March 25, 1927, the Pope had to warn against sophistic arrogance of intellect against the highest intellect.

The heaviest blow, however, fell upon the Jesuit Cardinal Billot, who protected the Actionists and congratulated Daudet for his integralist attitude. He was forbidden to appear at papal receptions and ceremonies, and his dismissal was announced by Fr. Ledochowski, General of the Society, on September 13. He subsequently retired in solitude to Galloro.

Pius XI knew that the danger of *Action Française* was not less than that Gallicanism with which Pius X dealt. Gallicanism's ultimate aim was to break the unity of the Catholic

Church, to bring the organization and the entire psychology of the Church under the domination and official control of the secular state. Jansenism, which Pius XI actually abhorred in every form, was there, too. Jansenism in the nineteenth century was "the spirit and practice of a cold, inhuman, ultra-puritanical spirit," which the Church had fought for centuries. The Pope saw all these dangers projected into the *Action Française*. Cardinal Billot probably did, too, but had another method of dealing with them.

When Billot was face to face with Pius XI he still argued. The Pope told the Cardinal his intentions: that excommunication was the only means to deal with the ill. Billot replied: "In such a case [namely, if *Action Française* members were excommunicated] I would be forced to give my Cardinal's hat back to you."

The Pope looked gravely at Billot for a second, and then said firmly: "You can do it immediately—right now." It was difficult for him to depose Billot, whom he personally liked. Ironically, it had been Billot who had put the tiara upon Pius XI's head when he was crowned in 1922.

Pope Pius XI put an end to this painful controversy in his consistorial speech of June 20, 1927, expressing his deep sorrow, his hope that the rebels would return, and said that above all he had to say what once was said by the Apostle John: "They have gone from us, because they did not belong to us."

This was a negative and polemical purging and defense of Catholicism in France. In a more positive sense, Pius XI welcomed and encouraged all symptoms of the true Catholic spirit in French letters, art, and thought, exemplified by the rise of a Catholic elite of men of letters and thought.

Pius XI was fully convinced that the Mexican revolution and its resultant ferocious persecution was an outcome of social ills and lack of really trained priests. He who knew the Italian Risorgimento so well was familiar with the dangers present in it for a priest who loved freedom, but did not know what freedom was. Pius XI was aware that religious, national and emotional issues mingled with the exploding social and racial issues, and the whole unrest was fomented, additionally, by deeply anti-Catholic foreign nationals. Communists and Catholic Church haters easily allied themselves against a Church that was shaken.

The Church in Mexico gave the most surprising testimony of its heroism. One can compare the Mexican persecution only with the Bolshevik persecution of religion in the 1920's and 1930's. Pius XI issued many statements about the Mexican situation. In this case he never tried to "appease" the persecutors, since he knew that he was not faced with genuine liberal forces, but with savage hate. The situation of the Church in Mexico started to improve when Pius XI, in 1929, sought and accepted the good offices of the government of the United States to obtain a respect for the hierarchy and the beginning of negotiations for a *modus vivendi*. The policy set down by Pius XI bore fruit in the subsequent years—a gradual pacification of that volcanic country.

Pius XI dealt with the Spanish problem with the same vigor. He was very much aware that Spain needed special treatment because of its unique historical role at the margin of Europe. Yet he refused to deal with the Spanish problem exclusively on Spanish terms and to accept the validity of a thesis that was totally outmoded and anti-human. The Church in Spain once had the function of defending the nation against the Moslems. As in many other countries of Europe, it became a feudal Church. King Alfonso XIII was a devout believer in the duties and privileges of a "knight" to defend the Church; full of enthusiasm, but with no true understanding of the social problems of his age. Since 1921 Alfonso had wanted to visit the Pope and express his undying loyalty. In the meantime, Benedict XV had died. Pius XI received Alfonso in November 1923.

The visit was a great revival of Spanish historical pomp. Alfonso prostrated himself before Pius XI in the presence of his own and the papal court, and kissed the feet and ring of the Pope, avowing that he was the first truly Catholic King of Spain in centuries ready to shed his own blood for the Church. Pius XI in his response called him a "Knight of God." Nevertheless, Pius XI was aware of the Spanish situation, pregnant with potential social upheaval and revolutionary violence.

The Pope believed in the sincerity of the king, but he complained to his advisers about the lack of social understanding in Spain. Pius XI had one of his best papal diplomats, Tedeschini (later a Cardinal) in Spain. When genuine liberal forces started to emerge in Spain and the old regime threw them in jail, Nuncio Tedeschini helped their families and visited them in prison, regardless of whether the politicians were Catholic or anti-Catholic.

The Holy See did not engage in partisan politics. But it refused to accept the views of King Alfonso and many others regarding the function of the Church. Pius XI favored a more genuine expression of willingness to help the Spanish people conduct their own affairs. He knew that the Holy See could not ally itself with the old regime, because this would have meant identification with reaction, and death for the Church in Spain.

Nevertheless, the revolution of 1931 had a distinct anti-Catholic tendency, too. However, the Pope did not break off diplomatic relations with the Spanish republic. He defended the rights of the Church, openly deplored the excesses, and gave orders to Nuncio Tedeschini to make an effort to convince the republican regime of the intentions of the Church and to convince them that they had chosen the wrong approach in attacking the Church. These intentions were: to live in peace with a new regime if it granted freedom for the Church and freedom for the individual. In his encyclical of June 3, 1933, he solemnly refused to recognize the anti-Church decrees of the government. But even in this encyclical Pius XI affirmed that the Holy See is not biased against any form of government, provided the state recognizes the divine rights of the Church.

The situation improved afterward, and in 1935 there were 120 Deputies of the Catholic Party in the coalition government, with five Catholic ministers as members of the cabinet. In 1936, Cardinal Pacelli negotiated personally in Barcelona on his trip back from the Eucharistic Congress of Buenos Aires, but the course of history could not be arrested. Communist infiltration was too widespread, and the Soviet had decided to make a test case of Spain.

The disappearance of the liberals and the overt terror and anti-religious attitude of the communists left no choice for Pius XI but to condemn the regime as evil and make the issue clear: the Church chose martyrdom rather than subservience.

The victory of Franco then made negotiation with the Holy See possible. It granted religious freedom, but the agreement did not mean that the Holy See backed all Franco's political aims.

Pius XI's fight with Hitler adds another dramatic chapter to his reign. Much has been written about the concordat that Pius XI concluded with Germany in 1934. Indeed the Pope and Holy See have been criticized, sometimes bitterly, for having negotiated the agreement with Hitler. Before describing the events and steps that led to the concordat with the nazis, we must consider some basic facts.

There was nothing necessarily surprising about the fact, seemingly paradoxical, that on the day of the election of Pius XI, the Italians, French and Poles hailed him as "our Pope." The history of the Church is replete with examples of nations that fancied the papacy defended their interests over those of other nations. The German press responded to the election of Achille Ratti with unconcealed hostility. The events in Oppeln were still fresh in the public mind and the Germans persisted in their unjustified anger against the alleged misdeeds of the Papal Commissioner to a greater extent than did the Poles. Pius XI was neither a Germanophile nor anti-Polish; in fact, he was completely devoid of nationalistic bias. The fickleness of public opinion was remarkably illustrated by the subsequent events that transpired at the Conference of Genoa and during the occupation of the Ruhr, when Pius XI, ever a defender of the truth and objectivity, was labeled a Germanophile. At the time, the overexcitable French chauvinists accused him of being in alliance with the armament manufacturer Krupp and the former Kaiser. Later, the atmosphere cleared, primarily because of the good offices of Nuncio Pacelli, an expert on German affairs and familiar with the psychology of the German people at all levels.

Nevertheless, the situation between the Holy See and Germany was not a completely happy one, because the relationship was based upon concordats signed in the nineteenth century. After World War I, when the German empire collapsed, the Weimar Constitution of the new democratic German government accorded more freedoms to the Church than did the old concordats entered into by the Holy See and the individual German states and kingdoms. After 1919 both the Vatican and the Germans were eager to restructure their relationships. It was not clear, however, who were properly authorized to carry out this revision of the concordats.

The Holy See had no Nuncio in Berlin before the new postwar Weimar republic came into being in 1919. A Nuncio was accredited to Bavaria and Pacelli was stationed there in Munich until his appointment as papal envoy to the Reich in 1921. In his speech at the ceremony in which he handed over his credentials, Pacelli, on behalf of the Holy See, expressed the hope that the federal government would sign a concordat with the Vatican. This was, of course, the official policy of Pius XI, transmitted to Nuncio Pacelli, who in turn carried it out brilliantly. The negotiations dragged on until 1924; in that year a complete draft of the concordat was prepared, but it was set aside because the Bavarians objected to it.

The Holy See had also been negotiating with the Bavarians

since 1922 and the text of a new concordat between Bavaria and the Holy See had been signed by Nuncio Pacelli and Bavarian Prime Minister Held on March 29, 1924. This was an important step because the last concordat signed with Bavaria dated from 1817. Since Bavaria was predominantly Catholic, the Holy See proceeded without hesitation to agree with the Bavarians and sign a concordat with them before an agreement was reached with the government of the Reich. This concordat regulated all pending financial questions between the Church and the state, particularly important for the Church in Bavaria because all the wealth and properties of the Church had been "secularized" at the beginning of the nineteenth century. The concordat contained important stipulations with respect to the appointment of professors of Catholic religion at the universities maintained by the state. One paragraph, for example, declared that only such teachers be authorized to carry out Catholic religious instruction in schools, including public schools, whose appointments had been approved by the bishops. The state was obliged to set up a preparatory school for religious instructors and give ample rights to the Church during the examination of the candidates. A last point declared that the Holy See was free to appoint bishops, but had to present their names to the government before publishing the appointments in order to ascertain whether the government had any objection on political grounds.

As was to be expected, the government of the Reich was not pleased with the concordat signed with Bavaria; it was urged in some expressions of public opinion to repudiate the concordat as a violation of the constitution of the Reich.

Since the Holy See had concluded an agreement with Bavaria and by this step had embarked upon the road of separate negotiations for concordats, the Nuncio tried to conclude concordats with the largest state of the German federation, Prussia. But he did not exclude the possibility of concluding a concordat with the Reich, too. There was strong opposition to the Prussian concordat. This was led by the German Evangelical Bund, by the Association of German Teachers, and by the Minister of Foreign Affairs, Stresemann. Stresemann was generally known as a genuine liberal who strongly opposed Prussian nationalism. Actually, Stresemann was a statesman in whom liberalism and strong nationalism (bordering on chauvinism) were allied with anti-clericalism. Many elements of this opposition objected on the ground that a concordat with Prussia, like any concordat, would increase the prestige of the Holy See. Pius XI replied that concordats were being concluded for the greater glory of God and for the salvation of souls. Finally, on June 14, 1929, a solemn convention was signed between the Holy See and the free state of Prussia. Its main points were: Complete freedom of religion was to be granted; the present territories of the dioceses were not to be changed; financial assistance was guaranteed by the Prussian state for Catholic religious purposes; financial benefits were to be granted to the clergy. One of the most important points was the right of "presentation," a survival of the nineteenth century. This meant that pastors, deans, canons and bishops could not be appointed by the Holy See unless their names were presented two weeks prior to publication of such appointments to the government.

The next concordat was the agreement between the Free State of Anhalt in June 1931. In October 1932, an agreement was also negotiated with Baden.

Württemberg and Hesse refused to enter into new agreements with the Holy See, despite the fact that their concordats with Rome, concluded in the nineteenth century, were outdated. The organization of all these agreements and concordats with the various German states was a most difficult, painstaking and unrewarding task for the person charged with it. At the end, Nuncio Pacelli necessarily became an authority on German geography, history and legislation, and became more knowledgeable about the country and its history than many Germans themselves.

After the signature of the concordat with Baden, the negotiations between the Holy See and the pre-Hitler German government came to a halt.

In the meantime, national socialism marched swiftly toward power and the governments of the Reich were unable to stop it. Since the program of national socialism was openly in conflict with Catholic principles, it was obvious that the Holy See was not happy about the result of the election which put Hitler in power. However, the fact that a government is not friendly to the Catholic Church, or is even antagonistic to it, has never been cause for the Holy See to refuse to enter negotiations for an agreement. It would be completely contrary to the essence of international law to assume that one international body, one sovereign, would enter into diplomatic relationship only with other sovereigns whose ideology is similar to their own.

Certain events are already forgotten or were not seen in a proper light in connection with the concordat signed with Hitler. First of all, it is obvious that the Holy See was in no hurry to conclude a concordat with the Reich because the new concordats with the federated states of Germany, which were autonomous, in many respects were already in effect. One could object that the Holy See, anxious to protect Catholic interests, might actually have been in a hurry and nobody could blame the Vatican for this.

Actually, the facts are quite different. Nuncio Pacelli, whom Pius XI appointed Secretary of State and promoted to Cardinal, arrived in Rome in 1931. The new Nuncio to Berlin, Orsenigo, was a saintly and prudent man, a friend of Pius XI from his student days in Milan. He had no instructions to start negotiations with the Hitler government. The Holy See understood that it would mean added prestige to Hitler if he could claim success in the question of the concordat.

Hitler followed Mussolini's example. He recognized that Mussolini had utilized the Lateran Treaty to strengthen his own prestige; Hitler wanted to do the same. He needed this not only for an international reputation, but also to lull the Catholics in Germany. Curiously enough, the dictators who rule against the people and never ask their opinion through the secret ballot are most anxious to be popular and boast before the world that it is a democratic consensus that keeps them in power. Hitler hated and despised the Catholics. Nevertheless, he wanted their applause and, if possible, their support. The best man to carry out Hitler's mission was former Reichschancellor von Papen, himself a Catholic, who belonged to a clique of Catholics unaffiliated with any party and thus useful for purposes of negotiation. Whether von Papen was in good faith remains to be seen; all the documents have not yet been published.

It was von Papen who approached the Nuncio and got in touch with former members of the Reichstag belonging to the Center Catholic Party (Zentrum), headed by Chancellor Bruening. The Zentrum was a party founded by Catholics and considered to be a Catholic party. In the 1920's Konrad Adenauer, at that time mayor of Cologne and an influential figure in Zentrum politics, wanted to transform the party into a non-denominational Christian democratic party. At the congress that decided this issue Adenauer remained in the minority and Dr. Bruening became the leader. Adenauer waited more than twenty years and after World War II his rise in German politics was providential. He then realized his aim that the Christian Democratic Union be built on non-denominational lines.

After the coming to power of Hitler, the German political parties manifested a peculiar behavior. The Social Democrats openly withdrew from the scene and their leader Loeb declared that he accepted Hitler. The Zentrum, the Catholic Party, dissolved itself in a plenary session.

There is only one sentence in the press release of the Zentrum that hinted at the real cause of its dissolution: "The withdrawal of the Zentrum Party from the stage of political history was caused by the same storms that raged at the birth of the party more than sixty years ago." It is difficult to determine just what this declaration meant—whether it meant the anti-Catholic policy of Bismarck or something else.

There was not a single dissenting vote at the session that dissolved the Zentrum Party. Reichschancellor Bruening was present. After the dissolution Bruening said that he went to the session determined that he was going to vote against it, yet he voted for it.

Leaders of the Zentrum Party later reported that the dissolution was hastened by a *mistake*. Msgr. Kaas, a leader of the Zentrum Party, who was not present at the session, telephoned Dr. Bruening and in the course of the conversation Kaas asked Bruening: "Are you still in existence?" Dr. Bruening understood this as a concealed warning for dissolution. Msgr. Kaas, who later lived in Rome and was responsible for the maintenance of St. Peter's Basilica (he died in 1954), said that it had not been his intention to warn the deputies of the Zentrum Party.

It was known in Rome, after the event, that Cardinal Bertram, leader of the German episcopate, had issued directives to German Catholics according to which they were told they might collaborate with the National Socialist Party. German Catholics were told that Cardinal Bertram withdrew his previous "grave concerns" regarding the party. The Cardinal did not consult the Holy See before he issued such a statement. The Nuncio in Germany learned of Bertram's declaration from the newspapers. Furthermore, Bertram did not consult most of the members of the German episcopate. The Cardinal thought that he would be able to appease Hitler.

On April 16, 1933, on Easter Sunday, von Papen arrived in Rome and told the Vatican that Hitler's government wished to sign a concordat with the Holy See. It is not true that the Holy See sounded out the German government first.

Other German politicians came to Rome, too. These were the formerly influential Zentrum deputies, Catholic political leaders, Stegerwald, Josef Wirth and Joos, trusted and vener-

THE FIGHT WITH THE GIANTS

able men. They told the Holy See that the concordats concluded with the German states no longer were valid as international treaties for German Catholics, now that Hitler had
taken over the Reich. Only a concordat with the Reich could
provide international and valid assurances that the rights of
the Church would not be violated. These Catholic leaders re-
peatedly declared that the German people wanted a concordat. Cardinal Pacelli, Secretary of State, answered that the
Holy See would conclude a concordat with the Reich only
if the German government took the initiative.

Since von Papen was in Rome, where he had declared with
authority that his government requested such a concordat,
Cardinal Pacelli, upon instructions of Pius XI, did not commit
himself, but let von Papen return to Germany with no promise. In the meantime, however, Cardinal Pacelli had started
a series of confidential conferences with German experts of
the Secretariat of State, on the subject of the future concordat
and the ones already in existence. This preliminary phase
lasted from May 16 to June 29.

In the meantime, the draft of the new concordat was sent
to the German bishops who were holding their traditional
Pentecost conference at Fulda. They agreed with the pro-
posals in the draft.

The Holy See thought that the draft of the concordat
would be too much for the nazis, and that they would reject
it. In such a case, the Holy See was prepared to conclude a
modus vivendi, thereby keeping the existing state concordats
in effect. It was hoped that since the nazis desired an agreement they would consent to this. But it was equally believed,
as has been said, that the nazis would first reject the draft of
a strong Reich concordat which would completely assure all
the rights and freedoms of the Church.

The turning point, and a most dramatic one, took place on
June 29. Von Papen arrived in Rome that morning and asked
to be received by Cardinal Pacelli, Secretary of State, on the
same afternoon. This move from von Papen was considered
reckless and a breach of diplomatic protocol. He should have

waited at least a day. Furthermore, von Papen knew quite
well that Cardinal Pacelli had participated in the long and
strenuous services connected with the feast of the Apostles
Peter and Paul.

Nevertheless, Cardinal Pacelli received von Papen June 29.

From this moment on, certain German Catholic circles, including the hierarchy, pressed the Vatican more and more
for a concordat. Cardinal Faulhaber declared that a concordat would help relations and would add to the security of
the Church. Since everybody concerned wanted the concordat, the Pope consented, since his aim was to protect people;
Hitler was already enjoying diplomatic relations with the
entire world.

Thus, negotiations between the Holy See and the Hitler
government officially began. This was the second phase of the
negotiations, lasting from June 29 to July 20, on which day
the concordat was signed. When the German government received the text of the draft delivered to its envoy in Rome,
the nazis published it immediately, before the Holy See. This
created an intolerable situation for the Catholic Church. The
nazis boasted, saying: We are full of good will because we
agreed to such a concordat, favorable to the Church. One
of the nazi leaders asked in public whether the Catholic
Church could afford to refuse to sign and launch a Kultur-
kampf as it had done during the Bismarck era. Pope Pius XI
and his advisers knew that this was impossible; the German
Church was unable to do so.

It was suspected, of course, that Hitler was in bad faith
because he had accepted so much without discussion. Obviously, he had no intention of keeping his word. Although Pius
XI feared this, he was acutely distressed when it became more
and more evident. The concordat was signed, nevertheless.
The Pope did it reluctantly.

The history of the diplomatic relations of the Holy See with
Germany from this point on was a continuous series of tensions and irritations. Significantly, the nazis for a while left

Ambassador von Bergen, appointed by the previous regime, at his post. Von Bergen was spied upon by a Gestapo agent who had the rank of minister. Inside Germany, the Hitler government slowly stripped the concordat of its contents and very soon only the skeleton remained. Nuncio Orsenigo protested, but in vain. It was at this time that a German underground was created that supplied the bishops with money and delivered to them books, papal speeches and encyclicals otherwise unobtainable in Germany. All this was carried out with the assistance of Pius XI, who was profoundly concerned over the developments. Pius XI took every occasion to speak against nazi ideology. First and foremost, he opposed oppression in any form, particularly for so-called reasons of "race." Pius XI declared that the term "race" describes animals and beasts; the expression *human genus* should be used to express the uniqueness of mankind. At the same time he told the Italians in many speeches that they have no reason to imitate German nationalism, in view of their great past, particularly their Risorgimento. Pius XI made such utterances frequently between 1933 and 1937. At the same time, he sent word on several occasions to Mussolini not to fall into Hitler's trap, because it would lead to a personal as well as a national catastrophe.

Pius XI refused to consider the existence of a so-called Jewish question. He said that this is a Christian question primarily, putting Christians to a test of their principles. "In no way whatsoever can a Catholic Christian become anti-Semitic," said Pius XI. On another occasion he added, "Spiritually, we all are Semites." Few Popes had ever made so clear the Catholic Christian attitude with respect to anti-Semitism. "In no way can a Catholic Christian become anti-Semitic" was a clear and clarion warning to those who fancied that they could be only "against the Jewish spirit." This was the thesis that erroneously interpreted the clear statement of St. Thomas that freedom should be given to the Jews.

It was during the reign of Pius XI that the Holy Office issued its declaration on anti-Semitism. It is obvious that a Christian cannot hate anyone; nevertheless, the question was brought before the Sacred Congregation of the Holy Office. Was anti-Semitism permissible for a Catholic? The answer, which was made on March 25, 1928, and which is an answer of the Church and binding upon each Catholic, was that the Holy Office condemned *"odium illud quod vulgo 'antisemitismi' nomine nunc significari solet"* (that hate which is now generally called anti-Semitism).

Pius XI with this dramatic pronouncement condemned all the "explanations" of a "spiritual" anti-Semitism fostered by certain small groups of Catholics all over the world, including Germany, who fancied that their so-called protective anti-Semitism was really harmless. He knew and said to his advisers that any kind of anti-Semitism ends in brutal, violent persecution.

During the Hitlerite persecution Pius XI identified himself with the persecuted by declaring: "Spiritually, we all are Semites." Yet the concordat with Hitler does not mention the Jews or "the Jewish question," because it is an agreement between the head of the Catholic Church and a foreign government regulating Church matters. Actually, the little freedom that the concordat left for the clergy and hierarchy was widely used to save as many persecuted Jews as could be saved.

Pius XI felt himself uneasy in the Vatican when the earth began to shake with political convulsions. He wanted to be on the spot. It will be remembered that when he was Nuncio in Warsaw and the Red army was approaching, he asked Pope Benedict XV that he be allowed to remain in Warsaw, even risking the chance of falling into the hands of the Bolsheviks. Now he wanted to help the persecuted personally.

Because of overwork, he fell ill. His illness, lasting four months—from December 1936 to March 1937—prevented him from issuing a pastoral letter at Christmas. But the moment he felt better Pius XI gave vent to his righteous anger over the crimes of the times. While convalescing, he had already been working on three encyclicals; the first was issued even before he was completely restored to health. This was *Mit Brennender Sorge* (March 14, 1937), a flaming denunciation of nazi persecution and bad faith. At this time the Pope did not care whether Hitler denounced the concordat or whether German Catholics would be able to conduct a new Kultur-kampf. His encyclical went to the heart of the matter. There are doctrine, faith, love, enthusiasm, and the wrath of an arch-angel in this magnificent document, written entirely by Pius XI:

"Take care, venerable brethren, that, above all, faith in God, the first and irreplaceable foundation of all religion, be preserved in Germany pure and unstained. The believer in God is not he who utters the name in his speech, but he for whom this sacred word stands for a true and worthy concept of the Divinity. Whoever identifies, by pantheistic confusion, God and the universe, by either lowering God to the dimen-sions of the world, or raising the world to the dimensions of God, is not a believer in God. Whoever follows that so-called pre-Christian Germanic conception of substituting a dark and impersonal destiny for the personal God denies thereby the wisdom and providence of God. . . .

"Whoever exalts race, or the people, or the state, or a par-ticular form of state, or the depositories of power, or any other fundamental value of the human community—however nec-essary and honorable be their function in worldly things—whoever raises these notions above their standard value and divinizes them to an idolatrous level distorts and perverts an order of the world planned and created by God: he is far from the true faith in God and from the concept of life which that faith upholds.

"Beware, venerable brethren, of that growing abuse, in speech as in writing, of the name of God as though it were a meaningless label, to be affixed to any creation, more or less arbitrary, of human speculation. Use your influence on the faithful, that they refuse to yield to this aberration. Our God is the personal God, supernatural, omnipotent, infinitely perfect, one in the Trinity of Persons, tri-personal in the unity of Divine Essence, the Creator of all existence, Lord, King and ultimate Consummator of the history of the world, who will not, and cannot, tolerate a rival god by His side.

"This God, this sovereign Master, has issued commandments whose value is independent of time and space, of country and race. As God's sun shines on every human face, so His law knows neither privilege nor exception. Rulers and subjects, crowned and uncrowned, rich and poor, are equally subject to His word. From the fullness of the Creator's right there naturally arises the fullness of His right to be obeyed by individuals and communities, whoever they are. This obedience permeates all branches of activity in which moral values claim harmony with the law of God, and pervades all integration of the ever-changing laws of man into the immutable laws of God.

"None but superficial minds could stumble into concepts of a national God, of a national religion; or attempt to lock within the frontiers of a single people, within the narrow limits of a single race, God, the Creator of the universe, King and Legislator of all nations, before whose immensity they are 'as a drop of a bucket' (Isa. 40:15)."

Hitler's answer was more vicious persecution, relaxed only for a few days when he was planning the absorption of Austria. It was March 1938. The Anschluss had gone down in history.

Hitler, the head of a state that had signed a concordat with the Holy See, came to Rome to visit Mussolini during the spring of 1938. No provisions were made to request a papal audience. And Pius XI for his part precluded even the possibility that Hitler's entourage might entertain the idea of visiting the Vatican. Pius XI took the only steps dignity called for: he left Rome for Castel Gandolfo on May 2, 1938. Hitler arrived on May 3. Never had the Popes left Rome so early for their summer residence; Rome in May is especially beautiful. The Vatican Museum was closed from May 3 to May 8 and the magnificent bronze gate of the Vatican Palace also was shut tight.

Pius XI received pilgrims in general audience in his summer residence at Castel Gandolfo on May 4. In his speech he deplored in a firm voice that "on the feast day of the Holy Cross [May 3] it was sacrilegious to elevate another cross that has nothing to do with the Cross of Christ." The Pope, of course, was referring to the swastika, called in Italian *croce uncinata*. *Osservatore Romano* totally ignored the visit of Hitler, printing no news of his arrival or stay.

But before the expression of his disdain of Hitler, the Pope made clear just how he felt about the occupation of Austria by the nazi dictator. The German episcopate never praised Hitler and, except for the isolated declaration of Cardinal Bertram, made no pro-nazi statement. The Austrian episcopate, on the other hand, issued—in good faith—statements that created great confusion. After the Anschluss, Cardinal Innitzer, Archbishop of Vienna, visited Hitler personally and lauded him in a public speech. Then the Austrian episcopate issued a collective pastoral letter, read from the pulpits on March 25, hailing the achievements of German National Socialism. The Holy See was alarmed and considered this collective letter and Cardinal Innitzer's behavior not only imprudent, but offensive to the feelings of the entire Catholic world. Within a week *Osservatore Romano* published two important items. One said that the Bishops' statement had to be understood as an expression of their right to state the Church's position. Another declared that the statement had been made without consultation with the Holy See. In other words, this meant the Holy See did not know about it and therefore disapproved.

Pius XI summoned Cardinal Innitzer to Rome. He entered the studio of the Pope shortly after 11:00 on the morning of April 6 and left, after a three-hour audience, at 2:00. When Bishop Hudal, Head of the Collegio dell' Anima, asked Cardinal Innitzer what had happened and how, all Cardinal Innitzer told him was: "I went in and greeted him with *'Laudetur Jesus Christus.'* When I left, I said, 'Thank you, Holy Father,' and kissed his hands. Everything between these two greetings was said by him."

After this audience the Austrian episcopate issued another collective pastoral letter which strongly reaffirmed Catholic principle, assuring the faithful that in their previous pastoral the bishops did not mean to give up any rights of the Church. Pius XI had acted resolutely, quickly and firmly.

The joint problem of Russia and communism had worried Pius XI since his days as Nuncio in Warsaw. The Soviets directed their attacks not only against the former orthodox state church and Christianity, whose bishops and priests were summarily shot or arrested *en masse,* but also against Catholic prelates. Archbishop Cieplak of St. Petersburg, after his arrest and sentencing in 1923, languished for another half year in jail; his vicar general, Budkiewicz, was martyred on Good Friday after having been accused, together with his Metropolitan, of violating Soviet laws and inciting to counter-revolution; Archbishop Von der Ropp of Mohilew was arrested and exiled, together with eighty priests; Bishops Sloskan and Matulis were accused of holding forbidden services and sent to Siberia; forty Catholic priests were sent along with 425 Orthodox priests to the notorious Solovki camp. In addition, priests were compelled to work on public labor projects and unreasonable work demands were made upon them. The seminary in St. Petersburg was made into a public school; the church of Smolensk changed into a radio tower. Many Catholic schools in Moscow were closed, the Caritas organization forbidden to function, foreign priests or Catholic writings prohibited. Thus, a monstrous poverty and a terrible shortage of priests weighed upon the Catholic communities that were left.

Pius XI, as heir and executor of the will of Benedict, tried as much as possible to stem this spiritual and material misery of terrible proportions. His letter of April 29, 1922, to Cardinal

Gasparri and the memorandum sent to Genoa by Monsignor Pizzardo on May 5 called upon the civilized world and the Christian powers to come to the aid of the peoples of the East, subject not only to religious persecution, but to hunger and plagues. As we have seen, the Pope requested guarantees from the Russians for the freedom of conscience, religious practices and the restitution of confiscated Church property. The Pope also requested the liberation of Patriarch Tychon and other Orthodox priests held in Moscow jails. The prestige of the Vatican saved fourteen priests who were arrested and awaited execution. Now the Soviet regime promised not to carry out the death sentence imposed upon Budkiewicz and others. He was executed later, however, because he allegedly supported Rome's plans to "interfere" in the inner affairs of the Soviet Republic and "compel" it to start negotiations.

While some emigré circles began to prattle about a papal alliance with the Bolsheviks for the alleged purpose of prose-lytization among the Russian masses, the Soviet press raised the question of a Russian representative at the Vatican in ex-change for papal recognition of the Soviet Union. What was behind this Soviet maneuver? The Pope had sent a purely charitable papal mission to Russia in 1922, consisting of twelve religious (Jesuits and members of the Society of the Divine Word). This mission had provisions for hundreds of thousands of hungry persons and medicines worth one mil-lion lire. The mission operated until 1926; then gave up its efforts in the face of governmental obstacles placed in its path, after making a complete distribution of its remaining provisions.

Meanwhile, Pius XI never ceased his efforts on behalf of Russia, ever urging aid, support and compassion for its peo-ple. These efforts were best expressed in his allocution of July 10, 1922, to the world episcopate, requesting two and one half million dollars on behalf of the hungry in Russia, regard-less of religion and nationality. In his consistorial speech of May 23, 1923 he deplored the sad and evil events in Russia,

and in his allocution of December 23 he again expressed his
anxiety and concern over the fate of Christians in Russia and
of Bishop Czieplak. In his encyclical of November 12, 1923,
dealing with St. Josaphat, he deplored the rising misery in
Russia and the persecution of Christians there. Again, in his
consistorial speech of March 24, 1924, he spoke of the victims
of hatred of Christianity, while on December 18 he expressed
his readiness to come to the aid of needy Russians without
thereby having to acknowledge the communist regime.

At the beginning of 1925 the Pope established a special Russian Commission within the Sacred Congregation for Easter
Rites. In the autumn of that year he sent Msgr. d'Herbigny,
S.J., its head, to Russia on three different occasions so that
he secretly could consecrate new bishops, appoint an administrator for the leaderless see of Leningrad, and divide the
immense territory into ten administrative districts. At that
time the Catholics of the Latin rite of Russia were estimated
to number 1,500,000, in eight dioceses. Many priests and
faithful in Russia were helped by zealous people outside
Russia, of various religious organizations. Great interest in
unification with the Catholic Church seemed to be rising, especially in southern Russia. But these efforts were again soon
crippled, and the Church in Russia had to give up its work
of conversion in the face of the attacks against it. Msgr.
d'Herbigny was ordered to leave Russia, and all his admin-
istrators and emissaries, as well as two-thirds of the priests—
except for the Bishop of Moscow—were condemned to im-
prisonment and forced labor.

Pius XI did whatever he could to help the persecuted and
hard-pressed Church and clergy. Through a personal letter
sent to Cardinal Pompili, on February 2, 1930, he authorized prayers in atonement for the outrages against divine
law committed in Russia. In another utterance of February 9 he urged the Catholic world to protest and to celebrate Masses of atonement against the persecution of religion
and the ridiculing of the Christmas holy day by the Russian

rulers. Pius XI established the Russicum in Rome in August 1929; its aim was to train missionaries to preserve the faith among the 140,000,000 inhabitants of Russia. The Pope also authorized the Russian Commission to establish a proper bishopric for White Russia in Harbin. Later, he issued instructions to the entire hierarchy about the Russians who had returned to the Catholic Church. In 1930 he detached the Russian Commission from the Oriental Congregation and made it into an independent body. Above all, he offered refuge to all Catholic as well as non-Catholic prelates, priests and Christians who sought freedom from the Bolshevik horror.

Pius XI was always deeply conscious of the missionary tasks and obligations of the Church. Mission activity was a distinct characteristic of his pontificate, and he practiced the most advanced methods for propagation of the faith within and beyond the confines of Christendom. In the first year of his pontificate three mission centennials were elaborately celebrated: the third centennial of the establishment of the Propaganda, the three-hundredth anniversary of the canonization of St. Francis Xavier, and the first centennial of the establishment of the Society for the Propagation of the Faith. On Pentecost Sunday he celebrated a pontifical Mass in St. Peter's, and from his throne he delivered a homily on missions before 30,000 persons. On this occasion he gave a historical account of the missionary work of the Church from its beginnings. Throughout, he stressed the "universal fatherhood" he felt in the presence of the "resplendent vision of the Christian apostolate," and the great masses of pagans yet to be converted.

This homily was an elaboration of an address he had made only a few days before, on June 3, at an International Conference of Missions which he had called in Rome. Here he had exhorted the missionaries to redouble their efforts, overcome all difficulties, and pay special attention to the establishment of a native clergy wherever and whenever possible.

Further evidence of the Pope's interest in mission work was
the founding of the Polyglot Propaganda College, in which
Church literature was prepared in thirty languages.

During the Holy Year of 1925 Pius XI gave a further im-
petus to world mission work. In that year he gave instructions
to the Director of Propaganda, Van Rossum, to erect a missionary exhibit illustrating the achievements and requirements in the mission lands, so that pilgrims coming to Rome
could return to their native countries with a greater awareness
of the obligations of the Church, and their own, with respect
to the missions. Eventually, this became the permanent "mis-
sionary-ethnological museum" in the Lateran.

On behalf of the world missions, Pope Pius XI, in the form
of letters, memoranda, exhortations and instructions, constantly urged the clergy and the laity, at all levels, to improve
the quality of their missionary activity, to coordinate their
activities, to improve their working methods, to meet modern
requirements, ever taking care to avoid the errors of exclu-
sivism, nationalism and secularism.

This constant strengthening of missionary organizations
and personnel and the increase in mission territories resulted
in an increase of 4,000 foreign missions in the first decade of
his pontificate. The number of domestic missions increased
from 2,670 to 4,000, missionary districts from 241 to 366, mission stations by twenty-five per cent. The number of converts
rose to 6,000,000.

Yet the greatest achievement in this field was the victorious missionary breakthrough, leading to the establishment of
a native clergy and missionary staff in Japan, China, India
and Africa. Pius XI, on the Feast of Christ the King in 1926,
consecrated six Chinese bishops; in 1927, one in Japan. In the
summer of 1933 he appointed three more Chinese bishops
and an Annamite (Indo-Chinese) bishop.

The reunification of the Eastern Church with that of Rome
was an idea close to the heart of Pius XI. In this, too, he
followed in the footsteps of his predecessors, Leo XIII and

Benedict XV. His view found principal expression in the two "Eastern" encyclicals, *Ecclesiam Dei*, November 1923, and *Rerum Orientalium*, September 1928, in which he made references to the previous papal invitations to unity, and again lovingly invited all the separated to return to the true Church.

His appeal was rejected both in Orthodox and in Protestant circles, and generated only slight interest in the world Catholic press and in many Catholic intellectual circles. In more practical terms, the Pope's interest in East-West unity found expression in the support of educational and cultural activities aiming in this direction. He sponsored, endorsed, and addressed many conferences and gatherings (as well as supported many organizations) dedicated to restoring the unity of the churches. It is enough to cite the conferences held in Velehrad (1924, 1927 and 1930), in Laibach (1925), in Vienna (1926), and the French and Belgian conferences held from 1926 to 1929.

Further, Pius XI encouraged the founding of uniate groups within the established orders (Redemptorists, Jesuits and Benedictines), the establishment of study circles and seminaries (such as the Ethiopian and Ruthenian in Rome), the holding of Eastern services, and triduums of prayer for church unity.

The attitude of Pius XI toward non-Catholic efforts and conferences on behalf of church unity was, of course, dogmatically determined. Yet Pius XI encouraged the "conversations" organized at Malines, Belgium, by Cardinal Mercier with the High-Church Anglicans led by Lord Halifax.

But he was more rigid in his attitude to the Protestant world conferences for church unity held in Stockholm (1925) and Lausanne (1927). Archbishop Soderblom of Upsala invited the Pope, through the Swedish pastor Neander, to send a delegation. The Pope received the pastor graciously and sent the bishop his personal blessing, but he refused the invitation, declaring that he could not be listed among the "seekers," since he had long since found himself.

In the meantime, British and American Protestantism made vigorous efforts at proselytism in the East, to tie the Russian and other Orthodox churches to Protestantism. Often, this was done with a clear, anti-Catholic tendency. Nevertheless, the Oriental missions increased in extent and membership during his pontificate. A total of 1,148 foreign and 2,400 native religious were active in eighty societies. They were active among the millions of uniate Catholics in this area encompassing Roumanians, Ruthenians, Albanians, Jugoslavs, Greeks, Bulgarians, Syrians and Armenians.

Four million Ruthenians living in Czechoslovakia and Poland remained loyal to the uniate Church, and in Jugoslavia 41,000 uniate Catholics held firm despite the oppression of the government allied with the Orthodox Church.

As a result of the concordat of 1929, the Church province and diocese of Bucharest, of Latin and Oriental rite, were organized like those in Transylvania and Bukovina and the relations between the Churches of both rites were improved. Redemptorist priests were active in Bulgaria; a vicariate was established in Salonika for Thrace and Macedonia; Jesuits and Franciscans worked in Albania and were responsible for many conversions and realizations of unity; while in Greece the Capuchin priests were most instrumental in effecting relations with uniate groups there as well as on the Ionian Islands and among Armenians.

It was difficult, however, to conduct such activities in Turkey after the 1929 victory of the Turks over Greece, because the Turkish government obstructed all Christian activity.

Pius XI also strove to defend Catholic interests in Palestine and Jerusalem. His efforts were best symbolized by the founding of the University of Beirut (1923) and the sending of the legate Giorgi to consecrate the basilicas in Gethsemane and Tabor.

Although Capuchin missions were not successful among Arabs, mass conversions occurred (about 30,000) to the uniate Coptic Church in Egypt. No less successful was the missionary progress in Abyssinia, when Emperor Haile Selassie visited Pius XI on June 21, 1924. A new missionary hierarchy was established, as well as new apostolic vicariates in Addis Ababa, Gondar, Tigrai and Dessie.

In contrast to the missionary tasks in the Near East, which were limited to attempts to achieve unity with the Eastern churches and exert thereby an indirect influence on Moslems, the Far East missions had two main concerns: the conversion of the natives and the establishment of churches, social and cultural agencies to be made independent as soon as possible so that they could be staffed by native personnel.

As early as 1923, Pius XI greatly encouraged such a development. He began with India proper by installing native bishops in the vicariates. At that time the tide of nationalism was steadily rising and that, together with the caste system, was a natural obstacle to efforts at conversion. For this reason Pius XI sent Cardinal Lepicier as Visitator to the Indian mission in 1924. Lepicier remained there for two years, visiting all the missions, paying special attention to the education of youth and the establishment of a native clergy. In 1926 he was succeeded by an American, Msgr. (now Archbishop) Mooney, who was made Apostolic Delegate to the Indian mission. Archbishop Mooney did yeoman work in reorganizing the extant dioceses and bringing new ones into being.

As a result of these efforts, the number of Catholics in India increased by 500,000, involving the activities of 1,200 European and 1,930 native missionaries. These achievements, of a cultural as well as a religious nature, were carried out primarily in the south, among the lowest social classes.

Just beyond India, the Indo-Chinese mission held fast against natural catastrophes and heathen opposition and reaction. This was exemplified by the figures on conversion. Conversions rose from 1,000,000 in 1922 to 1,568,000 in 1932. Here, as elsewhere, the chief problem and the ever-present crying need was to establish a native clergy.

It was the people on the Chinese mainland, however, who

were of special concern to Pius XI. On August 9, 1922, he
sent an Apostolic Delegate, Archbishop Constantini, to China.
Constantini arrived in Hong Kong in the autumn of that year,
warmly greeted by the Catholic population, and from there
he went to Hangkow and eventually to Peking, where he
presented his credentials to the President of the Chinese Republic.

Constantini's first task was to call a Chinese plenary or national council to discuss ways of strengthening and spreading
the Catholic religion in China. The general synod held in
Shanghai from May 15 to June 12, 1924, attended by forty-
five bishops, four prefects, and forty consultors, opened a new
era in the history of the Catholic Church in China. This was
an opinion expressed by the Pope himself in his communication to the delegates of the first plenary conference.

On June 15, 1925, when a group of professors of the University of Peking appealed to the Pope to protest against outrages committed against Chinese by Christians, the Pope
assured "the great Chinese people" of his sympathy and his
hope for the restoration of justice and love according to Christian principles.

On June 15, 1926, he sent a circular to mission authorities
in China, again outlining the religious aims of the missions.
In it he especially instructed them to keep free of any kind
of political nationalism (fostering the interests of the particular Western countries of the missionaries) and thereby refute
the charges that missionaries represented foreign interests. In
this connection he again stressed the special role to be played
by a native ecclesiastical body. And in August 1928, in a special message to the Chinese Republic, the Pope declared his
readiness, and that of the Church, to support the demands of
so great and ancient a nation whose future was rich with
promise.

The high point of the efforts to create the basis for a native
clergy and an independent Church structure was reached in
1926 when Pius XI, assisted by Archbishop Constantini, con-

secrated six Chinese bishops in St. Peter's. Thus, in China, despite civil wars, revolutions, and natural disturbances, by 1938 three million Catholics could be counted, a considerable increase over the 2,142,000 Catholics who had existed in 1922, at the beginning of the pontificate of Pius XI.

The picture in Japan was somewhat the same, though the pace and development of conversion were slower. There were about 80,000 converts in Japan, and 100,000 in Korea. As in China, a plenary council was held in Japan in 1924, under the guidance of Apostolic Delegate Giardini, where the tasks awaiting the missions were formulated and plans elaborated to solve them. In 1925, on the Feast of Christ the King, the Pope assigned twenty-seven Japanese priests to the old Christian center of Nagasaki. In 1931, Monsignor Mooney became the Apostolic Delegate in Tokyo. But Buddhist opposition at that time prevented the appointment of a Japanese representative to the Holy See, despite the general public sympathy toward the Vatican as a result of the Vatican gift of $25,000 to help earthquake victims.

In the Philippines, mission work was seriously set back by the shortage of priests, by Protestant influences, and by the secular school system, despite the zealous efforts of the old as well as new religious orders. Nevertheless, apostolic activity continued, Church provinces were reorganized, and the Pope's message radioed to the International Eucharistic Conference held in Manila in 1937 expressed his heartfelt concern for this Christian island.

The apostolate in Indonesia underwent a strong and steady development as a result of the younger missionary elements who took to the field. By 1934 the total of Christians rose to 230,000 from the original number of 60,000 recorded in 1922. The number of native clergy increased here, too. The original inhabitants of Africa, Australia and the two Americas—Eskimos and Indians—engulfed in the whirlpool of advancing civilization, with its industrialization, nationalism, urbanization, race tensions and conflicts, also felt the helping hand of Rome during the reign of Pius XI.

On December 7, 1922, the Pope established a South African delegation with its see in Capetown. The effectiveness of this activity was soon reflected not only by the existence of three Catholic newspapers, but by the opening, in July 1924, of the first South African general synod in Kimberley. Here, religious, church, social and political problems were on the agenda, with special attention to the burning race problem.

In 1927 a "Catholic African Union" was called into being, sponsored by Pius XI, in order to deal specifically with the Negro in Christian terms. Because of the far-sightedness and the long-range plans of the Pope, the Catholic missions in Africa were successful. The original ninety-four mission dioceses were increased to 133 districts in 1933, and the number of believers rose from 2,000,000 to more than 5,250,000, and catechumens numbered 2,177,083. All these were served by a total of 2,000 priests, 1,000 religious brothers and 5,000 sisters, many of them native Africans. By 1939 the African hierarchy (except for the Coptic dioceses in Egypt and Eritrea) included one patriarchate, two archbishoprics, sixteen bishoprics, 102 apostolic vicariates, forty-two apostolic prefects, as well as 171 Church dioceses. The Cameroons, Belgian Congo, Uganda and Central Madagascar with their millions of Catholics were fast becoming Christian lands during the pontificate of Pius XI.

In the South Sea islands, Catholic missions encountered economic crisis and other obstacles. Nevertheless, the number of South Sea Catholics rose from 110,000 to 200,000.

Catholic Action was not merely a slogan for Pope Pius XI. His spirit captured the faithful everywhere.

CHAPTER ELEVEN

Three Roses

THE good health that Pius XI enjoyed throughout his life was the result of his generally moderate habits, aided, probably, by his training as a mountain climber. He enjoyed smoking cigars, and drank beer or wine until the end of his life. He was a normal human being, endowed with much common sense and a great love in his heart for his fellow beings and God. Pius XI strengthened his constitution by constant physical exercise, hard work and—most important—a rare ability to forget his cares when it was necessary to forget them. He was a good and a sound sleeper.

His occasional nervousness, due to overwork, was the response of the human physique to fatigue. Pius XI fought back; he did not want to admit that he could become sick. When his strength started to fail, he set his mind determinedly to postpone the inevitable.

In June 1936, however, warning signs were visible. For the first time in his pontificate Pius XI complained about the pain in his legs and expressed a wish to lie down just for a minute during the day. This was quite different from his routine; he used to take a short break of five or ten minutes several times during the day, but he would never lie down. Now he said that he was looking forward to leaving Rome for the summer, for Castel Gandolfo. Pius XI admitted that he was very tired.

It should be borne in mind that for one who spoke so little about himself, and who never complained and who never felt tired, such words were fraught with significance, particularly in southern Europe where *sfogo* (the expression of one's true feelings) is an important part of hygiene. It is half a cure when people can liberate themselves by complaints of some sort or other. There is much to be said for the salutary effect of such frankness. But Pius XI was a different kind of man. If he admitted being tired this meant more. And he knew it, too.

During the spring, the Carmelite Sisters of Lisieux sent him their congratulations on his birthday. They told him that in their prayers they were asking the intercession of Saint Thérèse so that the Lord might grant him twenty more years. The Pope, who never lost his sense of humor, laughed and pointed out that for such an agreement one needs the consent of both parties, and it remained to be seen what the One in heaven would say to this request.

During the summer and the fall of 1936 the Pope twice complained about fainting spells. Once, he actually lost his equilibrium and fell backward, hurting his neck, which began to bleed. But he forbade anyone to call the doctor and next morning he seemed to be all right. Later, he said that the Pope could not permit himself the luxury of remaining in bed. On another occasion he said that he was now ready to suffer, to suffer in expiation for his sins as well as for the benefit of souls and for the peace of the world. But he hoped that it would be a suffering which would permit the total or at least partial discharge of his own duties as Pope.

In the meantime, however, he tried to "pull himself together," because he said that it was the Pope's duty to stay well and to be available to all. Despite the swelling in his legs, and despite the urging of his secretaries that he seek more medical attention, he did not pay enough attention to himself. On November 27, 1936, he received Admiral Horthy, regent of Hungary. The ceremonies exhausted the Pope and finally he asked for the doctor.

Pius XI primarily suffered from miocarditis, arteriosclerosis and varicose veins. As a result of the latter one of his legs became ulcerous. Prof. Milani visited him every day and treated him with all the medication required by his condition, including infra-red rays.

The Pope opposed consultation with other doctors. One afternoon he awakened and noticed that not only Prof. Milani but Fr. Gemelli, who was a physician and a psychiatrist, stood at his bedside. Pius XI turned to Fr. Gemelli, of whom he was very fond, and asked: "What are you doing here, Father? If I need Fr. Gemelli, the rector of the Catholic University, I can call him through the Congregation of Seminaries and Universities. If I want him as the president of the Pontifical Academy of Sciences, I call him through the Secretary of State. If I want him as a Franciscan, I can call him through the General of the Franciscans. If I want him as a friend, then I can call him by personal letter. But I don't need Fr. Gemelli the physician."

This objection was not due to any stubbornness. Once the Pope recognized that he was really sick, he did not want too much fuss made over his sickness. He did not like to put his own person in the limelight; this is obvious even from the fact that it was very difficult to get him to agree to pose for a photograph at any time during his pontificate. Doctors, consultations, people running around looking important, journalists waiting on the threshold for news—all this was most distasteful to him.

Eventually, the Pope consented to visits by other physicians, and Prof. Milani brought in numerous specialists. Finally, too, he agreed to take things more easily. Medical science and his own strength of will restored him for a while to a measure of health.

He first was put in a bed on wheels, which enabled him to do some work and to hold several important audiences. In January, he was able to sit in a wheel chair. On March 19, 1937, he was able to stand on his feet, and he celebrated Mass again in his private chapel. All through this period he had been preparing his three great encyclicals on Germany, Russia, and Spain, which were published that March. Late in the month he assisted at the Easter services in St. Peter's Basilica, and gave his benediction from the outer balcony. In April he again received newly married couples, a custom he had introduced, and he resumed his former physical exercises in the Vatican garden.

Despite the advice of the physicians, he continued to hold general audiences every day, for he felt that this did him no harm. His strength and vigor had been restored to such an extent that when Cardinal Bisleti, prefect of the Sacred Congregation of Seminaries and Universities, died, he kept that office for himself. This meant added work for him and not just the signing of papers. He liked Cardinal Bisleti and was satisfied with the Cardinal's handling of affairs. Yet, education, science and related problems were so close to the Pope's heart that the pace of work changed immediately when he took over the leadership.

The Pope was especially happy when he was notified that the new cathedral in Lisieux dedicated to St. Thérèse was completed and ready for consecration in July. He sent his most important associate, Cardinal Pacelli, Secretary of State, to represent him. He asked Pacelli to bring him back "a red rose, a white rose, and a pink rose." The meaning behind this request lay in the fact that the Sisters in Lisieux were constantly praying for the Pope. He had asked them to pray that he should behave with the dignity befitting a Pope should he again become ill and that he should follow and carry out the will of God to the end. Symbolically, the red rose meant that he conform to the divine will, the pink rose that he be able to work for the Church, and the white rose meant that God should present many and saintly priests to the world. After Pacelli left, the Pope asked that the statue of the Blessed Virgin that stood in the garden at Castel Gandolfo be decorated with masses of red, pink, and white roses.

In the meantime, he received more and more pilgrims in

audience. He returned to Rome on October 30, 1937. During
his stay in Castel Gandolfo the environs of St. Peter's Church,
between the piazza and Castel Sant' Angelo, underwent a
change. Until then, this section had been one of the most
ancient in Rome. This conglomeration of old houses, with its
labyrinthine streets, was demolished because the government
had decided, with the consent of the Vatican, that a new,
wide thoroughfare should lead from Castel Sant' Angelo to
St. Peter's, thereby providing an open vista of the church from
the distance. When the Pope returned, the work of demolition
was already completed, though the street was not yet paved.
The present Via della Conciliazione was not yet ready. Pius
XI, however, was the first to drive through this new road,
named after the reconciliation that was his work.

On December 13, 1937, the Pope held a consistory to create new cardinals. He reminded them that he was over eighty
years old and that this consistory could be his last. This
brought to mind, said the Pope, the words of St. John the
Apostle: "The one whom you will need is in your midst." But
he turned from this thought immediately and said: "But at
once I hear the sweet and loving word of the Divine Master,
the words he said to Peter, *Quid ad te*. This [the succession]
is not your concern. Just follow Him." Pius XI continued: "One
has to follow Him wherever and as long as He wishes. In the
tranquility of peace and in the troubles of great conflicts, one
should follow the Divine Master everywhere, at least with the
great desire to help, to do good to all those who turn to the
Pope, extending one's hand to all the suffering, towards all
their miseries; hoping that one could help them, or at least
comfort them or console them." Then, in a voice grave and
calm, he continued. He said one should act in the manner he
had just described, "provided that one is not required in the
least to sacrifice the sacred truth. That is the first charity
. . . provided that one is not asked to veil the truth, not even
in its smallest detail, by any confusion and alteration of ideas,

provided that one is not asked for tacit connivance, or a tacit complicity of silence in the face of superfluous repetitions of principles that are contrary to any religion or to any fear of God, and with it, contrary not only to all that which is Christian in the genuine sense of the word—and not in a certain contorted sense in which everything has its place, even the most despicable contradictions—but contrary also to any true good of civilized and human society."

The last year of his life was a great human drama. The Pope wanted to forestall the threatening events, because he was aware that the forces of evil were preparing a horrible conflagration. At the same time, he had to struggle with his own physical decline. He had had several heart attacks and had been on the verge of death a number of times. He had often told members of his entourage that he wanted to die with the words, "Jesus, Mary and Joseph," on his lips, as these had been taught to him by his mother. He requested that those close to him recite "Jesus, Mary and Joseph" with him when the time came.

Life for Pius XI in a physical sense became more and more difficult. Archbishop Confalonieri, his secretary, recorded all the utterances of the Pope during these years. They are truly the remarks of a man saintly in suffering. Once he said to Confalonieri: "It is really most comforting for me to have the Holy Sacrament. There Jesus in silence lives His divine life and governs the world. Even during the night He is an ineffable Companion. One prays, and so many problems are settled. It is almost like anticipating paradise."

While the Pope lived in complete union with God and was prepared to be taken to Him, Hitler prepared for war. The "pact of steel" of the Axis Powers was signed; the persecution of all adversaries of Hitler and Mussolini was intensified. Even Mussolini tried to introduce racial laws, despite the firm refusal of the population and the authorities in Italy to accept them. The ailing Pope found many occasions to condemn such actions. The most striking condemnation was his speech on July 28, 1938, when he received professors and students of the University of the Propaganda Fide in audience. He said that racism and exaggerated nationalism are barriers between man and man, between nation and nation, and he warned that those who fancied that they could attack Catholic Action and Catholic ideas without attacking the Pope and the Church are gravely mistaken.

Hitler and his associates, however, went on without heeding these warnings from the Vatican. Pius XI ordered prayers for peace. During the mounting tension in the summer of 1938 there were moments when he said: "Even I start to become a pessimist, I who am an optimist by nature." And he said to an audience composed of young people: "Never did I have such a desire to die than in these times. I hope that I will go first, but you younger people, I am afraid, will see sad things." He predicted the war and he predicted the great destruction in Europe.

On September 28, when the tension rose to its climax, the Pope said he wanted to offer his life or his death in exchange for the settling of the world's problems. He was terribly shaken. The Munich Conference was scheduled for September 29 and the Pope decided to speak the night before. In this most memorable radio message, directed to the whole world, he directed his greatest plea to God and man for peace. Since Czechoslovakia was the victim at that time, the Pope ended his radio message by recalling the heroic martyrdom of Saint Wenceslaus, the patron saint of Czechoslovakia.

Although the tension momentarily eased, the Pope no longer believed that human power could avoid war. His strength began to fail. His pulse weakened. For several months he had not taken injections for his cardiac condition, but in October 1938 they were again necessary. On November 25 Pius XI suffered two heart attacks, but the next day he had recovered. His doctors were surprised. His asthma worsened daily due to the cardiac condition, yet on December

18 he insisted on inaugurating the third year of the Pontifical
Academy of Sciences.

After an audience on February 1, 1939, he worked as usual
in his private library. But when his male nurse came on duty
in the evening (Brother Faustino of the German Franciscan
Tertiaries) he noticed that the Pope was not at all well. Although Prof. Milani was summoned and ordered the Pontiff
to bed, the Pope participated on February 3 in the celebration of the fiftieth anniversary of the foundation of the Pontifical Canadian College. Like so many of his speeches, the
one on this occasion was extemporaneous. His speeches have
still not been collected because many of those published were
not accurately transcribed, even from his rough notes, and
therefore need extensive editing.

On February 4 he decided to invite the entire episcopate
for an audience to be held February 11. He wanted to have
a more intimate non-official, paternal conversation with them
on February 12. No one expected this move from the Pope,
although it was known that he considered Mussolini's attachment to Hitler dangerous and fatal, not only for Italy but
for the relationship between the Holy See and Italy. Pius XI
recognized that, if Italy could remain neutral, other countries in Europe would be strengthened in their neutral attitude and this would have a calming effect on Hitler, too. Even
in case of war, Italian neutrality would help to localize the
conflict. Under the calm surface, punctuated by infirmity and
old age, the great and active mind of Achille Ratti was alive.
He was preparing an important stroke. It was his policy to
act immediately when action was needed. If an episcopal see
was vacant, he appointed the bishop at once. If he was asked
for a decision, he decided quickly. If the Church was attacked
or in danger, he responded at once, but he always held his
trump card, as it were, to the last minute. He believed in good
will and in the good faith of others. And he believed this until the contrary was proved. He liked to fight if there was a
chance to make an honest peace afterward, but he had no

liking for fighting for the battle's sake. He denounced racism, fascism and national socialism on every occasion. He sent warnings through diplomatic channels, delivered in a soft voice, warnings by special ambassadors and warnings spoken out clearly by himself—but to no avail.

As subsequent events proved, the idea of a major stroke against Hitler and Mussolini had been maturing in the Pope's mind for quite a long time. Now he gave orders for the convocation of the Bishops of Italy. February 11 was a day doubly important for him. This is the feast day of Lourdes, and on February 11, 1929, ten years before, the Lateran Treaty had been signed.

On February 4, the Pope's pulse was low, almost forty. Prof. Milani himself was sick with influenza and unable to come. And the confessor of the Pope was lying in a hospital, about to undergo an operation.

On February 5, the Pope was unable to celebrate Mass but he received Communion. Then he insisted on going to his library where he received Cardinal Pacelli. Afterward he received a group of children to whom he spoke for more than five minutes.

February 6 was the seventeenth anniversary of his election to the papacy. He received Communion and prayed in gratitude for the past seventeen years. In the afternoon two specialists, Drs. Rocchi and Bonanome, visited him. It was easier to keep him in his apartment because Monday was always a day of rest, so he did not protest. On February 7 he talked in his apartment with Cardinal Pacelli. Later, he insisted on getting up and going to his study, but as he tried to take a step he staggered and almost fell. Other doctors and Fr. Gemelli were notified.

The night between February 7 and 8 was a turbulent one. The Pope suffered and seemed to talk in his sleep or to be having nightmares. Some said that he was delirious.

From this day on there were persistent rumors in Rome—so typical of the Eternal City—that the Pope had even gone out of his mind. Since statements to the contrary could not be issued, the rumors persisted. It was even said that the situation would pose a difficult problem for the College of Cardinals should the Pope survive.

On February 8 a medical bulletin was issued which stated that his condition was such as to cause preoccupation and concern. He knew about his condition, because he talked with his doctors; he asked them to do everything possible to make him able to receive the Italian episcopate. The medical bulletin was not published. The Pope did not want to alarm the people. The Pope received Communion and was informed by Cardinal Pacelli and others about the state of affairs.

Osservatore Romano published only the news that the Pope was in good condition, that he was resting because he wanted to be fit to receive the Italian episcopate. Many cardinals besides Pacelli were worried about the proposed general audience. They thought this might injure the Pope's health. The Secretary of State took it upon himself to ask the Pope whether it would not be more advisable to postpone the audience. The Pope's response was quick and unmistakable. "No." As a matter of fact, Cardinal Pacelli stayed only one or two minutes at the sickbed, for the Pope did not discuss the matter further.

Pius XI hoped that he would be able to deliver the speech before the assembled Italian bishops on February 11. He had already prepared the speech and—as Archbishop Confalonieri has reported—the Pope intended to deliver his speech himself, but should he not be strong enough he said that one of the secretaries could read it in his presence. In addition to that, he decided that the speech should be printed and distributed to the bishops. This was an unusual provision and it showed the great importance that the Pope attached to this speech. He was determined to let the world know what he had to say (obviously against fascism and national socialism), because he had made provision even in case he could not get up from bed. He wanted a secretary to read the speech to the bishops.

He spent almost the entire night of February 8–9 in prayer, for he was unable to sleep. But he was in very good humor and hopeful about the prospective event.

On February 9 he received visitors and participated at the Mass that was celebrated at his bedside. He received Holy Communion, then became restless. He saw his physician, but wanted to know the names of those on the audience list. This list was always prepared and published in *Osservatore Romano*. Instead of the Pope, it was the Secretary of State, Cardinal Pacelli, who received those whose regular turn came. Pius XI still did not want the world to know that he was so ill.

High Vatican officials, headed by the Secretary of State, were alarmed, however, and wanted to give the world a sign without violating the Pope's orders, so a news release was prepared and issued announcing that the Vicariate of Rome asked the populace to hold triduums (three-day prayers) in all Roman churches to commemorate the tenth anniversary of the Lateran Treaty (the reconciliation with Italy), and to ask the Lord to restore the health of the Pope. The Pope, of course, was not told of this. This was how the world got the sudden news about the infirmity of the Pope. It was on the afternoon of February 9, 1939, that the wire services were authorized to flash the news to the entire world.

At noon the doctors visited him, and their report was discouraging. The cardiac condition, the arteriosclerosis, the vascular decomposition, had advanced. Pius XI was then told that his situation was grave. His answer was characteristic: "My soul is in the hands of God."

Despite the verdict of the doctors, Achille Ratti did not give up. He had often said since December 1936, when he first fell ill, that he did not mind. After all, he was eighty years old and this was the will of God. He could not read his breviary, or the Bible, but he kept them close by, touched them, and put them on his bed. His hands held the rosary of St. John Vianney, the Curé of Ars.

Around 3:00 in the afternoon of February 9, he asked those who were assembled at his bedside to recite the Rosary with him. The room was filled with the murmur of the prayer. The Pope's eyes were fixed on his crucifix. Everyone prayed for about thirty minutes, and then the Pope suddenly became paler than ever. Prof. Rocchi decided that a new injection might help. After the injection, the Pope fell asleep. As no immediate crisis was anticipated by the physicians, everybody left the room. Around 2:30 A.M. the next morning, Brother Faustino, who was alone in the sickroom with the Pontiff, became alarmed at his condition and called the doctor, the secretaries, and Cardinal Pacelli.

On February 10, at 3:00 in the morning, the end was obvious. The Cardinal Penitentiary of the Holy Roman Catholic Church, whose duty it is to administer the sacrament of extreme unction, could not be reached and Msgr. De Romanis, a high-ranking prelate with the title of Sacristan of the Holy Roman Catholic Church, administered the last rites and gave to the Pope the blessing that is given to the dying. Before 4:00 Prof. Milani arrived, too, but he could do nothing for the dying Pontiff. Pius XI never regained consciousness from the time he had fallen asleep around 3 P.M. the previous day.

At 4:00 Radio Vatican gave out the first bulletin reporting that the Pope's temperature was above 104 degrees. The bulletin also acknowledged that his condition was deteriorating rapidly.

While the bulletin was being broadcast one of his secretaries was celebrating Mass, and all those present prayed on their knees for the Pope. At 5:31 in the morning, February 10, 1939, Pope Pius XI was pronounced dead by his physicians.

In the meantime, all the Italian bishops summoned for the audience on February 11 had arrived in Rome, not for an audience with Pius XI, as they had supposed, but to pray at his bier.

The speech that might have changed the course of history remained undelivered and now rests in the secret archives of the Vatican.

Mussolini, whom Pius XI wanted to warn, not for the sake of Il Duce, or for fascism, but for the sake of the world, sent his condolences immediately to the Vatican. Secretly, he was happy that the speech had not been delivered. Most of the bishops did not know what was in that speech, but *Mussolini knew*. None of the Vatican officials, major or minor, disclosed it to him. Nevertheless, he knew it. For someone— as often happens—the existing power, even if it is evil, was more attractive than a man of the spirit who was dying.

For Achille Ratti, Pius XI, the world did not exist. He was already in the world of the Madonnina and St. Thérèse of the Infant Jesus.

Someone remembered his old request for the three roses, and inconspicuously put a red, a pink, and a white rose among the mountains of flowers disposed on the catafalque. Then silence fell upon the Vatican.

BIBLIOGRAPHY

Annuario Pontificio per L'anno 1957, Città del Vaticano, Tipografia Poliglotta Vaticana.

Aradi, Zsolt, *The Popes*, New York, Farrar, Straus and Cudahy, 1956.

Ardali, Paolo, *Mussolini e Pio XI*, Mantore, 1926.

Bendiscioli, M., *La Politica della S. Sede*, Firenze, 1939.

Bierbaum, Max, *Das Papstum. Leben und Werke Pius XI*, Köln, 1937.

Bouscaren, Anthony T., *Soviet Expansion and the West*, San Francisco, 1949.

Brezzi, Paolo, *Il Papato*, Rome, Editrice Studium, 1951.

Bruehl, Charles Paul, *The Pope's Plan for Social Reconstruction: A Commentary on the Social Encyclicals of Pius XI*, New York, Devin-Adair, 1939.

Castelli, L., *Quel tanto di territorio:* Ricordi di lavori ed opere eseguite nel Vaticano durante il pontificato di Pio XI (1922–39), Roma, 1940.

Cavagna, A. M., *Pio XI e L'azione Cattolica*, 1929.

Cecchetti, I., "Pius XI nella luce di una grande idea," *Bullettino Ceciliano*, 34 (1939), 3–92.

Chiesa e Stato: Studi storici e giurialici per il decennale della conciliazione tra la S. Sede e L'Italia, 2 vols., Milano, Univ. del S. Cuore di Milano, 1939.

Cianfarra, Camille, *The Vatican and the War*, New York, Dutton, 1945.

Claretta, G. R., *I papi e la gioventù*, Roma, 1944.

Confalonieri, C., "Nella luce di Pio XI," *La scuola cattolica*, 1941.

Confalonieri, C., "Pio XI nel decennio del beato transito," *L'Osservatore Romano*, February 10, 1949.

Confalonieri, C., *Pio XI Visto da vicino*, Torino, Edizioni S.A.I.E., 1957.

Cuddihy, Robert, and Shuster, George N., *Pope Pius XI and the American Public Opinion*, New York, Funk and Wagnalls, 1939.

Dalla Torre, G., *Azione Cattolica e Fascismo: Il Conflitto del 1931*, Roma, 1945.

Dalla Torre, G., "Pius XI di fronte al fascismo," *Idea*, 1945.

de Carli, Ferruccio, *La Corte Pontificia de il cerimoniale delle Udienze*, Roma, Bardi Editore, 1952.

de la Briere, Y., *L'Eglise et son gouvernement*, Paris, 1935.

Del Frate, Angelo, *Il Santuario del Sacro Monte sopra Varese*, Varese, La Modernografica, 1948.

Dezza, P., *Alle origini del neo thomismo*, Milano, 1940.

D'Herbigny, M., *L'aiuto pontificio ai bambini affamiti della Russia*, Roma, 1925.

Dietze, Hans-Helmut, *Die päpstlichen Nuntien*, Frankfurt am Main, Deutsche Kunst und Verlagsanstalt, 1943.

Dore, Renzo, *Il Vaticano* (La Corte Pontificia e Le Principali Cerimonie), Milano, Cavalotti, 1948.

Fontenelle, R., *Pie XI*, Paris, Editions Spes, 1939.

Fremantle, Anne, *The Papal Encyclicals in their Historical Context*, New York, Putnam, 1956.

Galbiati, G., *Papa P. XI*, Milano, 1939.

Galter, Albert, *Le Communisme et L'Eglise Catholique*, Paris, Editions Fleurus, 1956.

Gasquet, Francis Aidan, *His Holiness Pius XI: A Pen Portrait*, London, D. O'Connor, 1922.

Gemelli, Agostino, "La grandezza Storica di Pio XI," *Annuario del Università Cattolica del Sacro Cuore*, Milano, 1939.

Gessi, Leone, *La Citta del Vaticano*, Citta del Vaticano, 1937.

Giannini, A., *I concordati postbellici*, 2 vols., Milano, 1926–36.

Gwinn, Dennis-Rolleston, *Pius XI*, London, Holme Press, 1932.

Halecki, Oscar, *Borderlands of Western Civilization*, New York, Ronald Press, 1953.

Halecki, Oscar, and Murray, James F., Jr., *Eugenio Pacelli, Pope of Peace*, New York, Farrar, Straus and Young, 1954.

Hales, E. E. Y., *Pio Nono*, New York, Kenedy, 1954.

Hughes, Philip, *Pope Pius XI*, New York, Sheed & Ward, 1937.

Hughes, Philip, *A Popular History of the Catholic Church*, New York, Macmillan, 1949.

Jacquemet, M. Abbe G., *Tu es Petrus*, Paris, Librairie Bloud et Gay, 1934.

Ledrè, A., *Un Siècle sous la tiare*, Paris, Amiot-Dumont, 1955.

Linskey, Elizabeth, *The Government of the Catholic Church*, New York, Kenedy, 1952.

Maccarrone, M., *Il nazionalsocialismo e la S. Sede*, Roma, 1947.

Mella di Sant' Elia, A., *Istantanee inedite degli ultime 4 papi*, Modena, Edizioni Paoline, 1957.

Mella di Sant' Elia, A., "Ricordando P. XI," *Ecclesia,* 1946.

Meyer, Alfons, *Papstenekdoten,* Speyer, Pilger Verlag, 1954.

Morgan, Thomas B., *The Listening Post, Eighteen Years on Vatican Hill,* New York, Putnam, 1944.

Negro, Silvio, *L'Ordinamento della Chiesa Cattolica,* Milano, Bompiani, 1950.

Neundörfer, Karl, *Papst Pius XI, als Bergsteiger,* Breslau, Bergstadt, 1926.

Novelli, A., *Pius XI (A. Ratti),* Milano, 1923.

Olf, Lillian, *Pius XI: Apostle of Peace,* New York, Macmillan, 1938.

Olf, Lillian, *Their Name is Pius,* Milwaukee, Bruce, 1941.

Olgiati, Francesco, *L'Universita cattolica del Sacro Cuore,* Milano, 1955.

Oliver, Edmund, "The Pope's Mountaineering," *The Dublin Review,* 173 (1923).

A Papal Chamberlain: The Personal Chronicle of Francis Augustus MacNutt, New York, Longmans, 1936.

Pastor, Ludwig, *The History of the Popes,* London, 1906–33.

Pellegrinetti, E., *Pius XI: L'uomo nel pupa e il Papa nell'uomo,* Roma, 1940.

Pelzer, A., "Les iniciateurs italiennes de neo-thomisme," *Revue Neo Scholastique de Philosophie,* 18 (1911).

Restrepo, I. M., *Concordata regnante SS. D. Pio XI inita latine et gallice reddita et notis illustrata,* Roma, 1934.

Roucek, Joseph S. and others, *Central-Eastern Europe,* New York, Prentice-Hall, 1946.

Roux, R.-Ch., *Huit ans au Vatican* (1932–40), Paris, 1947.

Ryan, Joan, "Pope Pius XI the Scholar," *Studies* (March 1939), 13–23.

Salviucci, P., *La Politica vaticana e la guerra* (1937–42), Milano, 1943.

Sarkisyanz, Emanuel, *Russland und der Messianismus des Orients,* Tübingen, Mohr, 1955.

Scharp, Heinrich, *Wie die Kirche regiert wird,* Frankfurt am Main, Verlag Joseph Knecht Carolus Druckerei, 1950.

Schmidlin, J., *Papstgeschichte der neusten Zeit,* Munchen, Kösel und Pustet, 1939.

Spadolini, Giovanni, *Opposizione Cattolica da Porta Pia al '98,* Firenze, Vallecchi Editore, 1954.

Thinn, Gerhard, *Das Rätsel Russland,* Stuttgart, Scherz & Goverts Verlag, 1952.

Tisserant, Eugene, Cardinal, "Pius XI as Librarian," *Library Quarterly* (October 1939).

Townsend, Walter, *The Biography of His Holiness Pope Pius XI*, London, A. E. Marriott, 1930.

Van Riet, Georges, *L'Epistemologie Thomiste*, Louvain, Editions de L'Institute Superior de Philosophie, 1946.

Von Kienitz, Roderich, *Die katholische Kirche als Weltreich*, Oberursel, Europa-Archiv., 1948.

Von Lama, Frederich Ritter, *Papst und Kuria nach dem Weltkrieg*, 1926.

Williams, Michael, *The Catholic Church in Action*, revised by Zsolt Aradi, New York, Kenedy, 1957.

Williams, Michael, "Pope Pius XI," *Catholic World*, 115 (1922), 1–9.

INDEX